"A number of recent books have been writt
and so we might wonder if there is anything ιιεσιι α....
in Christ in Paul's theology. McFadden's book shows us that the answer is yes. ι ωα..
struck repeatedly by McFadden's careful and astute reading of the biblical text, a
reading in which he dialogues with scholarly interlocutors. McFadden demonstrates
that faith in Christ is constitutive of Paul's theology and central to it as well. Those
interested in Pauline theology, even those who disagree, will be provoked to consider
anew the role of faith in Christ in Paul's theology. We find here a remarkably close
and insightful reading of the Pauline letters, one that repristinates the theology of
the Reformers for our day."

Thomas R. Schreiner, James Buchanan Harrison Professor of New Testament
Interpretation, The Southern Baptist Theological Seminary

"Kevin McFadden has written an important book on a central theme of the New
Testament and of the theology of the apostle Paul more specifically. Interacting with
a wide range of scholarship, he forcefully defends the traditional understanding of the
phrase 'faith in Christ' as highlighting the necessity and the reality of faith in Jesus that
saves sinners. At a time when it has become fashionable to diminish the significance
of individuals in favor of corporate dimensions of the body of Christ, *Faith in the Son
of God* describes with admirable exegetical sensitivity how Paul uses the language of
faith when explaining what sinners do as God saves them on account of Jesus's death
on the cross. Thus, the book is as much about the gospel as it is about faith, and thus
about the effective witness of the church in an increasingly secular world."

Eckhard Schnabel, Mary French Rockefeller Distinguished Professor of New
Testament, Gordon-Conwell Theological Seminary; author, *Jesus in Jerusalem*

"McFadden presents a compelling case that Paul's letters emphasize the importance of
faith in Christ. His argument is that ἐκ πίστεως Χριστοῦ describes Christ-oriented
faith as the means ('instrumental cause') of salvation. This work is biblical theology at
its finest. Not content to merely tread the path well worn by others, McFadden presents
fresh arguments that I have not previously encountered. He writes as a scholar who is
consistently fair and irenic in his treatment of differing views and as a humble student
who is able to learn from those with whom he disagrees. More than anything else, he
writes as a faithful exegete who seeks to formulate his theology from the biblical text
rather than impose his preconceived theology on the text. I highly recommend this
book to scholars, students, and pastors."

Charles L. Quarles, Research Professor of New Testament and Biblical
Theology, Southeastern Baptist Theological Seminary

Faith in the Son of God

Faith in the Son of God

The Place of Christ-Oriented Faith
within Pauline Theology

Kevin W. McFadden

Foreword by Robert W. Yarbrough

:: CROSSWAY®

WHEATON, ILLINOIS

Faith in the Son of God: The Place of Christ-Oriented Faith within Pauline Theology
Copyright © 2021 by Kevin W. McFadden
Published by Crossway
       1300 Crescent Street
       Wheaton, Illinois 60187

Cover design: Lindy Martin, Faceout Studios
Cover image: Jordan Singer
First printing 2021
Printed in the United States of America

Trade paperback ISBN: 978-1-4335-7140-4
ePub ISBN: 978-1-4335-7143-5
PDF ISBN: 978-1-4335-7141-1
Mobipocket ISBN: 978-1-4335-7142-8

Library of Congress Cataloging-in-Publication Data

Names: McFadden, Kevin W., 1980– author.
Title: Faith in the Son of God : the place of Christ-oriented faith within Pauline theology / Kevin W. McFadden.
Description: Wheaton, Illinois : Crossway, 2021. | Includes bibliographical references and index.
Identifiers: LCCN 2020022105 (print) | LCCN 2020022106 (ebook) | ISBN 9781433571404 (trade paperback) | ISBN 9781433571411 (pdf) | ISBN 9781433571428 (mobi) | ISBN 9781433571435 (epub)
Subjects: LCSH: Bible. Epistles of Paul—Theology. | Jesus Christ—Spiritual life—Biblical teaching.
Classification: LCC BS2651 .M395 2020 (print) | LCC BS2651 (ebook) | DDC 227/.06—dc23
LC record available at https://lccn.loc.gov/2020022105
LC ebook record available at https://lccn.loc.gov/2020022106

Crossway is a publishing ministry of Good News Publishers.

VP		30	29	28	27	26	25	24	23	22	21
15	14	13	12	11	10	9	8	7	6	5	4	3	2	1

To my beloved Colleen,
διὰ πίστεως γὰρ περιπατοῦμεν, οὐ διὰ εἴδους·
(2 Cor. 5:7)

Contents

Analytic Outline

Foreword

THIS IS A BOOK WITH A CLEAR and striking central contention: "Paul significantly emphasizes Christ-oriented faith in his theology." This is a bombshell in an interpretive world in which "the faith/faithfulness of Christ" (hereafter FOC) has for many largely supplanted the older notion that "faith in Christ" was the key to salvation.

I confess that I never thought the FOC view (as a wholesale replacement for "faith in Christ") was convincing. So the exegesis and arguments of this book ring true to me.

But what will other readers think? Kevin W. McFadden certainly has his work cut out for him in this book.

For the FOC understanding has become a ruling paradigm for many, and no substantial correction is sought or allowed. After all, the FOC view[1] (sometimes in concert with the celebrated New Perspective on Paul) has the great virtue of calling into question not only the Reformation reading of Scripture but (more importantly) common evangelical preaching in the Reformation vein that calls the lost to personal and saving faith in Jesus. The mainstream "we" who eschew such preaching know how trite and wrong this preaching is!

Therefore, the FOC view functions for some as a bulwark against affirming the legitimacy of preaching that calls for saving faith *in* Christ all around the world. That's a pretty strong commendation if it upholds your status as a herald of the "gospel" that salvation is *not* by personal

---

[1] The FOC view is the central concern of this book, particularly as epitomized in Richard B. Hays's now-classic work *The Faith of Jesus Christ: The Narrative Substructure of Galatians 3:1–4:11*, 2nd ed. (Grand Rapids, MI: Eerdmans, 2002).

faith in Christ and never was—all you need is faith in a gracious "God" or participation in a community that celebrates Jesus (whoever he was) in ways analogous to how Paul and others in the early church framed and articulated their God consciousness. Or maybe it's that, additionally, you should affirm staunch "allegiance" to a regal Jesus.[2] Construals vary; what is constant is a rejection of the Reformation's *sola fide* conviction (salvation is through faith alone).

There is in too many cases an even more fundamental assumption at work in all this: *no one needs to be "saved"* in the New Testament and evangelical sense. Michael McClymond has shown how pervasive the doctrine of universal salvation has become—no one, in the end, will suffer eternal condemnation.[3] Humans have already been put right with God as a function of the goodness of God's creation or God's loving nature or God's covenant faithfulness or the total loyalty of God's saving agent Jesus Christ.[4] But isn't this, in the end, just a recapitulation, in key ways, of what H. Richard Niebuhr summed up as liberal theology's essence: "A God without wrath brought men without sin into a kingdom without judgment through the ministrations of a Christ without a cross"?[5]

This is not to say that all who support the FOC interpretation answer to "liberal" in Niebuhr's exact sense. But many tend in that direction. And there is no question about which way mainstream academic readings of Paul tend toward at present along the divide between a liberal understanding of human nature and religious "salvation," on the one hand, and an evangelical conviction of human sinfulness and proclamation of salvation through faith in the crucified and risen Christ, on the other.

---

2   See, e.g., Matthew W. Bates, *Gospel Allegiance: What Faith in Jesus Misses for Salvation in Christ* (Grand Rapids, MI: Brazos, 2019).

3   Michael J. McClymond, *The Devil's Redemption: A New History and Interpretation of Christian Universalism*, 2 vols. (Grand Rapids, MI: Baker Academic, 2018).

4   Repetition of "God" and avoidance of a masculine pronoun referring to God are intentional in this sentence, in keeping with the linguistic scruples that often attend these theological convictions.

5   H. Richard Niebuhr, *The Kingdom of God in America* (New York: Harper & Row, 1937), 193.

Yet change is in the air. Leading lights in Pauline interpretation like E. P. Sanders are passing from the scene, and their arguments and outlook have come to seem, in the end, unconvincing and unhelpful to many. So perhaps this book will be a guiding voice in a move away from Hays's FOC (and, where indicated, the New Perspective) and toward a fresh regard for the tried-and-true reading that McFadden seeks to rehabilitate.

Faith in the Son of God will certainly be a valuable resource and foundational for rereading Paul by a new generation of PhD students, seminarians, and intellectually active pastors who may be willing to admit that the FOC interpretation seems a bit thin and out of sync with too many New Testament passages, as McFadden shows. Some are bound to be asking, What's the alternative?

This book is an apt reply for those with an appetite for interpretation tethered to the whole of Scripture's witness. McFadden recovers a Pauline message true to historic gospel proclamation in the Reformation heritage that, while always subject to refinement, never deserved the dismissal it received in North American mainline circles. May gospel recovery among at least a few in those circles, and many elsewhere around the world, be among the outcomes of this understated but quietly brilliant book.

Robert W. Yarbrough
Professor of New Testament
Covenant Theological Seminary

Preface

PERHAPS NOTHING IS MORE axiomatic in the church than the idea that we believe in Christ. But as Martin Luther warned us, the doctrine of faith "is indeed easy to talk about, but it is hard to grasp; and it is easily obscured and lost."[1] While faith in Christ may seem axiomatic in the church, it has been highly debated in the academy, especially among those who study Paul's letters. Many have argued that Paul did not actually teach that we are justified by our faith in Christ but rather taught that we are justified by Christ's own faith or faithfulness. Others suggest that we have mistranslated the Greek word for "faith" in Paul's letters and thus misunderstood the concept. Add this to our broader cultural context in which unbelief has strangely taken the place of faith in our catalog of virtues, and it seems like plenty of reason to go back and examine carefully what exactly Paul's letters say about faith in Christ.

This book has taken a lot of time and work to write, and I have many to thank for their help along the way. First, I am grateful to the Lord for answered prayer, strength, and understanding. Thanks also go to my friends and family for praying for me and encouraging me. My former provost, Brian Toews, and my colleagues at Cairn University granted me a reduced class load for the 2016–2017 school year that enabled me to get my mind around this topic. Jonathan Master, my former dean, has supported me since then with a schedule

---

1   *Luther's Works*, ed. Jaroslav Pelikan (St. Louis, MO: Concordia, 1963), 26:114. Luther concludes, "Therefore let us with all diligence and humility devote ourselves to the study of Sacred Scripture and to serious prayer, lest we lose the truth of the Gospel." *Luther's Works*, 26:114.

that enabled continual chipping away at it. Stephanie Kaceli, Melvin Hartwick, Caleb Daubenspeck, and the staff at the Masland Library helped me secure needed resources. Thanks are also due to the staff at the Princeton Theological Seminary Library for their hospitality and the use of their resources. Several students, friends, and colleagues read drafts of the work and aided me in clarifying and sharpening my argument, including John Biegel, James Dolezal, John Hughes, Gary Schnittjer, Tom Schreiner, Claude Soriano, and Mike Stanislawski. Courtney Schlect helped me compile the bibliography. And my wife, Colleen, read a draft of the whole book and significantly improved it with her eagle eyes and perceptive feedback. Any remaining faults in the work, of course, remain my own. I also want to thank Crossway for accepting the book for publication, Justin Taylor for his valuable direction throughout the publication process, the Crossway team for their excellent work in publishing the book, Bob Yarbrough for taking time to write a foreword that sets this study in a broader context and thereby shows its importance, and David Barshinger for his exceptionally skillful work in editing the manuscript.

This book is dedicated to my beloved Colleen. All the Christian life until the resurrection is, as Paul says, an exercise in walking by faith and not by sight. Sometimes we feel this more acutely and sometimes less. But I am so grateful to be able to share this light and momentary journey with a fellow traveler like you.

Abbreviations

AB	Anchor Bible
AGJU	Arbeiten zur Geschichte des antiken Judentums und des Urchristentums
BCOTWP	Baker Commentary on the Old Testament Wisdom and Psalms
BDAG	Danker, Frederick W., Walter Bauer, William F. Arndt, and F. Wilbur Gingrich, *Greek-English Lexicon of the New Testament and Other Early Christian Literature*. 3rd ed. Chicago: University of Chicago Press, 2000.
BDB	Brown, Francis, S. R. Driver, and Charles A Briggs. *A Hebrew and English Lexicon of the Old Testament*. Oxford: Clarendon, 1906.
BDF	Blass, Friedrich, Albert Debrunner, and Robert W. Funk. *A Greek Grammar of the New Testament and Other Early Christian Literature*. Chicago: University of Chicago Press, 1961.
BECNT	Baker Exegetical Commentary on the New Testament
BNTC	Black's New Testament Commentaries
BZNW	Beihefte zur Zeitschrift für die neutestamentliche Wissenschaft und die Kunde der älteren Kirche
CBQ	*Catholic Biblical Quarterly*
CBR	*Currents in Biblical Research*
COQG	Christian Origins and the Question of God
EBC	Expositor's Bible Commentary
ETL	*Ephemerides Theologicae Lovanienses*

ExpTim	*Expository Times*
GKC	*Gesenius' Hebrew Grammar*. Edited by Emil Kautzsch. Translated by Arthur E. Cowley. 2nd ed. Oxford: Clarendon, 1910.
HALOT	Koehler, Ludwig, Walter Baumgartner, and Johann J. Stamm. *The Hebrew and Aramaic Lexicon of the Old Testament*. Translated and edited under the supervision of Mervyn E. J. Richardson. 4 vols. Leiden: Brill, 1994–1999.
ICC	International Critical Commentary
Int	*Interpretation*
JBL	*Journal of Biblical Literature*
JETS	*Journal of the Evangelical Theological Society*
JSNT	*Journal for the Study of the New Testament*
JTS	*Journal of Theological Studies*
LCL	Loeb Classical Library
LNTS	Library of New Testament Studies
LS	*Louvain Studies*
LSJ	Liddell, Henry George, Robert Scott, Henry Stuart Jones. *A Greek-English Lexicon*. 9th ed. Oxford: Clarendon, 1996.
LXX	Septuagint
n.b.	*nota bene* ("note well")
NICNT	New International Commentary on the New Testament
NICOT	New International Commentary on the Old Testament
NIGTC	New International Greek Testament Commentary
NKZ	*Neue kirchliche Zeitschrift*
NovT	*Novum Testamentum*
NSBT	New Studies in Biblical Theology
NTL	New Testament Library
NTMon	New Testament Monographs
NTS	*New Testament Studies*

OECS	Oxford Early Christian Studies
OTL	Old Testament Library
PNTC	Pillar New Testament Commentary
SJT	*Scottish Journal of Theology*
SNTSMS	Society for New Testament Studies Monograph Series
TDNT	*Theological Dictionary of the New Testament*. Edited by Gerhard Kittel and Gerhard Friedrich. Translated by Geoffrey W. Bromiley. 10 vols. Grand Rapids, MI: Eerdmans, 1964–1976.
TNTC	Tyndale New Testament Commentaries
TSK	*Theologische Studien und Kritiken*
TynBul	*Tyndale Bulletin*
VTSup	Supplements to Vetus Testamentum
WBC	Word Biblical Commentary
WUNT	Wissenschaftliche Untersuchungen zum Neuen Testament
ZECNT	Zondervan Exegetical Commentary on the New Testament

Introduction

The Πίστις Χριστοῦ Debate
and Pauline Theology

Belief is so important.
BLAISE PASCAL, *PENSÉES*

ON A FLIGHT SEVERAL YEARS AGO, I was reading a book titled *Paul and His Recent Interpreters* when the person in the seat next to me said, "Oh, people are writing about Saint Paul these days?" Yes, I assured her, they were, and if I had said what I was thinking, it would have been that I wish they would write a little less! The pens of Pauline scholars have not been idle. So many aspects of the apostle's theology have been questioned, reappraised, and debated in the last fifty years. These debates can become a "weariness of the flesh" to those trying to keep up and make sense of the various perspectives on Paul. But they can also force scholars and Christians from every perspective to reexamine Paul's letters more carefully and with new questions. This is what the πίστις Χριστοῦ debate has done for me. It has forced me to reconsider what Paul's letters actually say about faith, and this book is the fruit of that study.

For readers unfamiliar with this debate, it is a debate over the meaning of a Greek phrase that occurs eight times in Paul's letters: πίστις

Χριστοῦ.[1] While this phrase has historically been understood as a reference to Christ as the object of our faith (the "faith in Christ" view), many English-speaking scholars now understand it as a reference to Christ's own faith or faithfulness (the "faithfulness of Christ" view).[2] So much ink has been spilled over this debate in the last few decades that one might legitimately ask, Why does it really matter? At the level of grammar, these phrases can really be translated either way. And at the level of theology, both our faith and Christ's faithfulness are important, so the question may be simply which truth these eight phrases speak of.

But I have come to believe that this debate is significant because of the relationship of these eight phrases to Paul's entire theology and especially his view of justification and salvation (and thus, by implication, our view of salvation). Six of the phrases occur in the apostle's most important passages about justification: Romans 3:21–26 (2x); Galatians 2:15–21 (3x); and Philippians 3:2–11 (1x). Moreover, the grammar of the phrases in these passages indicates the role that πίστις plays in justification. This fact is obscured by the debate's unfortunate label. Technically, the words πίστις Χριστοῦ never occur in Paul's letters, because these words are always found within a prepositional phrase that indicates the means by which one attains salvific benefits (e.g., ἐκ πίστεως Χριστοῦ in Gal. 2:16).[3] That is, these eight phrases are part of Paul's common idiom "*by* faith," which he often sets in

---

1   In canonical order, the phrase occurs in Rom. 3:22, 26; Gal. 2:16 [2x], 20; 3:22; Phil. 3:9; Eph. 3:12. Scholars who dispute Paul's authorship of Ephesians would say the phrase occurs seven times in Paul's letters. Note also that πίστις Χριστοῦ is shorthand for phrases that have more variation in their actual wording—e.g., πίστεως Ἰησοῦ Χριστοῦ and πίστεως Χριστοῦ in Gal. 2:16, then πίστει . . . τῇ τοῦ υἱοῦ τοῦ θεου in Gal. 2:20.

2   These two positions are typically labeled the "objective-genitive view" and "subjective-genitive view," respectively, because the question is whether "Christ" is the object of πίστις ("faith in Christ") or its subject ("faithfulness of Christ"). Note that the "faithfulness of Christ," or subjective-genitive, view has had much less influence in German-speaking scholarship.

3   For this observation I am indebted to Karl Friedrich Ulrichs, *Christusglaube: Studien zum Syntagma πίστις Χριστοῦ und zum paulinischen Verständnis von Glaube und Rechtfertigung*, WUNT, 2nd ser., vol. 227 (Tübingen: Mohr Siebeck, 2007), 6. For a list of the eight prepositional phrases, see chap. 4, p. 184.

contrast with the attainment of salvific benefits "by works of the law" or "by the law" or "by works" (e.g., Rom. 3:28). All this means that the debate is not simply about the meaning of a few phrases; rather, as Karl Ulrichs rightly concludes, the debate "is about the basic principles of soteriology."[4]

This fact has been recognized by the advocates of the "faithfulness of Christ" view but has not been adequately addressed by scholars who hold the "faith in Christ" view. It is sometimes forgotten that the influential dissertation of Richard Hays, which convinced many scholars of the "faithfulness of Christ" translation, was concerned not primarily with the grammar of these phrases but with the shape of Paul's theology as a whole. In response, Barry Matlock, one of the most articulate advocates of the "faith in Christ" view, argued that we need to "dethcologize" the debate, setting aside theology so that we can concentrate on the meaning of the word πίστις.[5] I agree with Matlock's view in this debate. I also agree with him that the theological concerns of the "faithfulness of Christ" view have tended to cloud the debate through a lack of precision in defining the word πίστις in Paul.[6] Nevertheless, I think that Hays and others are correct that we cannot set aside theology in this debate, and I understand why he has faulted Matlock for failing to engage the argument "in the terms that [he has] tried to pose it."[7]

The goal of this book is to engage the theological argument of Hays and others and then to "retheologize" the debate by examining Paul's larger theology of Christ-oriented faith. The first step is to carefully articulate the theological argument of the "faithfulness of Christ" view,

---

4   Ulrichs, *Christusglaube*, 8 (my trans.).

5   R. Barry Matlock, "Detheologizing the Πιστις Χριστου Debate: Cautionary Remarks from a Lexical Semantic Perspective," *NovT* 42, no. 1 (2000): 1–23.

6   See Kevin W. McFadden, "Does Πιστις Mean 'Faith(fulness)' in Paul?," *TynBul* 66, no. 2 (2015): 251–70.

7   Richard B. Hays, *The Faith of Jesus Christ: The Narrative Substructure of Galatians 3:1–4:11*, 2nd ed. (Grand Rapids, MI: Eerdmans, 2002), xlvii.

which can be summarized as follows: *Paul does not teach that we are justified by our own faith in Christ but rather teaches that we are justified by Christ's faith or faithfulness.* This theological argument then propels us to reconsider what the apostle says about faith and Christ in the rest of the book. In contrast with those who have de-emphasized the importance of our faith in Paul's letters, I argue that Paul significantly emphasizes Christ-oriented faith in his theology.

The Theological Argument of the "Faithfulness of Christ" View

Rarely does a dissertation have as much influence as Richard Hays's *The Faith of Jesus Christ*, originally published in 1983 and then published in a second edition in 2002. Before Hays, many scholars had suggested the "faithfulness of Christ" translation in Paul,[8] most notably Karl Barth in his early commentary on Romans.[9] But it was Hays's careful argument that convinced many scholars in the English-speaking world to adopt this new translation, which has now had an effect even on some English Bible translations.[10] Because the "faithfulness of Christ" translation has become the enduring legacy of Hays's work, many may be surprised to learn that the primary concern of his dissertation was not about the phrase πίστις Χριστοῦ but about the story of Jesus that underlies the apostle's theology. In what follows I outline the theological argument

---

8   For a standard history of the debate, see Debbie Hunn, "Debating the Faithfulness of Jesus Christ in Twentieth-Century Scholarship," in *The Faith of Jesus Christ: Exegetical, Biblical, and Theological Studies*, ed. Michael F. Bird and Preston M. Sprinkle (Peabody, MA: Hendrickson, 2009), 15–31. Most histories go back to Johannes Haussleiter in 1891, but Schliesser's study has now unearthed the "faithfulness of Christ" translation among several early nineteenth-century German scholars. Benjamin Schliesser, "'Exegetical Amnesia' and Πίστις Χριστου: The 'Faith *of* Christ' in Nineteenth-Century Pauline Scholarship," *JTS* 66, no. 1 (2015): 61–76.

9   Barth specifically understood πίστις to be *God's* faithfulness in Jesus Christ, although in his later shorter commentary on Romans, he changed back to the "faith in Christ" translation. For the interesting backstory, see Schliesser, "Exegetical Amnesia," 83–86.

10 The "faithfulness of Christ" translation has been adopted by the New English Translation and the Common English Bible (with the exception of Rom. 3:26). The New Revised Standard Version offers "faith of . . ." as a footnote for the eight phrases, and the 2011 edition of the New International Version offers "faithfulness of . . ." as a footnote in Rom. 3:22; Gal. 2:16; and Phil. 3:9.

of Hays and its continuing trajectory in the "apocalyptic" school of Pauline theology. Not everyone who adopts the "faithfulness of Christ" translation accepts this theological argument in its entirety, but I aim to demonstrate that it was an important part of Hays's dissertation and is tightly bound up with the new translation.

Christology versus Anthropology

Those who hold to the "faithfulness of Christ" translation often label their position the *Christological* or *Christocentric* view, as opposed to the *anthropological* or *anthropocentric* view.[11] Framing the debate in these terms has led to some protest from the other side. Francis Watson, for example, comments that "it is disingenuous to play off a (virtuous) 'christocentric' reading against a (bad, protestant) 'anthropocentric' one. It is simply a matter of exegesis."[12] While I agree with Watson, I think that these labels can help us understand the argument of the "faithfulness of Christ" view—namely, that its advocates think of it not simply as a matter of exegesis but also as a matter of theology, something that has been true since the influential dissertation of Hays.

---

11 For example, a recent summary of the debate penned by a "faithfulness of Christ" advocate adopts these labels and notes that this "has become standard practice," although, he qualifies, he does not mean to suggest that "faith in Christ" advocates have a deficient Christology. Chris Kugler, "ΠΙΣΤΙΣ ΧΡΙΣΤΟΥ: The Current State of Play and the Key Arguments," *CBR* 14, no. 2 (2016): 244–55. Hays adopted the labels "christological" and "anthropological" in his famous debate with James Dunn, which is now included as an appendix to the second edition of his dissertation. Hays, *Faith of Jesus Christ*, 277. The more pejorative label "anthropocentric" is sometimes used by Douglas Campbell and his disciples; e.g., Douglas A. Campbell, "The Faithfulness of Jesus Christ in Romans 3:22," in Bird and Sprinkle, *Faith of Jesus Christ*, 61, 68, 70; Chris Tilling, "Campbell's Faith: Advancing the *Pistis Christou* Debate," in *Beyond Old and New Perspectives on Paul: Reflections on the Work of Douglas Campbell*, ed. Chris Tilling (Eugene, OR: Cascade, 2014), 240, 244.

12 Francis Watson, "By Faith (of Christ): An Exegetical Dilemma and Its Scriptural Solution," in Bird and Sprinkle, *Faith of Jesus Christ*, 159. See also the comments of Schliesser, "Exegetical Amnesia," 72n49; Jonathan A. Linebaugh, "Righteousness Revealed: The Death of Christ as the Definition of the Righteousness of God in Romans 3:21–26," in *Paul and the Apocalyptic Imagination*, ed. Ben C. Blackwell, John K. Goodrich, and Jason Maston (Minneapolis: Fortress, 2016), 235n52; and now Nijay K. Gupta, *Paul and the Language of Faith* (Grand Rapids, MI: Eerdmans, 2020), 173.

Reflecting on his work twenty years later, Hays recalls that his central thesis was that "*a story about Jesus Christ is presupposed by Paul's argument in Galatians, and his theological reflection attempts to articulate the meaning of that story.*"[13] Elsewhere he labels this approach "narrative theology" or the "narrative substructure" of Paul's theology. Hays observes that "the book's subtitle [*The Narrative Substructure of Galatians 3:1–4:11*] is a better guide to its content than the main title [*The Faith of Jesus Christ*]."[14] His argument about πίστις Χριστοῦ is an important but secondary thesis. And even this thesis is not simply about the translation of the phrase but more broadly about the meaning and function of the word πίστις in the argument of Galatians 3. Hays argues that Paul uses the phrase πίστις Ιησοῦ Χριστοῦ, and the word πίστις, as a way to refer by metonymy to the story about Jesus Christ—specifically, "to suggest and evoke that focal moment of the narrative," the cross. The cross was the place in which Jesus demonstrated his human "faithfulness" to God and in which God demonstrated his divine "faithfulness" to humanity. Thus, πίστις Ιησοῦ Χριστοῦ is an expression referring to the climactic event of Christ's gracious, self-sacrificial death.[15]

Hays's primary thesis about the "narrative substructure" of Paul's theology and his secondary thesis about πίστις, however, are closely intertwined. This is because his argument is that the "faith of Jesus Christ" is a reference to the "narrative substructure" that underlies Paul's theology in Galatians. Moreover, these two theses are both responding to the work of a German scholar whom Hays later refers to as the "great adversary whose shadow looms over *The Faith of Jesus Christ*"—Rudolf Bultmann.[16] Reflecting twenty years later, Hays says,

13   Hays, *Faith of Jesus Christ*, xxiv; emphasis original; cf. 6–9.
14   Hays, *Faith of Jesus Christ*, xxiv.
15   Hays, *Faith of Jesus Christ*, xxx–xxxi; cf. 161–62.
16   Hays, *Faith of Jesus Christ*, xxv. "Even where Bultmann is not mentioned explicitly, he is often the unnamed elephant in the room." Hays, xxvi.

In brief, it seemed to me that Bultmann had made two interrelated and fatefully mistaken hermeneutical decisions in his reading of Paul: he sought to "de-narrativize" Paul's thought world, and he understood the gospel principally as a message about human decision, human self-understanding. The theological burden of my argument is to show that Bultmann was wrong on both counts.[17]

We should observe how Bultmann's "two interrelated and fatefully mistaken hermeneutical decisions" are countered by Hays's two interrelated theses. Bultmann's famous project of demythologizing Paul's gospel (which Hays thinks is better termed "de-narrativizing") is countered by Hays's thesis that Paul rested his theology on a story about Jesus Christ. And Bultmann's understanding of faith as an act of decision, a new understanding of oneself, is countered by Hays's thesis that Paul's language about faith actually refers to Christ and not the human individual. This means that in order to understand Hays's two theses, we must understand Bultmann's two hermeneutical mistakes.

First, Bultmann refuses to allow faith to rest on the contingent facts of history: "Faith, being personal decision, cannot be dependent upon a historian's labor."[18] He strikingly admits that he disagrees with Paul on this point: in 1 Corinthians 15:1–11, Paul thinks he can "guarantee the resurrection of Christ as an objective fact by listing the witnesses who had seen him risen."[19] But Bultmann asks, "Is such a proof convincing?"[20] He clearly does not think so: "The resurrection cannot—in spite of I Cor. 15:3–8—be demonstrated or made plausible as an objectively ascertainable fact on the basis

---

17 Hays, *Faith of Jesus Christ*, xxvi; cf. 5–6 and especially 47–52.

18 Rudolf Bultmann, *Theology of the New Testament*, trans. Kendrick Grobel (New York: Scribner, 1951), 1:26.

19 Bultmann, *Theology*, 1:295. Bultmann views Paul as "pushed to do so by Gnosticizing objections to belief in any resurrection whatever." *Theology*, 1:295.

20 Bultmann, *Theology*, 1:295.

of which one could believe."[21] Faith cannot rest on the facts of the past but only on the proclamation of the present: "Insofar as it [the resurrection] or the risen Christ is present in the proclaiming word, it can be believed—and only so can it be believed."[22] Even to believe in the cross of Christ is not to believe on an objective historical event. "Rather," he says, "to believe on the cross means the cross of Christ as it overtakes the individual; it means to be crucified with Christ."[23] This is the kind of demythologizing or abstracting of the gospel from the story of Jesus that Hays is responding to in arguing for a "narrative substructure" to Paul's gospel.

Second, Bultmann's existential view of faith is very focused on the human self, or anthropology. As Hays observes, "Bultmann's exposition of Paul, in the effort to free God's action from mythological 'objectification,' inevitably tends to shift the weight of the emphasis away from God's action and onto the human faith decision."[24] Another way to put this is that Bultmann allows faith to rest on no external object other than the present proclamation (the kerygma). In so doing, he shifts the emphasis away from God's action in Christ and toward our faith itself. Bultmann also defines faith in existential terms, focusing on the individual self and the new self-understanding that one must submit to in light of the kerygma.[25] He argues that saving faith is not merely a belief that certain things are true about Jesus Christ but a "faith which is self-surrender to the grace of God

---

21 Bultmann, *Theology*, 1:305.

22 Bultmann, *Theology*, 1:305.

23 The original German reads, "Sondern an das Kreuz glauben, heisst das Kreuz Christi als das eigenen übernehmen, heisst sich mit Christus kreuzigen lassen." Bultmann, "Neues Testament und Mythologie," 46–47; quoted in Hays, *Faith of Jesus Christ*, 49.

24 Hays, *Faith of Jesus Christ*, 51. He continues, "This reading of Pauline theology stands in direct antithesis to the present work." Hays, 51.

25 It should be noted, however, that Bultmann does not focus on the self in terms of the individual's psychological process of faith: "The attention of the believer does not turn reflectively inward upon himself, but it is turned toward the object of his faith," that is, the confession of the kerygma. *Theology*, 1:319.

and which signifies the utter reversal of a man's previous understanding of himself."[26] Thus, faith is not merely agreeing with the kerygma but is embracing "that genuine obedience to it which includes a new understanding of one's self."[27] This is the self-focused view of faith that Hays responds to by shifting the meaning of πίστις from our faith to Christ's faith.

Hays, however, does not exclude our faith from Paul's thought entirely, a criticism he wisely anticipates at the beginning and ending of his influential argument about πίστις Χριστοῦ. He opens it by conceding that "Gal 2:16 speaks clearly and unambiguously of faith *in* Christ."[28] And he closes it by noting that "this interpretation should not be understood to abolish or preclude human faith directed toward Christ, which is also an important component of Paul's thought."[29] But it is important to observe that *in neither of these concessions does Hays concede that our faith in Christ is a means by which we obtain salvific benefits according to Paul.* In fact, he explicitly rejects this role for our faith in Galatians 3:1–4:11: "The positive thesis toward which this investigation leads may be summarized briefly as follows: Christians are justified/redeemed not by virtue of their own faith but because they participate in Jesus Christ, who enacted the obedience of faith on their behalf."[30] In his later debate with James Dunn, Hays argues again that "the central emphasis of the christological interpretation of πίστις Ἰησοῦ Χριστοῦ is precisely that we are saved by Jesus' faithfulness, not by our own cognitive disposition or confessional orthodoxy."[31] And Luke Timothy Johnson's foreword to the second edition of Hays's dissertation makes the same point:

---

26 Bultmann, *Theology*, 1:300. Cf. *TDNT*, 6:218: "Faith is thus obedient acceptance of the divine judgment on man's previous self-understanding."
27 Bultmann, *Theology*, 1:324.
28 Hays, *Faith of Jesus Christ*, 123.
29 Hays, *Faith of Jesus Christ*, 161.
30 Hays, *Faith of Jesus Christ*, 166.
31 Hays, *Faith of Jesus Christ*, 293.

"Paul does believe that humans are put into right relationship with God through faith. It is not through their own faith, however, but through the faith of Jesus. This book's argument, then, cuts to the very heart of Pauline theology."[32]

In sum, the influential dissertation of Richard Hays makes an argument not simply about Paul's grammar but about his theology. Bultmann took an *anthropological* approach to explaining Pauline theology: "Paul's theology can best be treated as his doctrine of man: first, of man prior to the revelation of faith, and second, of man under faith."[33] Hays countered with a *Christological* approach, emphasizing the story of Jesus Christ as foundational to Paul's gospel and reinterpreting the salvific role of faith in Paul's letters as a reference to the cross of Christ rather than an act of human decision. In Hays's view, Paul does not teach that we are justified by our faith in Christ but rather teaches that we are justified by Christ's own faith or faithfulness. This theological argument has now been picked up by other scholars and has gained rhetorical force, like a hurricane passing over the warm Atlantic, from its association with the school of Pauline theology known as "apocalyptic."

Divine Action versus Human Action

People sometimes ask if the "faithfulness of Christ" translation is a part of the New Perspective on Paul. On the one hand, it is closely related to the New Perspective, because it is a response to the "Lutheran view" of Paul and its emphasis on justification by faith alone.[34] Many scholars who hold to the "faithfulness of Christ" translation also hold to the

---

32 Hays, *Faith of Jesus Christ*, xii.

33 Bultmann, *Theology*, 1:191. His rationale for this approach was that "Pauline theology is not a speculative system. It deals with God not as he is in Himself but only with God as he is significant for man, for man's responsibility and man's salvation." *Theology*, 1:191.

34 See Karl P. Donfried, "Paul and the Revisionists: Did Luther Really Get It All Wrong?," *Dialog: A Journal of Theology* 46, no. 1 (2007): 31–40; Roy A. Harrisville III, "Πίστις Χριστοῦ and the New Perspective on Paul," *Logia* 19, no. 2 (2010): 19–28.

New Perspective on Paul.[35] On the other hand, this new translation is not technically a part of the New Perspective because, unlike the New Perspective, it is not built on the new view of Judaism proposed by E. P. Sanders. In fact, one of the more vocal critics of the "faithfulness of Christ" translation has been one of the most important advocates of the New Perspective, James D. G. Dunn.[36]

The "faithfulness of Christ" translation has been more closely linked with the "apocalyptic" school of Pauline theology. For our purposes the apocalyptic approach to Paul may be defined as a school of Pauline interpretation that emphasizes divine eschatological invasion in Paul's soteriology.[37] It emphasizes *God's* action in bringing about a new world order through Christ over against any human action.[38] If the New Perspective can be understood as a critique of the Lutheran view of

35 For example, Hays himself adopts the New Perspective in his interpretation of Rom. 4: "*The crucial issue in the chapter is not how Abraham got himself justified but rather whose father he is and in what way his children are related to him. The central thrust of Paul's argument is to affirm that Abraham is the father of Jews and Gentiles alike.*" Richard B. Hays, *The Conversion of the Imagination: Paul as Interpreter of Israel's Scripture* (Grand Rapids, MI: Eerdmans, 2005), 83; emphasis original. And N. T. Wright, one of the most well-known advocates of the New Perspective, has also adopted the "faithfulness of Christ" translation, which dovetails nicely with his claim that the "righteousness of God" in Paul refers to God's own covenant faithfulness; see N. T. Wright, *Paul and the Faithfulness of God*, COQG 4 (Minneapolis: Fortress, 2013), 836–51.

36 Dunn famously debated Hays on the translation of πίστις Χριστοῦ at the annual meeting of the Society of Biblical Literature in 1991. This debate is now included as an appendix in the second edition of Hays's dissertation. *Faith of Jesus Christ*, 249–71. See also James D. G. Dunn, "Ἐκ Πίστεως: A Key to the Meaning of Πίστις Χριστου," in *The Word Leaps the Gap: Essays on Scripture and Theology in Honor of Richard B. Hays*, ed. J. Ross Wagner, C. Kavin Rowe, and A. Katherine Grieb (Grand Rapids, MI: Eerdmans, 2008).

37 I am borrowing the term "eschatological invasion" from the helpful introduction in Blackwell, Goodrich, and Maston, *Paul and the Apocalyptic Imagination*. This introduction highlights two approaches to apocalyptic interpretation: "eschatological invasion," associated with J. Louis Martyn, Douglas A. Campbell, and Martinus C. de Boer, and "unveiled fulfillment," associated with N. T. Wright. But it also observes that the label "apocalyptic" is typically identified with the "eschatological invasion" approach. *Paul and the Apocalyptic Imagination*, 6.

38 Most scholars in the apocalyptic school emphasize divine action over human action. For example, de Boer observes that in apocalyptic eschatology the older order will be replaced by a new order "by God and God alone, which is to say that it cannot be initiated by human beings or effected by them." Martinus C. de Boer, "Apocalyptic as God's Eschatological Activity in Paul's Theology," in Blackwell, Goodrich, and Maston, *Paul and the Apocalyptic Imagination*, 50.

Paul, then the apocalyptic school can be understood as a radicalizing of the Lutheran view. The Protestant tradition emphasizes the Pauline dichotomy between works of the law and faith in Jesus Christ, excluding moral works as a cause of justification in favor of justification by faith alone. The apocalyptic school radicalizes this faith-works dichotomy into a dichotomy between divine action and any kind of human action, including faith. Thus it is a kind of "hyper-Lutheran" or "hyper-Protestant" view of Paul's soteriology.[39]

This radicalizing of the Protestant tradition can be seen already in Hays's dissertation. He introduces his argument about πίστις by presenting it as a solution to the risk that the Lutheran doctrine of justification turns "faith into another kind of work, a human achievement."[40] But the dichotomy between divine action and human action gained force through the later work of J. Louis Martyn, the father of the apocalyptic school. Although Pauline scholars had long appealed to Jewish apocalyptic as a background to explain the apostle's theology, Martyn gave scholars a new set of lenses by showing that apocalyptic themes are found not only in those letters that speak of God's invasion in the future but also in letters like Galatians that herald God's invasion of the world *already* in the cross of Jesus Christ (e.g., Gal. 1:4).[41]

Martyn explains this approach further in his powerful and compelling commentary on Paul's letter to the Galatians. In it he adopts the "faithfulness of Christ" translation, arguing that the phrase refers to "Christ's atoning faithfulness, as, on the cross, he died faithfully for

---

39 Matlock, too, observes the "hyper-Protestantism" in the "faithfulness of Christ" view. R. Barry Matlock, "'Even the Demons Believe': Paul and Πίστις Χριστοῦ," *CBQ* 64, no. 2 (2002): 312. And Thomas R. Schreiner says of Douglas Campbell's view of Paul, "If my view is Reformed, perhaps his can be labeled über-Reformed, or even hyper-Calvinist." In *Four Views on the Apostle Paul*, ed. Michael F. Bird, Counterpoints: Bible and Theology (Grand Rapids, MI: Zondervan, 2012), 144.

40 Hays, *Faith of Jesus Christ*, 120.

41 For his paradigm-shifting article, see J. Louis Martyn, "Apocalyptic Antinomies in Paul's Letter to the Galatians," *NTS* 31, no. 3 (1985): 410–24.

human beings while looking faithfully to God."[42] Moreover, he sees this interpretation as an important link in his understanding of Paul's soteriology:

> The result of this interpretation of *pistis Christou* is crucial to an understanding not only of Galatians but also of the whole of Paul's theology. God has set things right without laying down a prior condition of any sort. God's rectifying act, that is to say, is no more God's response to human faith in Christ than it is God's response to human observance to the Law. God's rectification is not God's response at all. It is the *first* move; it is God's initiative, carried out by him in Christ's faithful death.[43]

Here we see Martyn's conviction that justification is *unconditional* in Paul's theology, in the sense that it is not conditioned on any human action, including our faith in Christ. A similar argument about conditionality can be seen in Douglas Campbell's "apocalyptic rereading of justification in Paul." Campbell is concerned with the idea that faith is a human action that secures salvation in a kind of "generous contract."[44] Against this view he argues that πίστις is fundamentally Christological in Paul. Human beings respond in faith not as "a *condition* of participation in Christ but a *marker* that such participation is taking place."[45]

For Martyn it is important that justification is the "*first* move" by God and that human faith is a secondary response to justification.

---

42   J. Louis Martyn, *Galatians: A New Translation with Introduction and Commentary*, AB 33A (New York: Doubleday, 1997), 271.

43   Martyn, *Galatians*, 271.

44   Douglas A. Campbell, *The Deliverance of God: An Apocalyptic Rereading of Justification in Paul* (Grand Rapids, MI: Eerdmans, 2009), 24–28, 55–61.

45   This comes from Campbell's brief approving comments at the end of Tilling's helpful summary of Campbell's view of πίστις Χριστοῦ. "Campbell's Faith," 252. As Tilling observes, "The key issue for Campbell is that faith *not* be understood . . . as the *condition* for salvation." Tilling, 237.

Paul certainly speaks about faith in Christ but only *"in the second instance."*[46] From this point about order, Martyn draws a further conclusion about how works and faith are opposed in Pauline theology:

> The antinomy of Gal 2:16, then—*erga nomou* versus *pistis Christou*— is like all of the antinomies of the new creation: It does not set over against one another two human alternatives, to observe the Law or to have faith in Christ. The opposites, as one sees from Gal 1:1 onward, are an act of God, Christ's faithful death, and an act of the human being, observance of the law.[47]

This interpretation of Galatians seems to be a radicalizing of the Lutheran view of Paul. The dichotomy for Martyn is no longer between faith and works but between divine action and human action: "Paul draws contrasts not between two human alternatives, such as works and faith, but rather between acts done by human beings and acts carried out by God (1:1; 6:15)."[48] One can understand, then, why he viewed the πίστις Χριστοῦ debate as "what Paul would call a matter of life and death!"[49]

Hays wrote his dissertation before Martyn's influential work, but he later accepted Martyn's work on apocalyptic.[50] And this view seems to

---

46   Martyn, *Galatians*, 271. Martyn states, "For Paul, *God's* deed of rectifying us by the faith of Christ precedes *our* deed of placing our trust in that Christ." *Galatians*, 276.

47   Martyn, *Galatians*, 271. Cf. Hooker: "The true antithesis is not between works and faith, but between the works of the *Law* and the saving work of *Christ*." Morna D. Hooker, "Πίστις Χριστοῦ," *NTS* 35, no. 3 (1989): 341.

48   J. Louis Martyn, "The Apocalyptic Gospel in Galatians," *Int* 54, no. 3 (2000): 250. Cf. also Martyn, *Galatians*, 289.

49   Martyn, "Apocalyptic Gospel," 250. It is interesting that Martyn, like Hays, is responding to Bultmann's view that God's prevenient grace in the kerygma opens up the possibility for an obedient human response of faith. Martyn, 251.

50   Reflecting on his dissertation, Hays notes that he had originally "opined that Galatians 'lacks the apocalyptic themes that appear so prominently elsewhere in Paul. . . .' This is among the very few statements in the book that I would now repudiate" in light of Martyn's work. Hays, *Faith of Jesus Christ*, xxxviii.

have influenced his subsequent debate with Dunn. For example, in his explanation of Romans 3:21–26, he asks,

> What would it mean to say that God's justice has been made manifest through our act of believing in Jesus Christ? This, if it means anything at all, verges on blasphemous absorption in our own religious subjectivity. God's eschatological justice can only have been shown forth by an act of God: Paul's claim is that the death of Jesus is just such an apocalyptic event.[51]

Here the content of his explanation is not substantively different from what he originally said in his dissertation about Romans 3:21–26. And yet his argument seems to have gained force as the "faithfulness of Christ" view has been linked with the apocalyptic view of Paul's theology.

In conclusion, we should observe that Hays himself views his theological argument as essentially the same as Martyn's when he faults Matlock for failing to engage it: "He [Matlock] does not engage at all the arguments made by Martyn and by me that the whole point of the sentence [in Gal. 2:16] is to juxtapose futile human activity to gracious divine initiative."[52] In the view of Hays and Martyn, Paul teaches that justification is not by human action but by divine action. This means that not even our faith can be the means by which we are justified. It does not mean, however, that our faith is excluded entirely from Paul's theology. Rather, faith is rehabilitated via the category of participation.

Participation in the Faith of Jesus Christ

"Faithfulness of Christ" advocates often emphasize the centrality of participation with Christ in Paul's soteriology.[53] But the category of

---

51 Hays, *Faith of Jesus Christ*, 283.

52 Hays, *Faith of Jesus Christ*, xlvii.

53 Stubbs observes that one of the three legs of the Christological view is a "centering of soteriology around the concept of 'participation in Christ,'" along with a "christologically centred

participation, or even an emphasis on its centrality over justification by faith, is not really a contribution of this new translation. Participation or union with Christ has a strong pedigree in both Lutheran and Reformed theology. And several Pauline scholars over the years have attempted to argue that participation is more central in Paul than justification by faith.[54] Instead, the real contribution of the "faithfulness of Christ" translation is the idea that Christians participate not only in Christ's death and resurrection but also in his very faith or faithfulness. This contribution again goes back to Hays's dissertation.[55]

As I have observed, Hays rejects the idea that faith is the means by which we are justified but not the importance of our faith altogether. After rejecting its role in justification, he then rehabilitates the role of human faith in Paul's soteriology via the category of participation with Christ, or representative Christology. One can see this rejection and rehabilitation in his conclusion about the contours of Pauline theology:

> Because justification hinges upon this action of Jesus Christ, upon an event *extra nos*, it is a terrible and ironic blunder to read Paul as though his gospel made redemption contingent upon our act of deciding to dispose ourselves toward God in a particular way. . . .

---

understanding of the *pistis Christou* passages" and a "broader understanding of *pistis*," that is, one that includes the idea of "faithfulness." David L. Stubbs, "The Shape of Soteriology and the *Pistis Christou* Debate," *SJT* 61, no. 2 (2008): 139.

54 For example, Schweitzer famously argued, "The doctrine of righteousness by faith is therefore a subsidiary crater, which has formed within the rim of the main crater—the mystical doctrine of redemption through the being-in-Christ." Albert Schweitzer, *The Mysticism of Paul the Apostle*, trans. William Montgomery (1931; repr., Baltimore: Johns Hopkins University Press, 1998), 225; for a fuller explanation, see 220–26.

55 The idea that we participate in Christ's faith was perhaps anticipated by Jan Henrik Sholten, the father of the Dutch critical school, in which several scholars argued that πίστις Χριστοῦ refers to Christ as the author of our faith. Schliesser, "Exegetical Amnesia," 80–81. Cf. Torrance's similar suggestion, based on his interpretation of Rom. 1:17, that we participate in God's faithfulness: "God draws man within the sphere of his own faithfulness and righteousness and gives man to share in it, so that his faith is embraced by God's faithfulness." T. F. Torrance, "One Aspect of the Biblical Conception of Faith," *ExpTim* 68, no. 4 (1956–1957): 113.

Does this mean that the human faith-response to God's action in Christ is insignificant for Paul? By no means! It does mean, however, that "faith" is not the precondition for receiving God's blessing; instead it is the appropriate mode of response to a blessing already given in Christ. As such, it is also the mode of participation in the pattern definitively enacted in Jesus Christ: as we respond in faith, we participate in an ongoing reenactment of Christ's faithfulness.[56]

The order is very important for Hays, as it is for Martyn. Christ is the one who lives by faith, and then we participate with him as we also live by faith.[57]

Other scholars make similar arguments. Ian Wallis rejects the idea that our faith can bring about salvation in Paul: "If Paul maintains that salvation is mediated by a Christian's faith, faith is in danger of becoming yet another meritorious 'work.'" Then Wallis senses the problem of undermining the believer's faith: "However, if salvation is wrought by the faith of Christ, where is the place for human response?" Finally, he solves this dilemma by rehabilitating faith via the category of participation: "Reflection upon the corporate and inclusive nature of Christ's humanity in Paul suggests that, although all faith ultimately originates in Christ, at the point of conversion believers participate in that faith and, in some sense, make it their own."[58] Douglas Campbell similarly rejects the "contractual" model of justification by faith in favor of a "christocentric" paradigm. In this paradigm Christ himself possesses belief, trust, and fidelity, and *then* "the Spirit enables

---

56 Hays, *Faith of Jesus Christ*, 211.

57 See, e.g., Hays, *Faith of Jesus Christ*, 203, 212–13. It must be noted that Hays is not saying that Jesus's faith is "merely exemplary, as in nineteenth-century liberal theology, but vicariously efficacious." *Faith of Jesus Christ*, 210. For an example of some early nineteenth-century German scholars who viewed Jesus's faith as primarily an example for us to follow, see Schliesser, "Exegetical Amnesia," 64–68.

58 Ian G. Wallis, *The Faith of Jesus Christ in Early Christian Traditions*, SNTSMS 84 (Cambridge: Cambridge University Press, 1995), 68–69.

them [Christians] to participate in Christ's [n.b.] prior and definitive 'possession' of these actions and characteristics."[59] N. T. Wright is an exception to the scholars we are discussing because he does not reject a role for our faith in justification. Still, we see a similar pattern in his adoption of the "faithfulness of Christ" translation and rehabilitation of our faith by means of the category of participation. After arguing for the "faithfulness of Christ" translation in Romans 3:22, he then anticipates that this view may seem to downplay our faith but does not actually downplay it at all. Rather, just as faithfulness (πίστις) marks out Jesus as the true Israelite, so faith (πίστις) becomes the badge that marks out his followers.[60]

Finally, we should consider the category of participation in Morna Hooker's presidential address to the Society for New Testament Studies, which argued that πίστις Χριστοῦ should be translated "faithfulness of Christ." Hooker never categorically rejects the idea that our faith is a means of justification in Paul. But she does prioritize the faith or faithfulness of Jesus over the role of human faith. It is important for her that Christ's faith comes first and that believers then share in his faith:

> What about the belief that *leads* to righteousness? Is it a case of believing in him, and so entering into Christ? Or is it rather that, because we are in him, we share in his faith? The former interpretation, which understands the phrase πίστις Χριστοῦ as an objective genitive ["faith in Christ"], throws all the emphasis on the believer's faith. The second interpretation throws the emphasis on the role of Christ: it is his obedience and trust in God which are crucial, though of course the response of the believer is necessary; the faith which leads to righteousness is a shared faith.[61]

---

59 Douglas A. Campbell, *The Quest for Paul's Gospel: A Suggested Strategy* (New York: T&T Clark, 2005), 200.
60 Wright, *Paul and the Faithfulness of God*, 839–40.
61 Hooker, "Πιστις Χριστου," 337.

Hooker makes it clear that the "faithfulness of Christ" translation does not mean that our faith is undermined or downplayed.[62] And yet her emphasis on Christ's faithfulness does initially deemphasize our faith and then quickly rehabilitates it via the category of participation in Christ's faith, a category she appeals to repeatedly: "To believe is to share in the faith of Christ himself."[63] And again: "Believing faith depends on the faith/faithfulness of Christ: it is the response to Christ's faith, and claims it as one's own."[64]

This emphasis on participation with Christ is one of the reasons that advocates of the "faithfulness of Christ" view often argue that πίστις has both a double meaning and a double referent in Paul.[65] It has a double meaning in that it can be defined as both "faithfulness" and "faith" at the same time. Thus, it is often translated with glosses like "faith(fulness)" or "faith/faithfulness." And it has a double referent in that it can refer to both Christ's faith(fulness) and to our faith at the same time. For example, Hays suggests,

> Because the Christian's life is a reenactment of the pattern of faithfulness revealed in Jesus, it is futile to ask, in a formulation such as ἵνα ἐκ πίστεως δικαιωθῶμεν ([Gal.] 3:24), *whose* faith is meant. It is of course "the faith of Jesus Christ," but it is also the faith of the Christian.[66]

---

62 Hooker states, "However we interpret the phrase πίστις Χριστοῦ, we shall in no way undermine the believer's answering response to the activity of God." And later she says, "This interpretation in no way plays down the importance of the believer's faith; what it does do is to stress the role of Christ." Hooker, "Πίστις Χριστου," 337, 342.

63 Hooker, "Πίστις Χριστου," 342; cf. 323, 338, 339, 341.

64 Hooker, "Πίστις Χριστου," 340.

65 My use of *meaning* and *referent* correspond with the distinction between *sense* and *reference* in the field of lexical semantics. The meaning/sense of the word is the "mental content called up by that symbol or word"; the referent is the "extra-linguistic reality to which the word points." Charles Lee Irons, *The Righteousness of God: A Lexical Examination of the Covenant-Faithfulness Interpretation*, WUNT, 2nd ser., vol. 386 (Tübingen: Mohr Siebeck, 2015), 62.

66 Hays, *Faith of Jesus Christ*, 203.

And Hooker concludes that "it may well be that the answer to the question 'Does this phrase [πίστις Χριστοῦ] refer to Christ's faith or ours?' may be 'Both.'"[67] Wright's view is much more nuanced but similar at points. He typically distinguishes between the meaning "faith" and "faithfulness" and between a reference to Jesus's faithfulness and our faith. For example, in Romans 3:22, he says that πίστις means Jesus's "faithfulness" and *not* his "faith."[68] Further, the phrase "faithfulness of Jesus Christ" refers to *Jesus's* faithfulness, whereas the next phrase, "for all who believe," refers to *our* faith.[69] Still, in at least one verse, Romans 3:26, he does suggest a double meaning and referent for πίστις:

> Perhaps the point of the final dense clause, *ton ek pisteōs Iēsou*, literally, "the one out of the faith[fulness] of/in Jesus," is precisely to run together the elements of 3.22, namely Jesus' own faithfulness as the act whereby redemption is achieved and the faith of the believer which becomes the badge of members in the Messiah's people. If this is correct, we could perhaps paraphrase as "everyone who shares in the faithfulness of Jesus."[70]

This idea that we participate in Christ's faithfulness through our own faith is perhaps one reason Wright typically chooses to transliterate the word πίστις rather than define it.

Summary

In this section, I have attempted to articulate the theological argument of the "faithfulness of Christ" translation: *Paul does not teach that we*

---

67 Morna D. Hooker, "Another Look at πίστις Χριστοῦ," *SJT* 69, no. 1 (2016): 62. It should be noted, though, that in this more recent article she continues to emphasize the priority of Christ's faith: "Nevertheless, that faith/faithfulness is primarily that of Christ, and we share in it only because we are in him." Hooker, 62.

68 Wright, *Paul and the Faithfulness of God*, 839.

69 Wright, *Paul and the Faithfulness of God*, 839. Similarly, in Gal. 2:16, "faithfulness of Jesus Christ" refers to Jesus's faithfulness, and "we also have believed in Christ Jesus" refers to our faith. N. T. Wright, *Pauline Perspectives: Essays on Paul, 1978–2013* (Minneapolis: Fortress, 2013), 539.

70 Wright, *Paul and the Faithfulness of God*, 845.

are justified by our faith in Christ but rather teaches that we are justified by Christ's faith(fulness). Richard Hays responded to Rudolf Bultmann's anthropological view of faith with a strong Christological view. The phrase πίστις Χριστοῦ, and often the word πίστις, refers not to our faith but to Christ's own faith or faithfulness as the means by which we are justified. This view has gained more rhetorical force through its association with the apocalyptic school of Pauline theology. Paul teaches that we are saved not by our action, whether our works or even our faith, but by God's action in the faithful death of Christ. This does not mean, however, that our faith is excluded entirely from Paul's theology, for as we subsequently believe, we ourselves participate in Christ's faith(fulness). This theological argument has not been adopted (or fully adopted) by everyone who holds to the "faithfulness of Christ" view.[71] Nevertheless, I have attempted to show that the theological argument is closely bound up with the new translation.[72]

The Influence of the Theological Argument

This theological argument is probably one of the reasons that the "faithfulness of Christ" translation of πίστις Χριστοῦ has taken hold now in a way it has not in previous generations. It is important to observe that the theological argument is not only a *conclusion from* the new translation but is often given as a *reason for* this new translation. The best example is Wallis's study of the faith of Christ in early Christian traditions. Again and again he appeals to the theological argument as the basis of his exegesis. For example, he argues that the most important

---

71 I have observed that N. T. Wright is an exception. Frank J. Matera is another exception; see *God's Saving Grace: A Pauline Theology* (Grand Rapids, MI: Eerdmans, 2012), 102–8.

72 This theological argument is also seen in some who adopted the "faithfulness of Christ" translation before Hays's dissertation. For example, Howard says that "Paul's argument distinguishes justification by man (including his works, faith, and any other conceivable human act) from justification by God. Justification for Paul is a pure act of grace which created unity among all nations under one God." George Howard, *Paul: Crisis in Galatia; A Study in Early Christian Theology*, SNTSMS 35 (New York: Cambridge University Press, 1979), 65.

reason we should interpret "the righteous shall live by faith" in Romans 1:17 as a reference to Jesus's faith is that Paul's soteriology prioritizes grace and God's faithfulness over against our righteousness. Thus, to take this clause as a reference to our faith would be a "meritorious understanding of faith."[73] Hung-Sik Choi also uses this reason to argue that even the phrase "faith working through love" in Galatians 5:6 refers to Christ's faithfulness: "It seems unlikely that human faith has soteriological power in Pauline theology. It is probable, therefore, that Christ's faithfulness is an eschatological and apocalyptic power."[74] And Preston Sprinkle views the priority of divine agency over human agency in salvation as the main reason he does not adopt the "faith in Christ" translation:

> Is a person's faith the means through which God's saving power is apocalyptically revealed? Does faith in Jesus manifest God's saving power, here at the turn of the ages (νυνὶ δὲ, Rom. 3:21)? While some of course say "yes," I thought (and still think) that this puts a tremendous amount of stress on the human agent in the event of God's cosmic act of redemption.[75]

This same line of reasoning is also found in some of the commentaries that support the "faithfulness of Christ" view:

> I conclude, not least because of where the emphasis lies in Paul's thought when he discusses justification (namely on the Godward side

---

73   Wallis, *Faith of Jesus Christ*, 79–80. For similar arguments, see 67, 75, 82–83, 89, 90, 92, 106, 108. Note his conclusion: "Paul is not . . . [attributing] salvific efficacy to one human response over another. If believers are righteous by faith, Jesus need not have been crucified." Wallis, 110–11.

74   Hung-Sik Choi, "Πίστις in Galatians 5:5–6: Neglected Evidence for the Faithfulness of Christ," *JBL* 124, no. 3 (2005): 483–84.

75   Preston M. Sprinkle, "Πίστις Χριστοῦ as an Eschatological Event," in Bird and Sprinkle, *Faith of Jesus Christ*, 166.

of things, not on the side of the human response), that the phrase "faith of Christ" is a shorthand allusion to the story of the faithful one who was obedient even unto death on the cross, and so wrought human salvation.[76]

Within Pauline theology, moreover, the *instrumental* use of "faith of Christ" . . . is most appropriately read as a divine rather than a human action: human faith is not itself the means of bringing about the righteousness "derived from God," but merely the mode of its reception. It is certainly only the work of Christ which is in any theologically significant sense instrumental to the righteousness of God.[77]

And I should not pass up an opportunity to quote Matlock's parody of this line of thought:

"How," comes the urgent protest, "could Paul place such weight on human faith (and all just to score his point)?" How could the divine power of justification—how the very revelation of the righteousness of God!—lie in doffing the mental cap in the appropriate direction, in cultivating the proper spiritual disposition?[78]

There is, however, a genuine pastoral concern bound up with this debate. Markus Barth has asked, "If Christ's own faith counted nothing, and if men were totally delivered to the sincerity, depth, certainty of their own faith—how could any man ever be saved?"[79] Hays observes that

---

76 Ben Witherington III, *Grace in Galatia: A Commentary on St. Paul's Letter to the Galatians* (Grand Rapids, MI: Eerdmans, 1998), 182.

77 Markus Bockmuehl, *The Epistle to the Philippians*, BNTC (Peabody, MA: Hendrickson, 1998), 211.

78 Matlock, "Detheologizing," 22.

79 Markus Barth, "The Faith of the Messiah," *Heythrop Journal* 10, no. 4 (1969): 368.

the issues pursued here are of serious significance for the church. I have grown increasingly convinced that the struggles of the church in our time are a result of its losing touch with its own gospel story. We have gotten "off message" and therefore lost our way in a culture that tells us many other stories about who we are and where our hope lies. In both the evangelical and the liberal wings of Protestantism, there is too much emphasis on individual faith-experience and not enough grounding of our theological discourse in the story of Jesus Christ.[80]

And Wright suggests that we as evangelicals "have tended to stand closer to Bultmann than we like to realize, with his emphasis on faith as experience unconnected with history" and "his existentialist call for decision."[81] Wright observes that many now look for assurance of their salvation in their feelings and lose assurance the second God seems remote.[82] The solution to this pastoral problem for many scholars is to see that our salvation rests not in our own faith but in the faithfulness of God and Christ, in our participation with Christ, and in this apocalyptic revelation of God's saving action. But is this what the apostle really taught?

Evaluation and Prospect

Most readers will have guessed that my answer to this question is no, but I want to stress that it is a qualified no. There are many points on which Hays and others are correct but on which they have taken their reasoning a step too far and obscured what the apostle actually teaches. The primary thesis of Hays's dissertation, that Paul's

---

80 Hays, *Faith of Jesus Christ*, lii.
81 Wright, *Pauline Perspectives*, 38. My experience supports Wright's suggestion: I once heard a well-known, conservative Southern Baptist leader explain that he had studied Bultmann in his seminary days and appropriated Bultmann's emphasis on faith as "decision" in his revivalistic preaching.
82 Wright, *Pauline Perspectives*, 38.

arguments build on the story (or better, history) of Jesus Christ, is correct.[83] The apocalyptic school's emphasis on the priority of God's gracious action in Christ surely resonates with the apostle who so closely associates Christ with God's grace (e.g., Gal. 1:6; 2:21; 5:4). Participation with Christ is one of the most important topics in Paul's letters.[84] And the apostle does speak about the faithfulness of both God (Rom. 3:3) and Christ (2 Tim. 2:13). The goal of this book is not to deny any place for apocalyptic, participation, or the faithfulness of God and Christ in the theology of Paul. I think, however, that advocates of the "faithfulness of Christ" view have overreached with their theological argument and significantly de-emphasized the role of Christ-oriented faith within Pauline theology.[85]

First, advocates of the "faithfulness of Christ" view have significantly de-emphasized Christ's role as the object of our faith in Paul's theology. In this view of Paul's most important explanations of justification (Rom. 3:21–26; Gal. 2:15–21; Phil. 3:2–11), the apostle does not use πίστις Χριστοῦ to speak of Christ as the object of our faith. Further, it is often said that Paul rarely speaks about Christ as the object of our faith outside these debated phrases.[86] This role of Christ has not been rehabilitated in the idea that we participate in the faith(fulness) of Christ because Jesus continues to be the subject rather than the object of faith in this theological construct. Thus, one goal of this study is

---

83 Hays demonstrates the story in Gal. 3:13–14 and 4:3–6, but the story of Jesus Christ can also be found in Rom. 1:3–4; 3:25; 8:3; 15:8; 1 Cor. 11:23–25; 15:3–8; 2 Cor. 8:9; and Phil. 2:6–9.

84 For example, Paul speaks about the believer participating with Christ in his death and resurrection (Rom. 6:1–11; Phil. 3:10–11), in his sufferings (2 Cor. 1:5; Phil. 3:10), in his humility (Phil. 2:5–11), in his righteousness (2 Cor. 5:21), and in his glory (Rom. 8:17). The question is whether he ever speaks of the believer participating in Jesus's *faith*.

85 Williams, himself an advocate of the "faithfulness of Christ" view, perceptively observes that "although Hays does acknowledge that the faith of Christians is an important component of Paul's thought, his consistent tendency is to undervalue the faith of believers in the interest of emphasizing the faith of Christ and the salvific function of the Christian proclamation." Sam K. Williams, "The Hearing of Faith: Ακοη Πιστεως in Galatians 3," *NTS* 35, no. 1 (1989): 89.

86 For examples, see the introduction to chap. 2, p. 104.

to ask whether and how the apostle speaks about Christ as the object of our faith.

Second, advocates of the "faithfulness of Christ" view have set in opposition two things that seem to be closely associated for the apostle—grace and faith (e.g., Rom. 4:16). It is fascinating that Hays's dissertation considered whether the solution to faith being a work might be that it is a gift from God. He observes that sensitive exegetes who have seen this difficulty typically answer that "faith is not a product of human will but of divine agency, that it is a gift planted in the human heart by God."[87] But he dismisses this solution as not found in the text of Galatians.[88] In contrast, Douglas Campbell affirms that faith is a gift in Paul's theology.[89] But in Campbell's understanding of "grace," salvation must be entirely unconditional so that justification by our faith would not actually be grace at all.[90] But is this Paul's understanding of grace?[91] As Moisés Silva has observed, if "faith in Christ" is compatible with gracious divine initiative, then "the main (theological) motivation for arguing that πίστις Ἰησοῦ Χριστοῦ refers to Christ's own faith(fulness) turns out to be a phantom."[92] Thus, another goal of this study is to adjudicate the relationship between faith, grace, and Christ in Paul's theology.

Finally, advocates of the "faithfulness of Christ" view have rejected the very idea that we are justified by (our) faith according to Paul's

---

87 Hays, *Faith of Jesus Christ*, 121. Hays cites Adolf Schlatter's classic study on faith in the New Testament as an example.

88 Hays, *Faith of Jesus Christ*, 122.

89 Campbell, *Quest*, 196.

90 Campbell, *Deliverance of God*, 27, 59.

91 Barclay's work is key here in analyzing different definitions, or "perfections," of grace. John M. G. Barclay, *Paul and the Gift* (Grand Rapids, MI: Eerdmans, 2015), 70–75. Campbell insists that grace must be, among other things, a pure gift with no necessary response (noncircular), while Paul emphasizes especially grace given to the undeserving (incongruity). Barclay, 171–73, 569.

92 Moisés Silva, "Faith versus Works of Law in Galatians," in *Justification and Variegated Nomism*, vol. 2, *The Paradoxes of Paul*, WUNT, 2nd ser., vol. 140 (Grand Rapids, MI: Baker Academic, 2004), 234. So Harrisville: "It is only because Richard Hays could not conceive of faith as a gift that he thought he was compelled to offer up a creative reading." Roy A. Harrisville III, *The Faith of St. Paul: Transformative Gift of Divine Power* (Eugene, OR: Pickwick, 2019), 104.

theology.[93] It is *not* by means of our faith in Christ but by means of Christ's own faith(fulness). While Hays was right to criticize Bultmann's anthropological view of faith, he overcorrected by shifting the focus of πίστις entirely to Christology. Must we throw out the baby of our faith with the bathwater of existentialism?[94] A final goal of this study is to reexamine the role our faith plays in justification and salvation in Paul's letters.

The positive thesis for which this book is arguing is that *Paul significantly emphasizes Christ-oriented faith in his theology.* In the opening of this chapter, I observed that Paul's eight πίστις Χριστοῦ phrases have important implications for his entire understanding of salvation. But the apostle also has so much to say about Christ-oriented faith *outside* these phrases. In fact, most of this book focuses on texts outside the debate. The first chapter explores the historical context of Paul's understanding of Christ-oriented faith. The second chapter considers direct statements of Christ-oriented faith in Paul's letters. And the third chapter examines conceptual parallels to Christ-oriented faith in Paul's letters. The fourth chapter then addresses the translational debate head-on, interacting deeply with Hays's influential argument. And the final chapter of the book provides a theological synthesis of Christ-oriented faith within Pauline theology.

---

93 Irons justly observes that "one begins to wonder whether the proponents of this view actually believe that faith is the instrument by which we rest upon and receive Christ in order to be justified." *Righteousness of God*, 333.

94 Gupta also observes in the context of this debate that "we must be careful not to sell human faith in Paul too short." *Paul and the Language of Faith*, 176; see also 186.

1

Paul's Understanding of Christ-Oriented Faith in Historical Context

Truly, I say to you, if you have faith, . . . even if
you say to this mountain, "Be taken up and thrown
into the sea," it will happen. And whatever you ask
in prayer, you will receive, if you have faith.

JESUS OF NAZARETH

SOMETIMES BIBLICAL SCHOLARS and theologians can get so caught up with the Bible's literary beauty or theological power that they fail to step far enough back and consider the historical probability of their arguments. Thus, before I begin my exegesis of Paul's letters, we consider the broader historical context of Christ-oriented faith within Pauline theology.

But how broad should we go? A study of historical background could be almost limitless and could easily go beyond the aim of this study and my ability to complete it.[1] Thus, I have restricted the scope of this chapter to a study of sources that Paul explicitly refers to in

---

1   See now the exhaustive study of the concept of faith in Greco-Roman literature, Jewish literature, and Christian literature by Teresa Morgan, *Roman Faith and Christian Faith:* Pistis *and* Fides *in the Early Roman Empire and Early Churches* (New York: Oxford University Press, 2015).

the course of his teaching about faith, specifically those that use the word πίστις or one of its cognates. I do not want to conflate the meaning of the word πίστις with the apostle's theology of faith.[2] But Paul almost invariably uses the noun πίστις or one of its cognates in his teaching about faith.[3] And he refers to many sources that make use of these words as well. These sources can help put his teaching about faith in context. They include the tradition of Jesus's teaching about mountain-moving πίστις, a tradition that Paul briefly alludes to in 1 Corinthians 13:2 and that we now have recorded in Matthew 21:20–22 and Mark 11:20–24 (cf. Matt. 17:20; Luke 17:6). But most important are the Old Testament passages that Paul directly quotes in his teaching about faith: Genesis 15:6; Psalm 116:10; Isaiah 8:14; 28:16; 53:1; Habakkuk 2:4.[4] The focus of this chapter is on these Old Testament quotations.

Some may wonder if I am putting the cart before the horse by focusing on Paul's use of the Old Testament as the background of his own theology. For it is often suggested that Paul's theology affected his interpretation of these texts rather than the other way around. Surely it is true that the apostle interpreted Scripture in light of his encounter with the risen Son of God (see 1 Cor. 9:1; 15:8; Gal. 1:15–16). But it is also evident that these texts had an influence on his teaching about faith.[5] He describes Abraham as "a man of faith" (Gal. 3:9) because of Genesis 15:6. He adopts the logic of Psalm 116:10 as a rationale for his own faith-driven preaching of the gospel: "Since we have the

2   Cf. James Barr's classic critique of this problem in Gerhard Kittel's massive *Theological Dictionary of the New Testament*, which organized its discussion of biblical theology around word studies. James Barr, *The Semantics of Biblical Language* (London: Oxford University Press, 1961), 206–62.

3   One notable exception is 2 Cor. 1:9, in which Paul uses the second perfect of πείθω to speak about his trust or reliance not on himself but on "God who raises the dead." Cf. also his use of πείθω in Phil. 1:14 and 2:24.

4   It is interesting to observe that Gen. 15:6; Isa. 28:16; and Hab. 2:4 are three of only ten texts that are cited more than once in Paul's letters.

5   So David M. Hay, "Paul's Understanding of Faith as Participation," in *Paul and His Theology*, ed. Stanley E. Porter, Pauline Studies 3 (Leiden: Brill, 2006), 49.

same spirit of faith according to what has been written, 'I believed, and so [διὸ] I spoke,' we also believe, and so [διὸ] we also speak" (2 Cor. 4:13). Paul describes Israel as having "stumbled over the stumbling stone" in unbelief (Rom. 9:32) because of Isaiah 8:14 and 28:16. And his understanding of gospel preaching and his own specific vocation to proclaim Christ where he has not been named shows the deep impact of Isaiah 52–53 on his thinking.[6] Perhaps even his well-worn phrase "by faith" was originally derived from Habakkuk 2:4, as many now suggest.[7]

Therefore, my study of the historical context of Paul's teaching about faith focuses on these Old Testament passages. But it also keeps an eye on the broader historical context, especially other Jewish texts that appeal to these same passages, for the sake of comparison and contrast.[8] I first examine the concept of faith in these sources, then the subject and object of faith, and finally the relationship of faith and salvation. My argument is that Paul's teaching about faith refers to sources that speak about our faith in God, and even Christ, as a cause and condition of salvation. First, though, I discuss the meaning of the word πίστις in Paul, since this is not only a linguistic question but also a historical question.

---

6   See Rom. 10:15, which cites Isa. 52:7; Rom. 10:16, which cites Isa. 53:1; and Rom. 15:20–21, which cites Isa. 52:15. At the end of his survey of Isaiah in Romans, Wagner concludes, "Although his appeals to Isaiah serve Paul's own rhetorical ends, Isaiah's words also significantly shape Paul's understanding of his Gospel and mission." J. Ross Wagner, "Isaiah in Romans and Galatians," in *Isaiah in the New Testament*, ed. Steve Moyise and Maarten J. J. Menken (London: T&T Clark, 2005), 129.

7   See, e.g., Douglas A. Campbell, "The Meaning of Πιστις and Νομος in Paul: A Linguistic and Structural Perspective," *JBL* 111, no. 1 (1992): 101.

8   I do not give attention to Greco-Roman sources, since it is unlikely that these significantly influenced the apostle's teaching about faith. Morgan's study concludes, "We cannot tell whether Paul's vision of the relationship between God, Christ, and humanity draws consciously on contemporary Graeco-Roman models of conciliation and mediation. What is clear is that it resonates with a wide range of common operations of *pistis* and *fides* in the world around him, and so may have been intuitively easy for first-century listeners, whether Greek, Roman, or Jewish, to understand." *Roman Faith and Christian Faith*, 305.

The Meaning(s) of Πίστις

The meaning of the noun πίστις is a key part of Paul's teaching about faith. I agree with James Barr that biblical theology is better understood by the interpretation of sentences than the meaning of individual words.[9] That is why most of this book and even most of this chapter is devoted to the study of sentences, paragraphs, and larger discourse units. The meaning of individual words, however, is still important, and the meaning of the word πίστις is particularly pivotal in the πίστις Χριστοῦ debate.[10]

Πίστις is a word that has multiple related meanings (i.e., it is polysemic).[11] It was used in a number of ways in wider Greek literature over time.[12] But in the New Testament it typically means (1) "faithfulness," (2) "faith," or (3) the "body of faith."[13] The latter two definitions correspond with Augustine's distinction between "that which is believed" (*fides quae*, definition 3) and "the faith by which it is believed" (*fides qua*, definition 2).[14] These two definitions are also closely related

9   Barr, *Semantics of Biblical Language*, 263.

10 Barr himself spends an entire chapter evaluating Gabriel Hebert's and T. F. Torrance's arguments that the word πίστις in Paul has a "Hebrew meaning" rather than a "Greek meaning." Barr, *Semantics of Biblical Language*, 161–205.

11 Some linguists argue that we should begin with the assumption that words have one meaning (i.e., we should have a "monosemic bias"); see, e.g., Charles Ruhl, *On Monosemy: A Study in Linguistic Semantics* (Albany, NY: State University of New York Press, 1989). But these scholars still acknowledge that *some* words are polysemic—for example, Ruhl grants that the English noun *orange* is polysemic. *On Monosemy*, 5. This point seems to be missing in the recent discussion of monosemy in David J. Downs and Benjamin J. Lappenga, *The Faithfulness of the Risen Christ: Pistis and the Exalted Lord in the Pauline Letters* (Waco, TX: Baylor University Press, 2019), 26–41.

12 See the many definitions given in LSJ (s.v. "πίστις"), including "trust," "good faith," "credit," "faith," "assurance," "means of persuasion," "that which is entrusted," "protection," and "safe conduct." It can even mean "mortgage"; James H. Moulton and George Milligan, *The Vocabulary of the Greek Testament* (1930; repr., Peabody, MA: Hendrickson, 1997), s.v. "πίστις." See also the extensive study of πίστις and its cognates by Dennis R. Lindsay, *Josephus and Faith: Πίστις and Πιστεύειν as Faith Terminology in the Writings of Flavius Josephus and in the New Testament*, AGJU 19 (Leiden: Brill, 1993).

13 These glosses are from the three uses given in the standard Greek lexicon for the New Testament. BDAG, s.v. "πίστις."

14 Augustine, *On the Holy Trinity*, 13.2.5, in Philip Schaff, ed., *Nicene and Post-Nicene Fathers*, vol. 3 (Grand Rapids, MI: Eerdmans, 1978). See chap. 5, p. 242, where I interact with Morgan's questions about Augustine's distinction.

to each other in that "the body of faith" (or "the faith") is an extension of "faith," objectivizing the action of faith so that it refers not to belief itself but to the object that is believed.[15] For this reason it is sometimes difficult in Paul's letters to know if πίστις means "faith" or "the faith." An example can be found in 1 Corinthians 16:13, where Paul urges the Corinthians to "stand ἐν τῇ πίστει."[16] Is he calling them to stand in "the faith" (ESV), meaning the gospel itself, or to stand in "your faith" (NRSV)? It is difficult to decide.[17]

"Faith," the second definition, is often further subdivided by modern interpreters into intellectual "belief" (believing *that*) and relational "trust" (trusting *in*).[18] But such a distinction, although valuable for heuristic purposes, is not found in the way πίστις is used in the New Testament.[19] One possible exception is James, who distinguishes between an intellectual belief *that* God is one and a genuine, saving faith that is accompanied by works (James 2:14–26). But the point of his distinction seems to be that such a "faith apart from works" is not really faith at all; it is "dead" (James 2:17, 26).[20] The definition of πίστις as "faith" includes both belief and trust in the New Testament and in Paul.

---

15 BDAG observes that this "objectivizing of the term πίστις is found as early as Paul"; s.v. "πίστις," use 3. For example, "He who used to persecute us is now preaching the faith [πίστιν] he once tried to destroy" (Gal. 1:23).

16 Other examples include Eph. 4:13; Phil. 1:25; Col. 1:23; 1 Tim. 3:13; 5:8; 6:12; 2 Tim. 2:18; 3:8.

17 Most commentators think Paul means "the faith." Anthony C. Thiselton, *The First Epistle to the Corinthians*, NIGTC (Grand Rapids, MI: Eerdmans, 2000), 1336.

18 For example, Wright gives a fourfold typology of "trust," "belief," "the faith," and "faithfulness." N. T. Wright, "Faith, Virtue, Justification, and the Journey to Freedom," in *The Word Leaps the Gap: Essays on Scripture and Theology in Honor of Richard B. Hays*, ed. J. Ross Wagner, C. Kavin Rowe, and A. Katherine Grieb (Grand Rapids, MI: Eerdmans, 2008), 483–84.

19 Wright observes that "both [belief and trust] belong together in central New Testament formulations." "Faith," 483. Morgan's much wider study concludes that trust is often deferred to belief, "such that trust and propositional belief are everywhere entwined." *Roman Faith and Christian Faith*, 508.

20 Ernest De Witt Burton notes, "In Jas. 2:14–22, it is true also that πίστις is used of a purely intellectual holding of a religious proposition. But this usage is quite exceptional in the N. T., and, moreover, the whole argument of this passage is aimed at showing that such faith is

The definition of πίστις that has been of most interest to New Testament scholars recently has been the first definition, "faithfulness." It has always been clear that the noun occasionally means "faithfulness" in Paul: "What if some were unfaithful? Does their faithlessness nullify the faithfulness [πίστιν] of God?" (Rom. 3:3). What is new is the suggestion that it means "faithfulness" much more often than we previously thought.[21] Closely related to this suggestion is the idea that the word often has a double meaning—that is, it means both "faith" and "faithfulness" at the same time. This was one of Hays's original points about πίστις Ἰησοῦ Χριστοῦ, that it "has more than one level of meaning."[22] By "more than one level of meaning" Hays is suggesting that πίστις has both a double meaning ("faith" and "faithfulness") *and* a double referent (Jesus's faith/faithfulness and our faith).[23] This is the same thing T. F. Torrance suggested in an early contribution to the debate:

> In most of these passages the *pistis Iesou Christou* does not refer only either to the faithfulness of Christ or to the answering faithfulness of man, but is essentially a polarized expression denoting the faithfulness of Christ as its main ingredient but also involving or at least suggesting the answering faithfulness of man, and so his belief in Christ.[24]

---

futile." *A Critical and Exegetical Commentary on the Epistle to the Galatians*, ICC 34 (Edinburgh: T&T Clark, 1921), 479.

21 For example, Bates now argues that πίστις means "faithfulness" or "allegiance" in Rom. 3:22, 25; 5:1; Gal. 2:16, 20; 5:6; Phil. 3:9. Matthew W. Bates, *Salvation by Allegiance Alone: Rethinking Faith, Works, and the Gospel of Jesus the King* (Grand Rapids, MI: Baker Academic, 2017), 80–82. One of his main reasons is that Paul's gospel presents Jesus as the Lord or King, a context that calls for allegiance. Bates, 82–83. Certainly, Paul's gospel proclaims Jesus as Lord, but does this necessitate a wholesale redefinition of πίστις and its cognates in Paul? See my interaction with his view in chap. 5 under my discussion of both Christology (p. 243n11) and anthropology (p. 254).

22 Richard B. Hays, *The Faith of Jesus Christ: The Narrative Substructure of Galatians 3:1–4:11*, 2nd ed. (Grand Rapids, MI: Eerdmans, 2002), 228.

23 Hays, *Faith of Jesus Christ*, 203.

24 T. F. Torrance, "One Aspect of the Biblical Conception of Faith," *ExpTim* 68, no. 4 (1956–1957): 113. Cf. Hooker: "I suggest that we should think of it [πίστις Χριστοῦ] not as a polarized expression, which suggests antithesis, but as a *concentric* expression, which begins, always, from the faith

Torrance's argument was based on his idea that Paul's word πίστις followed the "Hebrew meaning" of faithfulness or steadfastness. But this position was laid to rest by James Barr's criticism that Torrance had freighted his larger theological construct into the meaning of the word πίστις.[25]

Barr's critique led Hays to wisely steer clear of the idea that Paul follows the Hebrew meaning of the word.[26] It did not steer him away, however, from the conclusion that πίστις in Paul refers to both our faith *and* Christ's faithfulness. This means that Hays's definition of πίστις is really subject to the same criticism Barr leveled against Torrance. It freights the word πίστις with a larger theological concept. John Murray criticized Torrance on this point as well. He granted the theological point that our faith is connected with the faithfulness of God and Christ. He even granted the possibility that in Paul's phrase ἐκ πίστεως εἰς πίστιν (Rom. 1:17), the first use of πίστις could refer to God's faithfulness and the second to our faith (cf. also Rom. 3:22). If this translation were correct, then the entire phrase would speak of a "polarized" situation in which God's faithfulness leads to our faith. Murray, however, states that "in no instance would the term πίστις itself be a polarized *expression*—in one instance it would refer to God's or Christ's faithfulness and in the other to the faith of man, but in no instance to both at the same time."[27] Murray's point is that Torrance is wrong to argue for a double meaning and especially for a double referent in one use of the word πίστις.

We can illustrate the lexical problem of the double-meaning argument by considering the use of πίστις in Romans 3:3: "What if some were unfaithful? Does their faithlessness nullify the faithfulness

---

of Christ himself, but which includes, necessarily, the answering faith of believers, who claim that faith as their own." Morna D. Hooker, "Πιστις Χριστου," *NTS* 35, no. 3 (1989): 341.

25 Barr, *Semantics of Biblical Language*, 161–203.

26 Hays, *Faith of Jesus Christ*, 146–47.

27 John Murray, *The Epistle to the Romans*, NICNT (Grand Rapids, MI: Eerdmans, 1959), 1:373–74.

[πίστιν] of God?" Almost everyone agrees that πίστις in this verse refers to God's faithfulness.[28] And no one that I know of argues that it means both God's "faithfulness" and his "faith." Why not? Because it is evident that "faithfulness" and "faith" are two different meanings of the word. In Romans 3:3, πίστις refers to God's fidelity to the oracles of Scripture, not his faith. It is strange that scholars can see this distinction of meanings in verses like Romans 3:3 but will then argue that we should not distinguish between these meanings in verses like Romans 3:22. For example, Matthew Bates observes that in Romans 3:3, the word πίστις "does not refer to God's belief, faith, or trust in something. Rather it intends God's *faithfulness* or *fidelity* to his people." So far so good. But his very next sentence refuses to apply this same distinction in Romans 3:21–26: "By what right, then, can we exclude this fidelity nuance the very next time we encounter *pistis* language in Romans, at verse 3:21 and following?"[29] Is it not by the very same right by which Bates excludes the faith nuance from Romans 3:3? "Faithfulness" and "faith" are simply different meanings of the word in different contexts.[30]

Another interesting example is found in Philo, the first-century Jewish philosopher. Reflecting on Abraham's faith in Genesis 15:6, Philo says that "God marveling at Abraham's faith in Him [τῆς πρὸς αὐτὸν πίστεως] repaid him with faithfulness [πίστιν] by confirming with an oath the gifts which He had promised."[31] Hays has appealed to this text throughout the years to show that πίστις can refer to both our

---

28 For an odd exception, see Harrisville's suggestion that πίστις in Rom. 3:3 refers to human faith in God. Roy A. Harrisville III, *The Faith of St. Paul: Transformative Gift of Divine Power* (Eugene, OR: Pickwick, 2019), 61–62.

29 Bates, *Allegiance Alone*, 81.

30 Similarly, Gupta sees that words like παῖς have different meanings in different contexts ("servant" or "child") but then suggests that πίστις is "far more complex," so that the meanings "belief" and "faithfulness" are often "blended or indistinguishable in usage." Nijay K. Gupta, *Paul and the Language of Faith* (Grand Rapids, MI: Eerdmans, 2020), 12. This seems like special pleading.

31 Philo, *On Abraham*, §273. All English translations of this work are from Philo, *On Abraham*, trans. F. H. Colson, LCL 289 (Cambridge, MA: Harvard University Press, 1935).

faith and God's faithfulness in the same sentence.[32] But it is crucial to observe that *Philo uses the word* πίστις *two times in this sentence, with two different meanings and two different referents.* The first use means "faith" and refers to Abraham's trust in God (Gen. 15:6), and the second use means "faithfulness" and refers to God's corresponding confirmation of the gifts he had promised with an oath (Gen. 22:16). In other words, this example actually demonstrates that "faith" and "faithfulness" are two different meanings of the word with two different extralinguistic referents that correspond with one another—Abraham's faith and God's corresponding faithfulness. Philo's translator has clearly seen that the word is used in two different ways in one sentence.[33]

How, then, can we determine whether the noun πίστις means "faithfulness" or "faith" (or "body of faith") in Paul? We can do so in the same way that Philo's translator has determined its two meanings: by considering each use of the word in its context. One important linguistic point for this determination is that the verb πιστεύω typically means "to believe" and never means "to be faithful."[34] This often helps us adjudicate the meaning of the noun πίστις. For example, in 2 Corinthians 4:13, Paul says, "Since we have the same spirit of faith [πίστεως] according to what has been written, 'I believed [ἐπίστευσα], and so I spoke,' we also believe [πιστεύομεν], and so we also speak." Here Paul's use of the noun πίστις most likely refers to his faith rather than his faithfulness, because he says it is like the psalmist who said,

---

32 In his dissertation, see Hays, *Faith of Jesus Christ*, 176n42; in his debate with Dunn, see Hays, *Faith of Jesus Christ*, 279; in his introduction to the second edition, see Hays, *Faith of Jesus Christ*, xlv–xlvi.

33 Cf. Philo, *On the Change of Names*, 181–84, where Philo contrasts Abraham's wavering πίστις with God's, which is complete (note that even though πίστις technically occurs only once here, the repetition of the article, τὴν . . . τῆς . . . , assumes a second use of the word). The πίστις of Abraham and God are closely compared in this argument, and yet still the first refers to Abraham's belief according to Gen. 15:6 and the second to God's faithfulness according to Deut. 32:4.

34 See Kevin W. McFadden, "Does Πίστις Mean 'Faith(fulness)' in Paul?," *TynBul* 66, no. 2 (2015): 260. Thus, Bates is certainly wrong when he translates πιστεύω as "give allegiance" in Rom. 1:16 and in 1 Cor. 1:21 and 15:2. *Allegiance Alone*, 44, 82.

"I believe," and because he then goes on to say, "We believe." I want to clarify that this is not an argument from etymology or what is sometimes called the root fallacy. Rather, it is an argument from context.

Faith as a Concept

Second Corinthians 4:13 also introduces a linguistic point that is important to my discussion of the concept of faith in Paul's Old Testament quotations. In this verse Paul quotes from Psalm 116:10, a passage that uses the hiphil stem of אמן, translated by the Greek verb πιστεύω. Similarly to πιστεύω, the hiphil stem of אמן typically means "to believe, think, trust," whereas the niphal stem of this verb typically means "to be faithful, reliable, permanent."[35] Thus, there is a linguistic distinction between the meanings "believe" and "be faithful" embedded in the different forms of the Hebrew verb אמן.[36] The significance of this point for my study is that Paul's teaching about faith consistently refers to Old Testament passages that use the hiphil of אמן ("believe") and not the niphal ("be faithful").

Genesis 15:6

Genesis 15:6 is probably the most important text quoted by Paul in his teaching about faith, because it is the one Old Testament text about this topic that the apostle explains at length (in Rom. 4). In Hebrew this verse uses the hiphil stem of אמן to describe Abraham's faith: "And he believed [וְהֶאֱמִן] the LORD, and he counted it to him as righteousness." Paul quotes this verse in Romans 4:3 and Galatians 3:6 from the Septuagint: "And Abram believed [ἐπίστευσεν] God, and it was reckoned to him as righteousness" (Gen. 15:6 NETS).[37] The original

---

35 See *HALOT*, s.v. "אמן."

36 To say there is a distinction in meanings is not to say that there is no relationship between the two meanings. Note the wordplay between the hiphil and niphal forms of אמן in 2 Chron. 20:20 and Isa. 7:9.

37 We know that Paul quotes from the Septuagint because he includes the subject "Abraham," has "God" rather than "the Lord," and has the passive verb "it was counted" rather than the active verb "he counted," as appears in the Hebrew. The passive voice may be a result of translation

context of Genesis 15:6 describes Abraham's faith in the Lord as a response to God's promise that his offspring would be like the stars: "And he brought him outside and said, 'Look toward heaven, and number the stars, if you are able to number them.' Then he said to him, 'So shall your offspring be'" (Gen. 15:5). And Paul picks up on this context in his explanation of Genesis 15:6: "In hope he believed against hope, that he should become the father of many nations, as he had been told, 'So shall your offspring be'" (Rom. 4:18, citing Gen. 15:5). This understanding of Abraham's faith in Genesis 15:6 can be usefully compared and contrasted with the history of Jewish interpretation.[38]

One trajectory of interpretation sees this verse as referring to the patriarch's faithful obedience when he was tested in Genesis 22. This trajectory is probably rooted in Israel's postexilic confession that summarizes the Abraham narratives in this way:

> You are the LORD, the God who chose Abram and brought him out of Ur of the Chaldeans and gave him the name Abraham. You found his heart faithful before you, and made with him the covenant to give to his offspring the land of the Canaanite, the Hittite, the Amorite, the Perizzite, the Jebusite, and the Girgashite. And you have kept your promise, for you are righteous. (Neh. 9:7–8)

The statement "You found his heart faithful before you" is most likely an interpretation of Genesis 15:6 in light of Abraham's sacrifice of Isaac

---

or may represent a different Hebrew *Vorlage*; see the evidence mustered by Benjamin Schliesser, *Abraham's Faith in Romans 4: Paul's Concept of Faith in Light of the History of Reception of Genesis 15:6*, WUNT, 2nd ser., vol. 224 (Tübingen: Mohr Siebeck, 2007), 215–19. Note that Paul uses the later form "Abraham" rather than "Abram," as in the Septuagint, but that using the full name for earlier texts is a practice also seen in Josephus and Philo.

38 In what follows, I am indebted to Yeung's analysis of two strands of Jewish interpretation of Gen. 15:6, although I am taking her analysis in a slightly different direction. Maureen W. Yeung, *Faith in Jesus and Paul: A Comparison with Special Reference to "Faith That Can Remove Mountains" and "Your Faith Has Healed/Saved You,"* WUNT, 2nd ser., vol. 147 (Tübingen: Mohr Siebeck, 2002), 232–64, especially 263.

in Genesis 22. It uses the verb אמן, which occurs in the Abraham narratives only in Genesis 15:6, and the phrase "you found" likely refers to
the outcome of Abraham's test (cf. "now I know," Gen. 22:12).[39] Instead
of using the hiphil of אמן as Genesis 15:6 does, this interpretation uses
the niphal participle referring to Abraham's faithfulness. Here we see
that while there is a linguistic difference between "faith" (hiphil of אמן)
and "faithfulness" (niphal of אמן), there is also a conceptual overlap
between Abraham's faith and faithfulness in biblical theology. We will
see that some Jewish interpreters exploit this conceptual overlap, but
Paul argues against this line of interpretation.

One Jewish interpreter who was probably influenced by Nehemiah
was Jesus, son of Sirach, in the second century BC. In a hymn in honor
of the ancestors, he says the following about Abraham: "Abraham was
the great father of a multitude of nations, and no one has been found
like him in glory; he kept the law of the Most High and was taken into
covenant with him; he established the covenant in his flesh, and when
he was tested he was found faithful" (Sir. 44:19–20). The words "he
was found faithful" seem to depend on Nehemiah 9:8 ("You found
his heart faithful").[40] And the connection to Genesis 22 is stated more
explicitly as the time "when he was tested" (cf. "God tested Abraham,"
Gen. 22:1).[41] In Sirach we also see a focus on Abraham's obedience:
"He kept the law of the Most High" (cf. Gen. 26:5). This trajectory of
interpretation goes a step further in the last words of Mattathias, the
father of the Maccabees (1 Macc. 2:49–68). Mattathias urges his sons to

---

39 I am indebted to my colleague Gary Schnittjer for helping me think through Neh. 9:8. Yeung
    suggests that Neh. 9:8 is "either an interpretation of Gen 15:6 alone or a cumulative reading of
    Genesis 15, 17, and 22. On both views, Gen 15:6 is understood along the line of faithfulness."
    Faith in Jesus and Paul, 239.

40 Both have the Hebrew verb "find" (מצא) and the niphal participle of אמן. See Pancratius C.
    Beentjes, *The Book of Ben Sira in Hebrew: A Text Edition of All Extant Hebrew Manuscripts and a
    Synopsis of All Parallel Hebrew Ben Sira Texts*, VTSup 68 (Leiden: Brill, 1997), 78.

41 Cf. Jubilees, a second-century-BC retelling of Genesis and Exodus, which presents the sacrifice
    of Isaac as the culmination of many tests in which Abraham had proved his faithfulness (Jub.
    17:15–18; cf. 18:16; 19:8–9).

show zeal for the law and give your lives for the covenant of our fathers. Remember the deeds of the fathers, which they did in their generations; and receive great honor and an everlasting name. Was not Abraham found faithful when tested, and it was reckoned to him as righteousness? (1 Macc. 2:50–52)

Like Sirach, Mattathias's speech focuses on Abraham's obedience ("deeds of the fathers, which they did"), depends on the wording of Nehemiah 9:8 ("found faithful"), and explicitly associates Abraham's faithfulness with the test of Genesis 22 ("when tested"). But it goes beyond Sirach in forging a more direct link between the reckoning of righteousness in Genesis 15:6 and Abraham's great deed in the binding of Isaac. Abraham was reckoned righteous *because* of his faithfulness in testing.[42] This line of interpretation probably represents the perspective Paul argues against in Romans 4:2: "If Abraham was justified by works, he has something to boast about, but not before God. For what does the Scripture say? 'Abraham believed God, and it was counted to him as righteousness'" (Rom. 4:2–3).[43]

Another line of Jewish interpretation does not follow the wording of Nehemiah 9:8 but instead relies directly on the language of Genesis 15:6. Both Philo and James quote from the Septuagint of Genesis 15:6 and focus on Abraham's faith in God. Philo, for example, notes the importance of the statement "he trusted in God [ἐπίστευσε τῷ θεῷ]" in the conclusion of his biography of the patriarch.[44] Rather than interpreting this as a statement about Abraham's faithfulness, Philo contrasts faith in God with faith in lesser things like fame, riches, health, and human strength, reminding his readers of how

---

42 Schliesser observes, "The scenes of Gen. 15 and 22 are for the first time completely merged" in 1 Macc. 2:52. *Abraham's Faith*, 202. So Yeung, *Faith in Jesus and Paul*, 251.

43 So Yeung, *Faith in Jesus and Paul*, 263; Simon J. Gathercole, *Where Is Boasting? Early Jewish Soteriology and Paul's Response in Romans 1–5* (Grand Rapids, MI: Eerdmans, 2002), 244–46.

44 Philo, *On Abraham*, §262. See Schliesser for a discussion of Philo's many references to Gen. 15:6. *Abraham's Faith*, 203–11.

precarious it is to trust in things like fame.[45] This is not to say that Philo ignores the traditional link with the binding of Isaac in Genesis 22. He closes his discussion by saying that God repaid Abraham's faith with an oath, "By myself have I sworn," and observes that "Moses adds this crowning saying 'that this man did the divine law and the divine commands.'"[46] The apostle James also follows the traditional link between Genesis 15:6 and Genesis 22 (James 2:21–23). But like Philo, he does not speak of Abraham being found faithful when he was tested. In fact, James clearly distinguishes Abraham's faith in God and his works that brought that faith to completion: "You see that faith was active along with his works, and faith was completed by his works" (James 2:22).

This second line of interpretation is similar to Paul, even though both Philo and James highlight Abraham's works positively. Paul, like Philo and James, quotes Genesis 15:6 rather than following the wording of Nehemiah 9:8. He focuses on Abraham's faith in God rather than his faithfulness in testing. But unlike Philo and James, Paul ignores the traditional connection between Genesis 15:6 and Genesis 22.[47] Surely he does this because of his contrast between justification by faith and justification by works (cf. Rom. 4:4–5). Paul not only follows the second line of interpretation that focuses on Abraham's faith in God but also argues against the first line of interpretation that views Abraham as the one who faithfully obeyed God. Thus, one problem with viewing Abraham as a model of faithfulness in Paul (whether of Jesus's faithfulness, of our faithfulness, or both) is that it seems to be the very trajectory of interpretation that the apostle is arguing against in Romans 4.

---

45 Philo, *On Abraham*, §§263–68.
46 Philo, *On Abraham*, §273 (quoting Gen. 22:16), §275 (cf. Gen. 26:5). For Philo, Abraham obeyed the unwritten natural law and was himself a "law and an unwritten statute." Philo, 276.
47 Yeung follows Ferdinand Hahn in arguing that Paul "looses Gen 15:6 from the traditional tie with Genesis 22." *Faith in Jesus and Paul*, 265.

Psalm 116:10

Psalm 116:10 uses the hiphil of אמן to declare the psalmist's faith, or confidence, in God in the midst of great affliction:

> I believed [הֶאֱמַנְתִּי], even when I spoke:
>   "I am greatly afflicted";
> I said in my alarm,
>   "All mankind are liars." (Ps. 116:10–11)

The psalmist does not declare his own faithfulness to God in this situation but rather his confidence that God will continue to be faithful to him, even when people are unfaithful. John Goldingay comments that "the speaker had to be trustful because there was nowhere else to turn."[48] Paul himself resonates with the psalmist's faith in the midst of his own apostolic suffering and claims to have the same "spirit of faith [πίστεως]" (2 Cor. 4:13).[49] In the context of Paul's use of Psalm 116:10, πίστις must refer to his confidence in God. His citation follows the Septuagint, which has several differences.[50] Most important for our study is the fact that the Septuagint tightens the connection between the psalmist's faith and speaking, presenting his faith as the very reason he speaks: "I believed [ἐπίστευσα]; therefore [διὸ] I spoke" (Ps. 115:1 [116:10] NETS). Paul follows the psalmist in viewing his faith, or confidence, in God as the very reason he can continue to speak the truth of the gospel in the midst of suffering: "We also believe, and so [διὸ] we also speak"

---

48 John Goldingay, *Psalms*, vol. 3, *Psalms 90–150*, BCOTWP (Grand Rapids, MI: Baker Academic, 2008), 343.

49 Some take "spirit" as the Holy Spirit, who gives faith; see especially Gordon D. Fee, *God's Empowering Presence: The Holy Spirit in the Letters of Paul* (Peabody, MA: Hendrickson, 1994), 323–24. This is possible, but in context Paul seems to be highlighting that he has the same mindset or attitude of faith as the psalmist (cf. "spirit of gentleness," 1 Cor. 4:21).

50 One major difference is that the Septuagint Psalter splits Ps. 116 into two psalms: Ps. 116:1–9 = 114:1–9 LXX; Ps. 116:10–19 = 115:1–10 LXX (except that "praise the Lord" in 116:19 is part of 116:1 LXX).

(2 Cor. 4:13).[51] Paul's faith is his confidence that God remains faithful, as he says in his one other allusion to Psalm 116: "Does their faithlessness nullify the faithfulness of God? By no means! Let God be true though every one were a liar" (Rom. 3:3–4).[52]

Isaiah 28:16

Isaiah uses the hiphil of אמן four times, and Paul appeals to two of these uses.[53] More than anything, the prophet gives the apostle language to describe Israel's unbelief in the gospel. Isaiah 28:16 occurs in a judgment oracle against Jerusalem warning the scoffers who rule the city and take refuge in lies that God will soon come in righteous judgment to sweep away their refuge of lies like a flood (Isa. 28:14–29). The language is elusive but perhaps refers to their attempt to seek shelter in an alliance with Egypt for protection from the coming flood of Assyria (cf. Isa. 8:7–8; 30:1–7). In any case, it is clear that the rulers of Jerusalem are trusting in their own wisdom and plans to avert the disaster coming on the city (Isa. 28:14–15). It is also clear that their wisdom and planning will not stop God's incomprehensible deed of judgment (Isa. 28:17–29). In the midst of this warning of judgment, the Lord God solemnly declares that he will lay the foundation of Jerusalem, just as he had founded it before (cf. Isa. 14:32):

> Behold, I am laying as a foundation in Zion
>   a stone, a tested stone,

---

51 Lambrecht rightly observes that Paul's use of the first-person plural ("we," "us") in 2 Cor. 4:7–15 "is most likely literary and points to Paul himself, although one cannot exclude a reference to his co-workers." Jan Lambrecht, "A Matter of Method (II): 2 Cor. 4,13 and the Recent Studies of Schenck and Campbell," *ETL* 86, no. 4 (2010): 447n44. It cannot refer to Paul and his audience, because he makes a clear distinction between the two in 2 Cor. 4:12, 14, and 15. Lambrecht, 447n44.

52 The allusion is clearer in Greek: πᾶς ἄνθρωπος ψεύστης (Ps. 115:2 LXX [116:11]); πᾶς . . . ἄνθρωπος ψεύστης (Rom. 3:4).

53 Those two uses include Isa. 28:16 in Rom. 9:33 and 10:11; and Isa. 53:1 in Rom. 10:16. The other two uses are Isa. 7:9 and 43:10.

a precious cornerstone, of a sure foundation.

Whoever believes [הַמַּאֲמִין] will not be in haste. (Isa. 28:16)[54]

This declaration calls the leaders of Jerusalem to trust in God's plan for the deliverance of the city rather than in their own ingenious plans.[55] It promises salvation for the one who *believes*. Paul quotes from the Greek translation of this verse two times in the course of Romans 9:30–10:21. His first citation is merged with Isaiah 8:14 and refers to Israel's "stumbling" over Christ rather than believing in him (Rom. 9:33). His second citation borrows the word "all" (πᾶς) from Joel 2:32 and gives hope to both Jews and Gentiles: "Everyone who believes in him will not be put to shame" (Rom. 10:11). These citations translate the hiphil participle of אמן with the participle ὁ πιστεύων, referring to faith in the stone, God's plan for the deliverance of Jerusalem, rather than one's own plans.

Isaiah 53:1

Isaiah 52–53 speaks of the good news that the Lord will return and redeem Jerusalem through the suffering of his servant. This passage has significantly influenced Paul's understanding of the preaching of the gospel:

---

54 I have changed the ESV's "has laid" to "laying," taking יסד as a participle, as in the Qumran scrolls, rather than a piel perfect, as in the Masoretic Text (the Great Isaiah Scroll [1QIsaᵃ] has מיסד; 1QIsaᵇ has יוסד). Childs notes that normally the Hebrew particle for "behold" calls for a participle. Brevard S. Childs, *Isaiah: A Commentary*, OTL (Louisville: Westminster John Knox, 2001), 208. I have also removed the ESV's quotation marks around "Whoever believes will not be in haste," since it is not clear from context that this is an inscription in the stone. So Childs, *Isaiah*, 209.

55 Cf. Isa. 30:15–16:

> For thus says the Lord God, the Holy One of Israel,
> "In returning and rest you shall be saved;
>   in quietness and in trust shall be your strength."
> But you were unwilling, and you said,
> "No! We will flee upon horses";
>   therefore you shall flee away;
> and, "We will ride upon swift steeds";
>   therefore your pursuers shall be swift.

How then will they call on him in whom they have not believed? And how are they to believe in him of whom they have never heard? And how are they to hear without someone preaching? And how are they to preach unless they are sent? As it is written, "How beautiful are the feet of those who preach the good news!" But they have not all obeyed the gospel. For Isaiah says, "Lord, who has believed what he has heard from us?" (Rom. 10:14–16, quoting Isa. 52:7; 53:1)

In Isaiah 53:1, the prophet laments that many have not believed this good news, and he uses the hiphil of אמן to speak of this unbelief. Here belief or unbelief is a response to the gospel message of the prophet. Paul follows the Septuagint's literal translation of the Hebrew text, which uses the verb πιστεύω.[56] His quotation of Isaiah 52:7 is looser and changes the singular participles of the Masoretic Text and the Septuagint into plurals in order to refer to the many who are now sent to preach the gospel. Thus, it seems likely that Paul also interprets the "us" in Isaiah 53:1 as a reference to the many who proclaim the good news like Isaiah and himself.[57] Isaiah's prophecy confirms for Paul both that the gospel must be proclaimed and that not all will believe its proclamation. In other words, Isaiah 53:1 gives Paul a category for Israel's unbelief.[58]

The word ἀκοή ("what is heard") in the Septuagint translation of Isaiah 53:1 has also influenced Paul's conclusion in Romans 10:17: "So faith comes from hearing [ἀκοῆς], and hearing [ἀκοή] through the word of Christ." In this conclusion, ἀκοή could mean the act of

---

56 The Septuagint also specifies the addressee of the prophet's complaint by adding the word "Lord" (κύριε).

57 See J. Ross Wagner, *Heralds of the Good News: Isaiah and Paul in Concert in the Letter to the Romans* (Leiden: Brill, 2003), 173, 179–80. Oswalt comments that "the prophet is probably identifying himself with his people and speaking for them." John N. Oswalt, *The Book of Isaiah, Chapters 40–66*, NICOT (Grand Rapids, MI: Eerdmans, 1998), 381.

58 The context of Rom. 10:16 makes it likely that Paul is thinking specifically of Israel's unbelief. So Wagner, *Heralds*, 178.

"hearing" (ESV) or the object of hearing ("what is heard," NRSV), just as πίστις can mean the act of faith ("believing") or the object of faith ("body of faith"). In Paul's citation of Isaiah 53:1 (Rom. 10:16), ἀκοή clearly means "what is heard," so perhaps it should be translated this way in Romans 10:17 as well. On the other hand, it seems like a tautology to say "what is heard comes through the word of Christ" (i.e., what is heard comes by what is heard), so perhaps we should understand ἀκοή in Romans 10:17 to mean the "act of hearing" that comes about when someone hears the word of Christ.[59] This translation also fits the context in which believing follows from hearing, which follows from preaching (Rom. 10:14–16).[60]

But in either case, Isaiah 53:1 has clearly influenced the language of Romans 10:17, which probably means that it has also influenced the similar phrase ἐξ ἀκοῆς πίστεως in Galatians 3:2 and 5. This phrase is an important piece of evidence in Hays's Christological understanding of πίστις, which I address in chapter 4.[61] Here I simply observe that Isaiah 53:1 speaks about faith (or unbelief) as the response to the gospel that has been proclaimed and heard.

Habakkuk 2:4

Each of the passages we have examined so far uses the hiphil stem of the verb אמן, translated with the verb πιστεύω. But in Habakkuk 2:4, which Paul quotes in Romans 1:17 and Galatians 3:11, we find the noun אֱמוּנָה, translated with the noun πίστις in Paul. Whereas πίστις can mean "faith" or "faithfulness" depending on its context, אֱמוּנָה typically means "steadfastness" or "faithfulness," in line with the niphal stem of אמן ("to be faithful"). B. B. Warfield suggests that Habakkuk 2:4 is

---

59 Cf. the use of ἄγρα in Luke 5, which means the act of catching (fish) in 5:4 and then the object that was caught in 5:9.

60 So Williams, who also notes the cognate verb in the following verse: "Have they not heard [ἤκου-σαν]?" (Rom. 10:18). Sam K. Williams, "The Hearing of Faith: Ακοη Πιστεως in Galatians 3," *NTS* 35, no. 1 (1989): 84–85.

61 See chap. 4, p. 202.

the only place in the Old Testament that requires the word to mean "faith."[62] But the standard Hebrew lexicons do not even list the definition "faith" as a possible rendering.[63] Thus we must question whether it is special pleading to argue that אֱמוּנָה means "faith" in Habakkuk 2:4.

Richard Longenecker, an advocate of the "faithfulness of Christ" translation, says that the word πίστις in Paul's debated πίστις Χριστοῦ phrases should be read "in terms of the Hebrew noun אמונה, *'emûnâh*, which includes the nuances of both 'faith' and 'faithfulness.'"[64] The problem with this argument is that the Hebrew noun does not have the double meaning "faith" and "faithfulness." For example, it does not mean "faith" and "faithfulness" when David prays,

> Hear my prayer, O LORD;
>> give ear to my pleas for mercy!
>> In your faithfulness [בֶּאֱמֻנָתְךָ] answer me, in your righteousness!
>> (Ps. 143:1)

Or when Jeremiah calls to mind his confession about the Lord:

> Great is your faithfulness [אֱמוּנָתֶךָ]. (Lam. 3:23)

Or when Isaiah says of the Messiah,

> Righteousness shall be the belt of his waist,
>> and faithfulness [הָאֱמוּנָה] the belt of his loins. (Isa. 11:5)

---

62 Benjamin Breckinridge Warfield, "Faith," in *Biblical and Theological Studies* (Philadelphia: Presbyterian and Reformed, 1952), 431.

63 *HALOT*, s.v. "אֱמוּנָה." BDB lists the definition "faithfulness, trust." BDB, s.v. "אֱמוּנָה." But in this context the English word "trust" means not "faith" or "belief" but the quality of being "trustworthy." See *Oxford English Dictionary*, s.v. "trust, *n*.," use 2.

64 Richard N. Longenecker, *The Epistle to the Romans*, NIGTC (Grand Rapids, MI: Eerdmans, 2016), 410. He makes the same argument in Richard N. Longenecker, *Galatians*, WBC 41 (Dallas, TX: Word Books, 1990), 87.

Rather than suggesting a double meaning, we must choose the best meaning of the word in its context. The word typically means "faithfulness," which is how several English translations render it in Habakkuk 2:4.[65] If this is correct, then the prophet's meaning is that the righteous person is faithful to God in contrast with the arrogant pride of the Chaldeans or Babylonians, who had been raised up to destroy Jerusalem.

The translator of Habakkuk in the Septuagint probably also understood אֱמוּנָה to mean "faithfulness," although instead of seeing a reference to the righteous person's faithfulness, it is taken as a reference to God's faithfulness. The Hebrew has a third-person suffix: "by his faithfulness" (בֶּאֱמוּנָתוֹ). But the Greek translation has a first-person pronoun: "by my faithfulness" (ἐκ πίστεώς μου).[66] This was probably a simple error of sight by the Greek translator. It would be easy to mistake a *waw* (וֹ, "his") for a *yod* (י, "my"), and it is not uncommon for the translator of Habakkuk 1–2 to have different pronouns than the Hebrew text.[67] In any case, the Septuagint translation probably lends more credence to the idea that Habakkuk is making a statement about "faithfulness," though the Septuagint wrongly sees a reference to God's faithfulness rather than to human faithfulness. The righteous person will live as God is faithful to judge the wicked and deliver his people.[68]

---

65 E.g., NET, NIV 2011. The ESV, NASB, and NRSV list "faithfulness" as a marginal reading. Cf. the CEB: "The righteous person will live honestly."

66 Note that a few have taken the translation of ἐκ πίστεώς μου to mean "by faith in me"; e.g., Charles Lee Irons, *The Righteousness of God: A Lexical Examination of the Covenant-Faithfulness Interpretation*, WUNT, 2nd ser., vol. 386 (Tübingen: Mohr Siebeck, 2015), 305. But this seems unlikely when one considers the typical meaning of אֱמוּנָה.

67 Examples include μου (1s) for the 3ms suffix in Hab. 1:11 (the example most like 2:4), αὐτά (3np) for a 3ms suffix in 2:2, αὐτόν (3ms) for a 2ms suffix in 2:7, and σε (2s) for a 3fp suffix in 2:17. Typically, however, the translator renders the suffixes of the Hebrew text correctly. Note that it is likely that a different person translated Hab. 3 in the Septuagint; see the preface to the Twelve Prophets in NETS.

68 Note that we have also discovered a fragmentary Greek translation of the Minor Prophets (8HevXIIgr) that is independent of the Septuagint tradition and reads ἐν πίστει αυτοῦ in Hab. 2:4. See Joseph A. Fitzmyer, *To Advance the Gospel: New Testament Studies*, 2nd ed. (Grand

Perhaps it is possible that אֱמוּנָה, which typically means "faithfulness," simply means "faith" in Habakkuk 2:4, in line with the hiphil stem of אמן.[69] There was no other Hebrew noun available to mean "faith."[70] And this translation makes good sense of the context in Habakkuk. The prophecy divides rather neatly into Habakkuk's two complaints (Hab. 1:1–11; 1:12–2:20) and Habakkuk's confession of faith (Hab. 3:1–19).[71] The first complaint about wickedness in Israel is answered with a call to faith in the Lord's unbelievable work, using the hiphil of אמן. The Lord will certainly punish the violence and injustice of Judah but in an astonishing way:

> Look among the nations, and see;
>> wonder and be astounded.
> For I am doing a work in your days
>> that you would not believe [לֹא תַאֲמִינוּ] if told.
> For behold, I am raising up the Chaldeans,
>> that bitter and hasty nation,

Rapids, MI: Eerdmans, 1998), 240–41; Desta Heliso, *Pistis and the Righteous One: A Study of Romans 1:17 against the Background of Scripture and Second Temple Jewish Literature*, WUNT, 2nd ser., vol. 235 (Tübingen: Mohr Siebeck, 2007), 59–61. Paul is clearly not dependent on this separate tradition.

69 Some think that the interpretation, or pesher, of Hab. 2:4 in the famous Qumran Habakkuk commentary (1QpHab) understands אֱמוּנָה as "faith" in the Teacher of Righteousness because it provides an object with the preposition בְ; e.g., Barr, *Semantics of Biblical Language*, 202. This seems possible since the pesher on Hab. 1:5 says that the verse speaks of those "who will not believe when they hear all that is going [to happen t]o the final generation, from the mouth of the Priest whom God has placed wi[thin the Commun]ity." 1QpHab, 2.6–8, in *The Dead Sea Scrolls Study Edition*, ed. Florentino García Martínez and Eibert J. C. Tigchelaar (Leiden: Brill, 1997), 1:13. But this preposition could just as likely present the Teacher of Righteousness as the object of their "faithfulness" or "loyalty." Cf. Ps. 78:37, which uses the niphal of אמן with בְ: "They were not faithful to his covenant [נֶאֶמְנוּ בִּבְרִיתוֹ]." I am indebted to Bruce Clark for this reference.

70 Barr calls this "the most important fact in this whole question [about the meaning of 'faith'], and one which is almost entirely ignored by both Hebert and Torrance: Hebrew usage, as far as the Old Testament evidence shows (with some possible qualification for Hab. 2:4), had developed no substantive meaning 'believing, faith' to correspond with its well known verb . . . 'trust, believe' [the hiphil of אמן]." *Semantics of Biblical Language*, 201.

71 Yeung, *Faith in Jesus and Paul*, 200.

who march through the breadth of the earth,

to seize dwellings not their own. (Hab. 1:5–6)

Habakkuk's second complaint about how God can rightly punish Israel with a more wicked nation is answered by a judgment oracle against Babylon.[72] In the introduction to this answer, Habakkuk is found waiting at his post for an answer, and he is told that the revelation awaits the end of time and that it "will not lie. / If it seems slow, wait for it; / it will surely come; it will not delay" (Hab. 2:3). The point seems to be a message of assurance: "Habakkuk, you can trust the vision." Thus, it makes good sense in context that Habakkuk 2:4 refers to the righteous person living by "faith" in the prophetic word of God as he awaits its fulfillment.[73] In fact, this is exactly what Habakkuk resolves to do in his final prayer (Hab. 3:16).[74]

Even if אֱמוּנָה means "faithfulness" in Habakkuk 2:4, however, it is still more likely that Paul understood the word to mean "faith." It is important to observe that Paul has chosen to *not* follow the Septuagint in his citation of Habakkuk 2:4. I have observed that the Septuagint has the first-person pronoun, "by my faithfulness," whereas the Hebrew has the third-person pronoun, "by his faithfulness." Paul has decided to leave the pronoun out of his two citations. Why? Most likely because he knew the translation problem in the Septuagint and did not follow it in seeing a reference to God's faithfulness.[75] Rather, the immediate contexts of Paul's citations of

---

72 Seen in the fivefold "woe" of Hab. 2 (vv. 6, 9, 12, 15, 19).

73 Watson helpfully observes that Hab. 2:4 formalizes the waiting of Hab. 2:3 (although he translates אֱמוּנָה as "faithfulness"). Francis Watson, *Paul and the Hermeneutics of Faith*, 2nd ed. (New York: Bloomsbury T&T Clark, 2016), 143.

74 Note as well how the wicked Chaldeans (Babylonians) are depicted as worshiping their strength (Hab. 1:11), sacrificing to their dragnets by which they capture the nations (Hab. 1:16), and trusting (בטח) in their idols instead of in the Lord (Hab. 2:18–20).

75 Compare Paul's rendering with the approach of the author of Hebrews, who apparently moves the pronoun "my" (μου) in the Septuagint so that it does not modify "faith" but rather

Habakkuk 2:4 use the verb πίστευω, indicating that the apostle understood אֱמוּנָה/πίστις as a reference to our faith.[76] In Romans 1:16–17, Paul quotes Habakkuk 2:4 as part of the ground of his claim that the gospel is "the power of God for salvation to everyone who believes [τῷ πιστεύοντι]" (Rom. 1:16). And in Galatians 3:6–7, he associates the ἐκ πίστεώς principle of Habakkuk 2:4 with Abraham's faith in God: ". . . just as Abraham 'believed [ἐπίστευ-σεν] God. . . .' Know then that it is those of faith [ἐκ πίστεως] who are the sons of Abraham" (Gal. 3:6–7; cf. 3:11). Thus it seems likely that Paul understood Habakkuk's statement about the role of πίστις in salvation to be a reference to our faith.

There is one other clue we have to the apostle's understanding of Habakkuk 2:4. According to Acts, Paul quoted Habakkuk 1:5 in his sermon at Pisidian Antioch (Acts 13:13–43). This sermon concludes with a call for faith and a warning about unbelief:

Let it be known to you therefore, brothers, that through this man forgiveness of sins is proclaimed to you, and by him everyone who believes [πᾶς ὁ πιστεύων] is justified from everything from which you could not be justified by the law of Moses. Beware, therefore, lest what is said in the Prophets should come about:

"Look, you scoffers,
  be astounded and perish;
for I am doing a work in your days,
  a work that you will not believe [οὐ μὴ πιστεύσητε], even if
    one tells it to you." (Acts 13:38–41)[77]

"righteous one": "But my righteous one will live by faith" (ὁ δὲ δίκαιός μου ἐκ πίστεως ζήσεται, Heb. 10:38).

76 Fitzmyer similarly suggests that Paul omitted the word "my" (μου) "because of the sense in which he wanted *pistis* to be understood." *To Advance the Gospel*, 242.

77 I have adopted the ESV's marginal translation of the verb δικαιόω in Acts 13:38 and 13:39, "justified," rather than "freed," since "justified" is the normal translation of the verb and most likely Paul's meaning.

The warning about unbelief is a loose citation from the Septuagint of Habakkuk 1:5, which translates the hiphil of אמן with the verb πι-στεύω. Here the apostle understands Habakkuk's warning about God's judgment in the exile as a foreshadowing of his judgment of those who reject Christ. What God has done in Christ is so astonishing that Israel will not believe that God has done it, even though Paul is telling them. This clue makes it more plausible that Paul also understood Habakkuk 2:4 to be calling readers to faith in God's unbelievable work of judgment and salvation, although it is not as important as the immediate context of Paul's citations in Romans 1 and Galatians 3.

Has Paul misquoted the prophet? Joseph Fitzmyer argues that Paul "fills that word [πίστις] with his own Christian meaning of 'faith.'"[78] Others suggest that the concepts of faith and faithfulness overlap so much that Paul has not misquoted the text.[79] It is true that the concept of faithfulness and faith overlap, as we saw in Nehemiah 9:8's interpretation of Genesis 15:6: Abraham's faith in God resulted in his being found faithful when he was tested.[80] It is also true that Paul calls people to both faith and faithful obedience. But this conceptual solution still faces the problem that Paul has a different meaning of the word אֱמוּנָה/πίστις from that generally assumed to be in Habakkuk 2:4, since the word means "faithfulness" in

---

78 Fitzmyer, *To Advance the Gospel*, 242.

79 For example, Watson says, "Within the text of Habakkuk, there is no faithfulness without what Paul and the [Qumran] pesherist call 'faith'—just as, for Paul, there is no faith without faithfulness. If 'faith' has been substituted for 'faithfulness' in the citation of Habakkuk 2.4, the semantic loss is minimal." *Hermeneutics of Faith*, 148; so Moisés Silva, "Galatians," in *Commentary on the New Testament Use of the Old Testament*, ed. G. K. Beale and D. A. Carson (Grand Rapids, MI: Baker, 2007), 802; Thomas R. Schreiner, *Romans*, 2nd ed., BECNT (Grand Rapids, MI: Baker Academic, 2018), 80–81. Seifrid has a different spin on this approach because he sees Hab. 2:4 as a reference to the faithfulness of the prophecy/God. And yet Paul has not misquoted the prophet because "faith has its source in the faithfulness of God who promises and fulfills." Mark A. Seifrid, "The Faith of Christ," in *The Faith of Jesus Christ: Exegetical, Biblical, and Theological Studies*, ed. Michael F. Bird and Preston M. Sprinkle (Peabody, MA: Hendrickson, 2009), 140.

80 Note that Keil appeals to Neh. 9:8's interpretation of Gen. 15:6 to argue that אֱמוּנָה in Hab. 2:4 combines the niphal and hiphil meanings of אמן. Carl Friedrich Keil, *The Twelve Minor Prophets*, trans. James Martin (Grand Rapids, MI: Eerdmans, 1954), 2:73.

Habakkuk 2:4 and "faith" in Paul's citations of Habakkuk 2:4. It seems more consistent to argue that perhaps אֱמוּנָה actually does mean "faith" in Habakkuk 2:4, both for the reasons mentioned above and because of the apostle's own interpretation of this verse.

Even if I am wrong, however, about the meaning of אֱמוּנָה/πίστις in Habakkuk 2:4 and Paul's citations, we should be careful about putting too much weight on this one verse. Many appeal to this verse to argue for the importance of Christ's faithfulness or our faithfulness in Paul's theology. But no matter what אֱמוּנָה/πίστις means in this verse and its citations, it should not overwhelm the more important point that all the other Old Testament texts referred to in Paul's teaching about faith use the hiphil of the verb אמן ("believe").

Jesus's Teaching

Paul rarely appeals directly to Jesus's teaching, but his first letter to the Corinthians contains several direct references to the teaching of the Lord (1 Cor. 7:10; 9:14; 11:23–25). This fact combined with the verbal resemblance of 1 Corinthians 13:2 and Jesus's teaching about mountain-moving faith make it likely that Paul was influenced by this tradition now recorded in Mark 11:20–24 // Matthew 21:20–22 (cf. also Matt. 17:20 // Luke 17:6):[81]

> If I have all faith [ἐὰν ἔχω πᾶσαν τὴν πίστιν], so as to remove mountains [ὄρη] . . . (1 Cor. 13:2)

> If you have faith [ἐὰν ἔχητε πίστιν] like a grain of mustard seed, you will say to this mountain [τῷ ὄρει τούτῳ], "Move from here to there," and it will move. (Matt. 17:20)

---

81 Yeung, *Faith in Jesus and Paul*, 30–31. Yeung surveys many other suggested parallels but concludes that outside Jesus and Paul, only two texts combine mountain removal with faith (Zech. 4:6–7; Josephus, *Jewish Antiquities*, 2.333). Yeung, 21–30. Even the similar sayings of Jesus about mountain moving in the gnostic Gospel of Thomas (vv. 48, 106) do not connect mountain removal with faith.

Have faith [ἔχετε πίστιν] in God. . . . Whoever says to this mountain [τῷ ὄρει τούτῳ], "Be taken up and thrown into the sea" . . . (Mark 11:22–23)

Jesus's teaching about faith in Mark 11:20–24 // Matthew 21:20–22 is really teaching about prayer. His call for "faith" (Matt. 21:21) or "faith in God" (Mark 11:22) is a call to believe God in prayer: "And whatever you ask in prayer, you will receive, if you have faith" (Matt. 21:22); "Therefore I tell you, whatever you ask in prayer, believe that you have received it, and it will be yours" (Mark 11:24). In another version of this tradition, Jesus rebukes his disciples for their "little faith." He apparently means their total lack of faith, because he goes on to say, "For truly, I say to you, if you have faith like a grain of mustard seed, you will say to this mountain, 'Move from here to there,' and it will move, and nothing will be impossible for you" (Matt. 17:20).[82]

Paul seems to know both the mustard-seed and the mountain-moving aspects of Jesus's teaching. He exaggerates both these aspects in 1 Corinthians 13:2 when he speaks about "all faith" (rather than mustard-seed faith) and a faith that removes not only one mountain but many mountains.[83] The apostle's point is actually about love: even if someone has such exaggerated faith, he or she is nothing without love. But Paul relies on Jesus's teaching about faith that describes it as believing or trusting in God that he will answer our prayers.[84]

Summary

We have seen that most of the sources Paul references in his teaching about faith describe various aspects of faith (and not faithfulness).

---

82   In the parallel saying in Luke 17:6, mountain-moving faith is changed to faith that can uproot a mulberry tree and plant it in the sea.

83   Here I am indebted to Yeung's observation of Paul's hyperbole. *Faith in Jesus and Paul*, 49.

84   Note also that πίστις in Mark 11:22 // Matt. 21:21 is defined with the verb πιστεύω in Mark 11:23 // Matt. 21:22.

This is true at the linguistic level in that most of these texts use the hiphil (rather than the niphal) stem of אמן, which is translated in the Septuagint and Paul with πιστεύω ("believe"). The Jesus tradition uses the same verb to explain Jesus's teaching about mountain-moving faith. The one exception to this linguistic pattern is Habakkuk 2:4, which uses the noun אֱמוּנָה, translated with πιστίς in the Septuagint and Paul. This Hebrew noun typically means "steadfastness" or "faithfulness," and thus there is strong reason to translate it so here. But it is possible to translate it as "faith," and Paul seems to understand it this way. Beyond the linguistic level, we have seen that faith is described as belief or trust in God's promise (Gen. 15:6); confidence in God's faithfulness in the midst of suffering (Ps. 116:10); trust in God's saving plan rather than one's own (Isa. 28:16); a response to the preaching of the gospel, which many have not given (Isa. 53:1); waiting for the fulfillment of God's unbelievable, prophetic word (Hab. 2:4, probably); and trusting in God to answer prayer (Jesus's teaching). We also observed that Romans 4 seems to be arguing against an interpretive trajectory that merged Genesis 15:6 with Genesis 22 and focused on Abraham's faithful obedience when he was tested. Thus, the concept of faith captures Paul's understanding of these passages much better than the concept of faithfulness.[85] But whose faith, confidence, waiting, and so on is in view in these texts? The next section considers whether these texts refer to our faith or the faith of the Christ.

Faith's Subject and Object

Teresa Morgan has observed that Greco-Roman literature speaks much more often about faith between fellow human beings than the Septuagint and especially the New Testament do.[86] Scripture typically speaks of faith as a part of the divine-human relationship in which

---

85 This is not to deny that faith results in faithful obedience in Paul and biblical theology more broadly (e.g., Neh. 9:8).

86 Morgan, *Roman Faith and Christian Faith*, 187, 205, 209–10, 215, 217–18, 255–56, 278.

people (the subject) trust in God (the object).[87] I argue in this section that all the passages Paul appeals to in his teaching about faith reflect this pattern. One theological issue that makes the πίστις Χριστοῦ debate interesting and complex, however, is the incarnation, the reality that Jesus Christ is both human and divine. This means that we must ask whether Paul sees in these passages a reference to Jesus Christ as a human being who trusted in God or to Jesus Christ as God, who is worthy of our trust—or to Jesus Christ as both. Related to this is the question whether the Old Testament speaks at all about the Christ as the object of our faith. Martyn suggests that "as far as we know, there is no Jewish background for the expression 'to believe in the Messiah'" and that this idea arose as a result of Christ's faithful death and resurrection.[88] But I observe in this section that while most of the Old Testament passages that Paul quotes in his teaching about faith refer to our faith in God, two speak in a veiled way about faith in the Christ who is God.

Genesis 15:6

Genesis 15:6, one of the most important passages Paul quotes in his teaching about faith, speaks of the Jewish patriarch (the subject) believing in God (the object): "Abraham believed God" (Rom. 4:3; cf. Gal. 3:6). The object of Abraham's faith in Genesis 15:6 stood out to Philo, who reflects at length on the insecurity of trusting in other things, such as fame, wealth, and beauty, concluding that "belief in the former things is disbelief in God, and disbelief in them belief in God."[89] Philo observes that Abraham is the first person spoken of as having believed in God, "since he first grasped a firm

---

87 Exceptions often include faith in the representatives of God, such as Moses (Ex. 4:1–9; 14:31; 19:9), the Lord's prophets (2 Chron. 20:20), King Hezekiah (2 Chron. 32:15), and Philip the evangelist (Acts 8:12).

88 J. Louis Martyn, *Galatians: A New Translation with Introduction and Commentary*, AB 33A (New York: Doubleday, 1997), 275n179.

89 Philo, *On Abraham*, §§263–69.

and unswerving conception of the truth that there is one Cause above all."[90] Like Philo, Paul notices not simply Abraham's faith in general but his faith in God. Unlike Philo, however, Paul does not highlight Abraham's philosophical insight into the first cause but rather highlights Abraham's belief in God's promise and his confidence that God was able to fulfill that promise:

> In hope he believed against hope, that he should become the father of many nations, as he had been told, "So shall your offspring be" [Gen. 15:5]. . . . No unbelief made him waver concerning the promise of God, but he grew strong in his faith as he gave glory to God, fully convinced that God was able to do what he had promised. (Rom. 4:18, 20–21)[91]

It is clear that Paul understands Abraham's faith in God as a paradigm for our faith in God.[92] He is "the father of all who believe," both Gentiles and Jews (Rom. 4:11–12). Like father, like son. Paul speaks of Abraham's faith as the "footsteps" in which we now walk (Rom. 4:12). And he tells the Romans that "the words 'it was counted to him' [Gen. 15:6] were not written for his [Abraham's] sake alone, but for ours also. It will be counted to us who believe in him who raised from the dead Jesus our Lord" (Rom. 4:23–24). Most commentators have also seen a clear comparison between our faith and Abraham's faith in Galatians 3:5–7, indicated by the word "just as" (καθώς):[93]

---

90 Philo, *On the Virtues*, trans. F. H. Colson, LCL 341 (Cambridge, MA: Harvard University Press, 1939), §216.

91 Schliesser observes in his own exegesis of Gen. 15:6 that "faith denotes a relationship between two persons, between Yahweh and Abraham, which is located in a 'word-event.'" *Abraham's Faith*, 137.

92 Hays acknowledges this as well, citing Rom. 4:12 and 24: "Clearly there is an analogy between Abraham's faith and the faith of the Christian believer." Richard B. Hays, *The Conversion of the Imagination: Paul as Interpreter of Israel's Scripture* (Grand Rapids, MI: Eerdmans, 2005), 81.

93 An older example is J. B. Lightfoot, *The Epistle of St. Paul to the Galatians* (1865; repr., Grand Rapids, MI: Zondervan, 1971), 136. A current example is Schreiner: "The point of comparison

Does he who supplies the Spirit to you and works miracles among you do so by works of the law, or by hearing with faith—just as Abraham "believed God, and it was counted to him as righteousness"?

Know then that it is those of faith who are the sons of Abraham.

Does Paul also see in Genesis 15:6 a paradigm for Jesus's faith in God? Richard Hays has argued that Paul presents Abraham as a paradigm for Jesus's faith in Galatians 3:6–9.[94] He begins by suggesting that the phrase "by hearing with faith [ἐξ ἀκοῆς πίστεως]" in 3:5 cannot refer to our faith because "the accent in verse 5 falls heavily upon the action of God" (n.b. the theological argument).[95] This means καθώς in 3:6 cannot be making a comparison between the Galatians' faith and Abraham's faith.[96] In 3:7, οἱ ἐκ πίστεως is an allusion to Habakkuk 2:4, which Hays takes as a reference to Christ's faith. This means that it refers to "those who are given life on the basis of [Christ's] faith."[97] Finally, this leads to Hays's interpretation of Galatians 3:8: "The Scripture, foreseeing that God would justify the Gentiles by faith [ἐκ πίστεως], preached the gospel beforehand to Abraham, saying, 'In you shall all the nations be blessed.'" Hays argues that because the Gentiles are blessed "in Abraham," we should take "by faith" as a reference to Abraham's faith, which has a vicarious effect for others, foreshadowing the vicarious effect of Christ's faith.[98] Hays compares this idea with the rabbinic teaching about the "merits of the fathers" and with Genesis 22:18, in which the nations are blessed because of Abraham's faithful obedience.[99]

---

is that both Abraham and the Galatians exercised faith." Thomas R. Schreiner, *Galatians*, ZECNT (Grand Rapids, MI: Zondervan, 2010), 191.

94 Hays, *Faith of Jesus Christ*, 168–77.

95 Hays, *Faith of Jesus Christ*, 170.

96 Hays, *Faith of Jesus Christ*, 170.

97 Hays, *Faith of Jesus Christ*, 172.

98 Hays, *Faith of Jesus Christ*, 173–77.

99 Hays, *Faith of Jesus Christ*, 174–76. He makes a similar argument about Rom. 4, concluding that because the chapter focuses on Abraham's representative fatherhood, we should view Abraham's

Hays's argument that Paul presents Abraham's faith as a paradigm for Christ's faith depends heavily on his idea that πίστις refers not to our faith but to Christ's faith (and Abraham's faith too). But it is important to observe that Paul nowhere *explicitly* draws an analogy between Abraham's faith and Christ's faith as he does between Abraham's faith and our faith. Even Hays himself has backed away from his original argument by allowing that Paul also compares our faith to Abraham's faith in Galatians 3:6–9.[100] At the very least, we can say that it is unclear that Paul understands Genesis 15:6 to present a pattern for Jesus's faith, but it is clear that he understands it to present a pattern for our faith in the God who raises the dead.

Psalm 116:10

The suffering psalmist does not spell out the object of his faith in Psalm 116:10, but in context his confidence is clearly in the Lord.[101] Goldingay observes the similar wording in Psalm 116:9 and Psalm 27:13 and suggests that the psalmist is specifically confident in "seeing good from Yhwh in the land of living."[102] Paul is also confident in God in the midst of suffering, "knowing that he who raised the Lord Jesus will raise us also with Jesus and bring us with you into his presence" (2 Cor. 4:14). For the psalmist and the apostle, faith in God means faith that God will bring good out of affliction, life out of death.

An intriguing suggestion by advocates of the "faithfulness of Christ" view is that Paul reads Psalm 116 as a messianic psalm, so that Paul's own faith is a participation in Christ's faith. Paul's participation in the

---

faith/obedience as a paradigm for Jesus's faith/obedience, which has a vicarious soteriological effect on believers. Hays, *Conversion of the Imagination*, 79–84.

100 In his debate with Dunn, Hays retracts his argument that Paul does not see Abraham as a paradigm for the believer, but he continues to see Abraham in Gal. 3:8–9 as a representative figure who prefigures Christ. The change is that Hays allows Abraham's faith to be a paradigm for our faith as well. *Faith of Jesus Christ*, 290.

101 "No doubt Yhwh is the object of the trust, but the emphasis lies on the confidence despite pressures." Goldingay, *Psalms*, 3:343.

102 Goldingay, *Psalms*, 3:343–44.

death and resurrection of Christ is an important theme in the context
of 2 Corinthians 4:13. He describes his afflictions as "always carrying
in the body the death of Jesus, so that the life of Jesus may also be
manifested in our bodies" (2 Cor. 4:10). Morna Hooker concludes
from this description that in his citation of Psalm 116:10, Paul is "surely
referring to the spirit of faith which enabled Jesus to be given up to
death."[103] Douglas Campbell also appeals to the theme of participation
with Christ in 2 Corinthians 4:1–5:17 as a major reason to read Paul's
citation of Psalm 116:10 as messianic.[104] The early Christians, including
Paul, sometimes read the Psalms as speaking for the Christ (e.g., Rom.
15:3; Heb. 10:5–7), and Psalm 116 is a good candidate for such an
interpretation.[105] But the sticking point for this interpretation is that
there is simply no indication from the immediate context of 2 Corinthians 4:13 that Paul understands this psalm as the words of Jesus.[106]
Here we may draw a contrast with Paul's messianic citation of Psalm
69:9, which clearly presents that psalm as the words of Jesus: "Let each
of us please his neighbor for his good, to build him up. For Christ did
not please himself, but as it is written, 'The reproaches of those who
reproached you fell on me'" (Rom. 15:2–3). Thus we should listen to
Jan Lambrecht's critical response to Campbell, which pleads for us to

---

103 Hooker, "Πιστις Χριστου," 335. Hooker does not technically see Paul reading Ps. 116:10 as
    messianic but rather sees Jesus, the psalmist, and Paul as all sharing the same faith.

104 Douglas A. Campbell, "2 Corinthians 4:13: Evidence in Paul That Christ Believes," *JBL* 128,
    no. 2 (2009): 348–53.

105 Schenck suggests a messianic allusion to Ps. 116:6–9 in Heb. 5:7. Kenneth Schenck, "2 Corinthians
    and the Πίστις Χριστοῦ Debate," *CBQ* 70, no. 3 (2008): 532. There also seems to be a messianic
    allusion to Ps. 116:3 in Acts 2:24. One problem with Schenck's argument is that Paul is quoting
    from the Septuagint, in which these allusions are a part of Ps. 114, whereas Paul's citation is the
    first verse in Ps. 115. Lambrecht, "Method [II]," 447. Campbell avoids this problem by arguing
    only from Ps. 116:10–19 [115:1–10 LXX], which speaks of the "vindication of a righteous suf-
    ferer." Campbell, "2 Corinthians 4:13," 343. Hays also notes that the plot of Ps. 116 [115 LXX]
    moves "from abasement to praise," and he even suggests that the "cup of salvation" in Ps. 116:13
    [115:4 LXX] could be seen as prefiguring the Lord's Supper. Hays, *Conversion of the Imagination*,
    108–9.

106 I owe this observation to Lambrecht, "Method [II]," 447.

see that Paul is simply making a comparison between his faith and the psalmist's faith in 2 Corinthians 4:13.[107] Both are confident that God will deliver them from their affliction.

Isaiah 8:14 and 28:16

Paul's citations from Isaiah 8:14 and 28:16 follow the pattern of human faith (the subject) trusting in God (the object). But Isaiah also calls readers to faith in the Christ who is God, albeit in a veiled way. The apostle's first citation calls for faith in the "stone" of Isaiah 8:14 and 28:16 (Rom. 9:33). Here Paul merges these two texts by inserting Isaiah 8:14 within a citation of Isaiah 28:16.[108] This allows him to replace the positive description of the stone in Isaiah 28:16 with the negative description found in Isaiah 8:14, associating the stone with judgment for unbelief: "a stone of stumbling, and a rock of offense" (Rom. 9:33).[109] In contrast, Isaiah 28:16 speaks about believing on the stone for salvation: "And whoever believes in him will not be put to shame" (Rom. 9:33). Paul clearly depends in some way on the Septuagint translation of Isaiah 28:16 because he includes the prepositional phrase "in him" (ἐπ' αὐτῷ), which is not found in the Hebrew.[110] This phrase was probably an addition made by the Greek translator to make better sense of

---

107 Lambrecht, "Method [II]," 448. He concludes that "refusing such an accumulation of hypotheses is a matter of sound method." "Method [II]," 448. See also Jan Lambrecht, "A Matter of Method: 2 Cor 4,13 and Stegman's Recent Study," *ETL* 84, no. 1 (2008): 175–80.

108 Paul is probably relying on a Christian tradition that associated these two texts, because 1 Peter's citation of the two texts follows the unique wording of Paul's citation yet without merging them together. This makes it likely that they were relying on the same source. Frank Thielman, "Paul's View of Israel's Misstep in Rom 9.32–3: Its Origin and Meaning," *NTS* 64, no. 3 (2018): 364–65.

109 Paul's citation of Isa. 8:14 follows the syntax of the Hebrew, although some of his lexical choices are probably dependent on the Septuagint: λίθος, πρόσκομμα, and πέτρα; σκάνδαλον is perhaps from a revised Septuagint similar to Aquila, Symmachus, and Theodotion. BDAG, s.v. "σκάνδαλον," use 2.

110 That said, there are also several differences between Paul's citation and the Septuagint in Paul's citation—for example, οὐ rather than οὐ μὴ, which is closer to the Hebrew, and the future passive indicative καταισχυνθήσεται, rather than the Septuagint's aorist passive subjunctive (καταισχυνθῇ).

the statement in its context, identifying the stone more clearly as the object of faith.[111] But how should we identify the stone of Isaiah 28:16?

In Isaiah 8:14, the stone is the Lord himself, who is to be feared rather than the nations coming against Jerusalem (Isa. 8:11–13). In the Septuagint of Isaiah 8:14, which Paul was familiar with, there is an even clearer call for faith in the Lord than in the original Hebrew, because it begins with a conditional clause not found in the Hebrew text: "And if you trust in him [ἐὰν ἐπ᾽ αὐτῷ πεποιθὼς ᾖς], he will become your holy precinct, and you will not encounter him as a stumbling caused by a stone" (Isa. 8:14 NETS). This appears to be the translator's attempt to make sense of the verse's strange juxtaposition of both positive and negative descriptions of the Lord.[112] In Hebrew the text reads, "And he will become a sanctuary and a stone of offense and a rock of stumbling" (Isa. 8:14). Interpreters recognize that the first description is positive and the second and third are negative, but their direct juxtaposition is jarring to the reader. This is probably why the Greek translator added a clarifying conditional statement that is actually picked up from 8:17, in which Isaiah resolves, "I will trust in him [πεποιθὼς ἔσομαι ἐπ᾽ αὐτῷ]" (Isa. 8:17 NETS). My point is simply that the Septuagint of Isaiah, which Paul was clearly familiar with, explicitly calls for faith in the Lord in Isaiah 8:14. This resonates with the larger context of Isaiah 7–8, in which Ahaz is warned not to fear threats against Jerusalem but to trust in the Lord:

> If you are not firm in faith,
>   you will not be firm at all. (Isa. 7:9)

---

111 A similar move is made by the translator in Isa. 8:6, who adds the phrase ἐφ᾽ ὑμῶν, a phrase from Isa. 8:7, in order to make sense of the verse.

112 The Aramaic Targum attempts to clarify the Hebrew with a conditional clause as well, although it removes any positive description and focuses on the negative (this edition uses italics to show expansions of the Hebrew text): "*If you do not attend*, his Memra will become *among you an avenger*, and a stone of *smiting* and a rock of stumbling." Bruce D. Chilton, *The Isaiah Targum* (Collegeville, MN: Liturgical Press, 1990), 19.

Isaiah 28:16 calls for faith not in the Lord per se but in the stone he is laying in Zion. This stone is clearly a foundational element in the Lord's salvation and establishment of Jerusalem. But what is it? Isaiah's prophecy is elusive, leading to disagreement among commentators.[113] The association of the stone's founding with the establishment of justice and righteousness in Isaiah 28:17, however, make it likely that he refers to the establishment of the Davidic monarchy (cf. Isa. 9:6; 16:5).[114] This is also the way that Paul understands the object of faith in Isaiah 28:16 when he talks about Israel stumbling over the "stumbling stone" (Rom. 9:32).[115] His second citation of the verse is even clearer:

> If you confess with your mouth that Jesus is Lord and believe in your heart that God raised him from the dead, you will be saved. For with the heart one believes and is justified, and with the mouth one confesses and is saved. For the Scripture says, "Everyone who believes in him will not be put to shame." (Rom. 10:9–11)

In this citation, the "him" who is to be believed is the risen Lord, Jesus himself. Thus, Paul's merging of Isaiah 8:14 with 28:16 allows him to speak of Jesus as both the Lord himself and as the Davidic King placed in Zion by God. This interpretation does not come from thin air but is rooted, in a veiled way, in the ancient prophecy that calls readers to faith in the Lord, the stone, and in the stone that he will lay as the foundation of Zion's salvation.

---

113 Childs comments, "The interpretive proposals are numerous and extend from a reference to the temple, to Zion, to the Davidic monarchy, to the remnant, or to faith itself." Childs, *Isaiah*, 209.

114 Some see support for this suggestion in the Aramaic Targum, which identifies the stone as a king—e.g., Childs, *Isaiah*, 208. But in the flow of the Targum, the king is probably the Gentile king who will bring them into exile. So Wagner, *Heralds*, 143n80.

115 Cf. "We preach Christ crucified, a stumbling block to Jews" (1 Cor. 1:23). Most commentators see Paul identifying the stone with Christ in Rom. 9:32. It is unlikely that he meant his audience to see a reference to both the Torah *and* Christ. Pace N. T. Wright, *Paul and the Faithfulness of God*, COQG 4 (Minneapolis: Fortress, 2013), 1179.

Isaiah 53:1

Isaiah 53:1 stands out among these Old Testament texts in that the object of human belief (here, unbelief) is "what he has heard," or the message of salvation. The broader content of this message in its larger context is the good news about the peace, salvation, and reign of God (Isa. 52:7; cf. Rom. 10:15). But Isaiah 53:1 is also tied in lexically to the immediately preceding verse, which says,

> Kings shall shut their mouths because of him,
> for that which has not been told them they see,
>   and that which they have not heard they understand.
>   (Isa. 52:15)

In this verse the kings of the earth are silent because the suffering servant of the Lord has been exalted so highly that they now understand what they had not previously heard. Thus, "what he has heard" in Isaiah 53:1 refers to what the kings "have [previously] not heard" (Isa. 52:15)—namely, the message of the suffering and exalted servant. The Septuagint translation of Isaiah 52:15, which Paul quotes verbatim in Romans 15:21, makes the content of the message even clearer. Instead of the original "that which has not been told *them*," the Septuagint has "those who were not informed about *him*" (NETS), identifying the content of the message as "him," or the servant. It is no wonder, then, that Paul was influenced by this verse to preach the gospel where Christ had not been named (Rom. 15:20–21). My point here, however, is to observe that the object of disbelief in Isaiah 53:1 is the message that has been heard about the suffering and exalted servant, which is explained in Isaiah 53:2–12.

Habakkuk 2:4

The Septuagint translation of Habakkuk 2:4 seems to view it as a statement about God's own faithfulness (the subject), but the Hebrew text, which Paul follows, sees it as a reference to the faith (or faithfulness) of a righteous human being (the subject). There is no stated object of faithfulness or faith. If אֱמוּנָה means "faithfulness," then it probably refers to faithfulness to the Lord and perhaps to his law.[116] But if I am correct that the word means "faith," corresponding to the hiphil stem of אמן, then the object of faith is probably the prophetic vision of the Lord that is introduced in 2:2–3 and explicated in 2:6–20. Habakkuk himself resolves to wait quietly for the day when this judgment oracle comes on the Chaldeans who have invaded Judah (Hab. 3:16–19).

Habakkuk 2:4 is a key text in the πίστις Χριστοῦ debate not only because the word אֱמוּנָה normally means "faithfulness" but also because Hays and others have argued that Paul understands it as a statement about Christ's own faithfulness.[117] Several arguments are put forward in support of a messianic interpretation of "the righteous shall live by faith." First, "the righteous one" is a title sometimes used by the early Christians for Jesus Christ (e.g., Acts 7:52; 1 Pet. 3:18; 1 John 2:1).[118] One difficulty with this argument is that "the righteous one" is not *exclusively* a messianic title (e.g., James 5:6; 1 Pet. 4:18).[119] Another is that the title is likely an allusion not to Habakkuk 2:4 but rather to Isaiah 53:11 ("By his knowledge shall the righteous one, my servant, / make

---

116 Note that Hab. 2:4 was considered a summary of the 613 precepts of the law in the Babylonian Talmud (Makkot 24a). The interpretation of the Qumran pesher is similar but is influenced by their sectarian interests: "Its interpretation concerns all observing the Law in the House of Judah, whom God will free from the house of judgment on account of their toil and of their loyalty to the Teacher of Righteousness." 1QpHab 8.1–3, in Martínez and Tigchelaar, *Dead Sea Scrolls*, 17.

117 Hays, *Conversion of the Imagination*, 119–42; Douglas A. Campbell, *The Deliverance of God: An Apocalyptic Rereading of Justification in Paul* (Grand Rapids, MI: Eerdmans, 2009), 610–16. Hays's original argument was actually that Paul views Hab. 2:4 in Gal. 3:11 as a reference both to Jesus's faith(fulness) and to our faith. Hays, *Faith of Jesus Christ*, 140. I address this argument in chap. 4, p. 205.

118 Hays, *Conversion of the Imagination*, 124–31; cf. Campbell, *Deliverance of God*, 614. Hays also observes that the Son of Man figure in the parables of 1 En. 37–71 is identified as "the Righteous One" (1 En. 38.2, 3; 53.6). *Conversion of the Imagination*, 122–23.

119 Hays makes the interesting argument that James 5:6 is an allusion to Wis. 2:12–20, which early Christians would have viewed as a prefiguration of Jesus. *Conversion of the Imagination*, 130. But this interpretation of James and Wisdom of Solomon is unclear.

many to be accounted righteous, / and he shall bear their iniquities"), since the early Christians used the title with reference to Jesus's vicarious suffering:[120]

> . . . the Righteous One, whom you have now betrayed and murdered. (Acts 7:52)

> Christ also suffered once for sins, the righteous for the unrighteous, that he might bring us to God. (1 Pet. 3:18)

> We have an advocate with the Father, Jesus Christ the righteous. He is the propitiation for our sins. (1 John 2:1–2)

A second line of evidence in favor of Christ as the righteous one who lives by faith in Habakkuk 2:4 is that the author of Hebrews interprets Habakkuk 2:3 as messianic:

> For you have need of endurance, so that when you have done the will of God you may receive what is promised. For,
>
>> "Yet a little while,
>>   and the coming one will come and will not delay [Hab. 2:3];
>> but my righteous one shall live by faith [Hab. 2:4]."
>>   (Heb. 10:36–38)

Here the author of Hebrews quotes from the Septuagint with a few minor differences. In the original Hebrew, the clause "it will surely come" refers to the "vision" (Hab. 2:3) of the Chaldeans' destruction

---

120 Watson considers the evidence and concludes that "there is no indication in these or other relevant passages that [ὁ] δίκαιος is drawn from Habakkuk 2:4 or is influenced by it in any way." Francis Watson, "By Faith (of Christ): An Exegetical Dilemma and Its Scriptural Solution," in Bird and Sprinkle, *The Faith of Jesus Christ*, 158.

that has not yet happened but will surely take place. But in the Septuagint rendering of this clause, the referent of what "will come" is not clear. "Vision" in Greek is feminine, but "coming" is a masculine participle. Perhaps the translator was simply slavishly literal and followed the Hebrew gender, in which "vision" is masculine.[121] Or perhaps "coming" is a reference to the "time" in which the vision comes, since "time" in Greek is masculine.[122] In any case, the author of Hebrews takes the masculine participle "coming" as a reference to "the coming one," Christ himself, by adding the article "the" (ὁ). Thus, there is a Christian tradition of reading Habakkuk 2:3 with reference to Christ.[123] It is important to observe, however, that the author of Hebrews interprets "the righteous one" in Habakkuk 2:4 *not* as a reference to Christ but rather as a reference to "those who have faith and preserve their souls" (Heb. 10:39).[124]

The major difficulty with the argument for a messianic interpretation of Habakkuk 2:4 is that Paul simply gives no indication in either Romans 1:17 or Galatians 3:11 that he understands "the righteous one" as a reference to Jesus Christ.[125] We can contrast this with his messianic interpretation of Genesis 17:8: "Now the promises were made to Abraham and to his offspring. It does not say, 'And to offsprings,' referring to many, but referring to one, 'And to your offspring,' who is

---

121 Rikki E. Watts, "'For I Am Not Ashamed of the Gospel': Romans 1:16–17 and Habakkuk 2:4," in *Romans and the People of God: Essays in Honor of Gordon D. Fee on the Occasion of His 65th Birthday*, ed. Sven K. Soderlund and N. T. Wright (Grand Rapids, MI: Eerdmans, 1999), 10.

122 This is how the NETS renders the Greek.

123 Hays, *Conversion of the Imagination*, 131–34.

124 Hays rightly sees that the author of Hebrews takes the "righteous one" as a direct reference not to Christ but to Christians, although he observes that, theologically, "Hebrews presents Jesus as the paradigm for the life of faith," meaning that it has some reference to Jesus. *Conversion of the Imagination*, 134. Campbell, in contrast, argues that both "the coming one" and the "righteous one" in Heb. 10:37–39 refer to Christ. *Deliverance of God*, 614.

125 Indeed, as Ulrichs concludes in an excursus on Hab. 2:4 in Paul, the messianic reading seems to be foreign to the context of both Rom. 1:17 and Gal. 3:11. Karl Friedrich Ulrichs, *Christusglaube: Studien zum Syntagma πίστις Χριστοῦ und zum paulinischen Verständnis von Glaube und Rechtfertigung*, WUNT, 2nd ser., vol. 227 (Tübingen: Mohr Siebeck, 2007), 190.

Christ" (Gal. 3:16).[126] Here Paul clearly explains that the offspring of
Abraham "is Christ." Would his audience have understood that "the
righteous one" is Christ in Romans 1:17 and Galatians 3:11 without a
similar explanation? It seems unlikely. At the end of the day, the messianic reading of Habakkuk 2:4 is almost entirely dependent on the
"faithfulness of Christ" view of πίστις Χριστοῦ.[127]

Jesus's Teaching

Jesus's teaching about mountain-moving faith follows the typical pattern in Scripture in which human beings look to God. In Matthew
21:20–22, Jesus does not name the object of faith, but the context of
prayer makes it clear that he is calling his disciples to trust in God.
Mark's record of Jesus's teaching spells out the object of faith explicitly: "Have faith in God" (Mark 11:22). It is interesting to observe
that this verse is often mentioned in the grammatical debates about
πίστις Χριστοῦ, with both sides typically acknowledging that Mark
11:22 is a clear example of πίστις with an objective genitive (πίστιν
θεοῦ).[128] The context of this verse supports this rendering because
in the following verses Jesus calls his disciples to believe and pray to
God.[129] My point here, however, is not grammatical but historical:
Jesus's teaching about mountain-moving faith, which Paul alludes to

---

126 Hays himself asks, "If Paul has in mind a messianic interpretation of Hab. 2:4, why does he not
    say so more clearly, as he does in the case of Gen. 17:8?" *Conversion of the Imagination*, 141.

127 In a monograph arguing for the plausibility of the Christological reading of Hab. 2:4, Heliso
    concludes, "Admittedly, the pre-Pauline and Pauline evidence in favour of reading ὁ δίκαιος in
    the Habakkuk citation as Christ seems to be insufficient and the christological meaning of ἐκ
    πίστεως is heavily dependent on the disputed subjective genitive interpretation of πίστις Χριστοῦ.
    However, that this reading is internally coherent and has some degree of argumentative cogency
    cannot be denied." *Pistis and the Righteous One*, 254.

128 For example, Hays acknowledges that this is an example of πίστις with an objective genitive. *Faith
    of Jesus Christ*, 149.

129 This makes it very unlikely that Jesus in Mark 11:22 means "You have the faithfulness of God"—
    contra Peter G. Bolt, "The Faith of Jesus Christ in the Synoptic Gospels and Acts," in Bird and
    Sprinkle, *The Faith of Jesus Christ*, 210–14. Note also that the parallel statement in Matt. 21:21
    cannot refer to God's faithfulness but must be a call for the disciples to believe in God.

in 1 Corinthians 13:2, is a call for his disciples (the subject) to believe in God (the object).[130]

Finally, I make two less certain observations concerning how Jesus's teaching about faith may have historical significance for Paul's understanding of Christ as the object of faith. I want to stress that these points are not as clear as the others in this section. First, Maureen Yeung's carefully controlled study of faith in Jesus and Paul concludes that Paul may have actually been influenced by Jesus's understanding of Habakkuk 2:4. Her argument is that Jesus's saying "Your faith has saved you" has no close parallels except for Habakkuk 2:4 and that in this saying Jesus was calling for faith in his own person, just as we see Paul calling for faith in Christ in his use of Habakkuk 2:4.[131] Second, Paul's use of Isaiah 28:16 was likely influenced by Jesus's identification of himself with the rejected stone of Psalm 118:22 (Mark 12:10).[132] These observations suggest that Paul's understanding of Christ as the object of faith may have been influenced by Jesus's own exegesis of these Old Testament passages.

Summary

All the passages referenced by Paul in his teaching about faith view it as a one-way street in which human beings (the subject) trust in God (the object). Nuances of this theme include faith in the God who promises life (Gen. 15:6), confidence that God will deliver from affliction (Ps. 116:10), and waiting on the fulfillment of the prophetic word of God (Hab. 2:4). Scholars who hold to the "faithfulness of Christ" view have argued that in each of these three texts, Paul sees a reference to Jesus's own faith. Abraham's faith had vicarious soteriological effect, foreshadowing Jesus's vicarious faith (Gal. 3:6–9); the afflicted psalmist

---

130 Perhaps an implication is that the disciples are to follow Jesus in his own faith in God. Ian G. Wallis, *The Faith of Jesus Christ in Early Christian Traditions*, SNTSMS 84 (Cambridge: Cambridge University Press, 1995), 42–46. But this point is never clearly made in Matthew or Mark. Certainly, though, the fact that Jesus prayed to God indicates that he had faith in God.

131 Yeung, *Faith in Jesus and Paul*, 225.

132 E. Earle Ellis, *Paul's Use of the Old Testament* (Grand Rapids, MI: Eerdmans, 1957), 87.

speaks for the suffering Christ (2 Cor. 4:13); and Christ is the righteous one who lives by faith (Hab. 2:4). But I have argued that each of these interpretations is, at best, unclear in Paul's citations and is heavily dependent on the "faithfulness of Christ" translation. Moreover, two of the texts referenced by Paul in his teaching about faith present Christ not as the subject of faith but as the object of our faith, the Davidic foundation stone of the restored Jerusalem (Isa. 28:16) and the suffering and now exalted servant associated with the good news of God's reign (Isa. 53:1). Although the messianic referent is veiled in Isaiah's prophecy, these two texts call for faith in the Christ, at least according to Paul's interpretation.

Faith and Salvation

Thus far I have observed that the passages referenced by Paul in his teaching about faith speak about our faith in God or even in Christ. Now I must ask the soteriological question. For the sake of clarity I want to observe that I tentatively understand justification in Paul's theology to be a subset of the larger category of salvation. But the apostle can also speak of the two almost interchangeably: "With the heart one believes and is justified, and with the mouth one confesses and is saved" (Rom. 10:10). Thus I often speak of the two interchangeably throughout this study, which Hays also does in his dissertation. Hays and many others have claimed that Paul does not teach that we are justified by our own faith in Christ but rather by the faith or faithfulness of Christ. But is it out of bounds historically to imagine that Paul would see a causal link between human faith and divine salvation? This is the question that drives the final section of the chapter.[133]

In two of these passages, faith is associated with salvation, but the relationship between faith and salvation is unclear. Psalm 116:10 depicts

---

133 It is important to note that I use the term *cause* in this section and throughout the book in a general way and not in a way that is intended to deny the imputation of Christ's righteousness.

the psalmist as believing and speaking in the midst of his affliction, but it quickly turns to the psalmist thanking the Lord for salvation, for deliverance from death,[134] and for the breaking of the psalmist's bonds (Ps. 116:13, 15, 16). The most we can say of the relationship of faith and salvation in this context is that the psalmist's faith *precedes* his salvation and is not simply a result of his salvation. Isaiah 53:1 is even less clear about the relationship of faith and salvation. Faith (or unbelief) in the message is associated with the revelation of "the arm of the LORD" (Isa. 53:1), a way of speaking about his salvation (cf. Isa. 52:10).[135] It is also associated with the justification of the many through the suffering of the servant (Isa. 53:11). But the exact relationship of faith to salvation and justification is unclear. The other passages, however, speak of a causal or conditional relationship between faith and salvation.

Genesis 15:6

Paul quotes Genesis 15:6 from the Septuagint, which clarifies the relationship between Abraham's faith and righteousness or justification. In Hebrew the ambiguous clause "He counted it to him as righteousness" could refer to either Abraham counting the Lord to be righteous or the Lord counting Abraham to be righteous.[136] But this ambiguity is removed in the Greek translation by the transformation of the active verb into a passive, making it clear that righteousness was reckoned to Abraham.[137] It is this translation that Paul uses to make his famous

---

134 Regarding the statement "Precious in the sight of the LORD / is the death of his saints" (Ps. 116:15), Goldingay comments that "the people in danger of death who are committed to Yhwh are valuable to him. The implication is that Yhwh would therefore not let their death come about." *Psalms*, 3:346.

135 The Septuagint of Isa. 53:1 uses the verb "reveal" (ἀποκαλύπτω). Cf. "The righteousness of God is revealed by faith" (Rom. 1:17, my trans.).

136 It is more likely that the Hebrew means that the Lord counted Abraham to be righteous; see Schliesser, *Abraham's Faith*, 110–17.

137 This difference was perhaps due to the translator's attempt to clarify the meaning of the verse, just as the NRSV and NET translators add a subject ("the LORD") to clarify the meaning. Or it may reflect a different Hebrew *Vorlage* that may also be preserved in 4QPseudo-Jubilees (4Q225),

argument about Abraham and righteousness by faith. The key point for my argument is that the logic of Genesis 15:6 is an action that leads to a result. "Abram believed God, and it was reckoned to him as righteousness" (Gen. 15:6 NETS) means "Abram believed God, and [the result was that] it was reckoned to him as righteousness." Thus, in what is probably the most important text referenced by Paul in his teaching about faith, the patriarch's faith is said to be a cause of his justification.

Isaiah 8:14 and 28:16

Isaiah 8:14 and 28:16 both speak a word about faith and salvation in the midst of a judgment oracle against Jerusalem. The contexts of these two stone texts are so similar that it is not really surprising that the early Christians associated them.[138] The most important parallel for this section is that both call on Israel to trust in the rock for salvation.

Isaiah 8:14 is introduced by a call for the prophet to fear the Lord alone (Isa. 8:12–13; cf. 7:9), and it continues with the statement that "he will become a sanctuary" (Isa. 8:14). The idea seems to be that if one fears the Lord, he will become a sanctuary of refuge. Paul's brief citation picks up on the rest of the verse, in which he will also become a "stone of offense and a rock of stumbling to both houses of Israel, a trap and a snare to the inhabitants of Jerusalem" (Isa. 8:14). I observed above that Paul's brief citation of Isaiah 8:14 does not follow the Septuagint but that Paul was clearly familiar with the language of the Septuagint. Thus, he probably knew that the translator, by borrowing language from 8:17, attempted to disambiguate

---

which has a Hebrew form of Gen. 15:6 closer to the Old Greek. J. A. Fitzmyer, "The Interpretation of Genesis 15:6: Abraham's Faith and Righteousness in a Qumran Text," in *Emanuel: Studies in Hebrew Bible, Septuagint, and Dead Sea Scrolls in Honor of Emanuel Tov*, ed. Shalom M. Paul, Robert A. Kraft, Lawrence H. Schiffman, and Weston W. Fields, VTSup 94 (Leiden: Brill, 2003), 265–68; see also Schliesser, *Abraham's Faith*, 215–19.

138 Note three similarities: (1) Both Isa. 8:1–18 and 28:1–22 use flood imagery to warn about a coming invasion. (2) These warnings are the only ones in Isaiah that combine the verbs "snared" (niphal of יקשׁ) and "taken" (niphal of לכד) (Isa. 8:15; 28:13). (3) These are also some of the only oracles in Isaiah to repeatedly use the anticovenant formula "this people" (Isa. 8:6, 11, 12; 28:11, 14)—as opposed to "my people."

the surprising juxtaposition of "sanctuary" and "rock of stumbling": "And if you trust in him, he will become your holy precinct, and you will not encounter him as a stumbling caused by a stone" (Isa. 8:14 NETS). The Greek translator makes explicit what was implicit in the Hebrew text. What makes the difference of whether one encounters the Lord in salvation or judgment is whether one trusts in him or not. Faith is the condition of salvation. And Isaiah resolves to wait on the Lord (Isa. 8:17).

The conditional relationship between faith and salvation is spelled out more clearly in both the original Hebrew and the Greek translation of Isaiah 28:16: "Whoever believes will not be in haste." The Hebrew verb "will not be in haste" (literally, "hurry," חוש) means that this person will not hurry away or "panic" (NRSV). He or she will have a rock to stand on in the coming storm of judgment. The logic of this statement is conditional and essentially means that *if* someone believes, he or she will not panic. Both of Paul's citations of this verse follow the Greek translation: "The one who believes in him will not be put to shame" (Isa. 28:16 NETS). The Greek translator probably did not know the exact meaning of the rare Hebrew verb but pieced it together from context.[139] Being "put to shame" in Isaiah is one way to speak of the coming dismay of the Lord's judgment.[140] Conversely, the hope that one "will not be put to shame" speaks of the relief of God's salvation.[141]

---

139 This Hebrew verb חוש is used three times in Isaiah, and each time the Septuagint translates it with a different verb that makes sense in its context (ἐγγίζω in Isa. 5:19; καταισχύνω in Isa. 28:16; and συνάγω in Isa. 60:22). If the translator was using the translation of the law as a guide, the Hebrew verb occurs there only twice, and it is not clear that the Pentateuch translator knew its meaning either (see Num. 32:17; Deut. 32:35).

140 Note especially Isa. 42:17: "They are turned back and utterly put to shame, / who trust in carved idols." Cf. Isa. 1:29; 26:11; 41:11; 44:9, 11; 45:16, 24; 65:13; 66:5. The Hebrew verb "to be ashamed" (בוש) is typically translated with αἰσχύνω in Isaiah, except in 54:4, where it is translated with the synonym καταισχύνω (i.e., the verb used in Isa. 28:16 LXX).

141 Note especially Isa. 45:17:

But Israel is saved by the LORD
with everlasting salvation;
you shall not be put to shame or confounded
to all eternity. (cf. Isa. 29:22; 49:23; 50:7; 54:4)

In the midst of the judgment oracle of Isaiah 28, the translator recognized that the prophet was forecasting a ray of hope, salvation for the one who trusts in the rock. Thus, the Greek translation of Isaiah 28:16 also sees a conditional relationship between faith and salvation. Paul's second citation of the verse exploits the open-ended nature of this conditionality and universalizes it as a promise of salvation to all, both Jew and Greek: "Everyone who believes in him will not be put to shame" (Rom. 10:11).

Habakkuk 2:4

I have spent a lot of time on Habakkuk 2:4 because this little verse is often considered the source of Paul's "by faith" idiom, including his ἐκ πίστεως Χριστοῦ phrases. It is thus an important factor in the πίστις Χριστοῦ debate.[142] It is not certain that Paul derived the phrase from Habakkuk 2:4. Ulrichs observes that according to Galatians 2:16, the phrase "by faith" existed in Antioch before Paul was making use of it.[143] It is still significant conceptually, however, because it is a part of the "by faith" idiom in Paul.

The phrase ἐκ πίστεως presents faith as a cause or instrument of salvation.[144] But scholars disagree about whether it modifies "the righteous" or "shall live." The Masoretic accents in the Hebrew text connect the phrase with "shall live." The syntax of the Hebrew probably supports this reading as well in that "his" is probably part of the second half of the sentence pointing back to the

---

142 Scholars from both sides of the debate tend to agree about this; e.g., Campbell, "Πιστις and Νομος in Paul," 101–3; Watson, "By Faith (of Christ)," 148–49, 162–63.

143 Thus, he rightly cautions against making Hab. 2:4 the *shibboleth* in the πίστις Χριστοῦ debate. Ulrichs, *Christusglaube*, 31–32. He also observes that in Gal. 2:16, Paul uses διὰ πίστεως before ἐκ πίστεως, which calls into question Campbell's argument that ἐκ πίστεως is more fundamental. Ulrichs, 118; see Campbell, "Πιστις and Νομος in Paul," 99–101.

144 In systematic theology, cause and instrument are sometimes distinguished, but in grammar, they are similar, overlapping categories. For example, Moule discusses this use of ἐκ under the category "*Causal* or *Instrumental*." C. F. D. Moule, *An Idiom Book of New Testament Greek*, 2nd ed. (Cambridge: Cambridge University Press, 1959), 73.

subject ("the righteous").[145] Thus, in Hebrew the meaning is probably "The righteous shall live by his faith." Faith is the means by which the righteous escapes the judgment of God and lives.

The Greek is more ambiguous. Paul may have understood "by faith" as modifying "the righteous" (ὁ δίκαιος), because he commonly uses the verb "justify" (δικαιόω) with "by faith" (Rom. 3:26, 30; 5:1; Gal. 2:16; 3:8, 24) and the noun "righteousness" (δικαιοσύνη) with "by faith" (Rom. 1:17; 3:22; 9:30; 10:6; Phil. 3:9).[146] The most important example is Romans 1:17, because in this verse Paul cites Habakkuk 2:4 as scriptural support that "the righteousness of God is revealed ἐκ πίστεως." Galatians 3:11 is important as well, because Habakkuk 2:4 is quoted as a positive counterpart to the statement that "no one is justified before God by the law." We would expect Paul then to say that it is those who are righteous by faith who will live.[147] The difficulty is that Paul goes on to say that "the law is not of faith, rather 'The one who does them shall live by them'" (Gal. 3:12). In this verse "by them" modifies "shall live," which would lead us to think that "by faith" in the antithetical statement modifies "shall live" too. Perhaps, then, we are being overly precise. Paul speaks of life and righteousness as synonyms for salvation: "For if a law had been given that could give life, then righteousness would indeed be by the law" (Gal. 3:21). Thus, perhaps his citation of Habakkuk 2:4 refers to faith as a cause of both righteousness and life.[148]

---

145 This is a compound sentence with a subject juxtaposed to an independent verbal clause that has a retrospective pronominal suffix. *GKC*, §143b. For this argument I am indebted to O. Palmer Robertson, *The Books of Nahum, Habakkuk, and Zephaniah*, NICOT (Grand Rapids, MI: Eerdmans, 1990), 177.

146 See Watson, "By Faith (of Christ)," 159–60. In my view Watson places too much weight on this issue for solving the πίστις Χριστοῦ debate.

147 Watson, "By Faith (of Christ)," 161–62.

148 On this point I am close to Hays. He argues that "by faith" modifies "shall live," but he adds that "the *meaning* of this statement is substantially identical to the affirmation that 'the one who is righteous [= justified] by faith shall live.' If there is any material distinction to be found between

Jesus's Teaching

New Testament scholars have often drawn a contrast between Jesus's miracle faith and Paul's salvation faith, but Yeung has now shown that this is a false dichotomy: "Both Jesus and Paul are seen to adhere to the Jewish biblical tradition and to understand faith as consisting of both the miraculous and the salvific elements."[149] Jesus's teaching about mountain-moving faith may be simply a proverb that faith in God is able to work the impossible (including salvation).[150] But the placement of this tradition alongside the cursing of the fig tree and the cleansing of the temple in Matthew 21 and Mark 11 may suggest that in some versions of his teaching about mountain-moving faith, Jesus was referring to the destruction of the Temple Mount. In this case the saying should be understood "against the Jewish tradition of linking eschatological judgment and salvation with mountain removal" (e.g., Isa. 40:4; 42:15; Ezek. 38:20; Zech. 14:4–5, 10).[151] But in either case, the salvation that mountain removal represents is conditioned on the disciples' faith. The saying in Matthew begins with a conditional clause: "If you have faith and do not doubt . . ." (Matt. 21:21; cf. 17:20 // Luke 17:6), and thus we should probably understand the participle "believing" (πιστεύοντες) in Matthew 21:22 to be conditional as well, meaning "if you believe."[152] The parallel saying in Mark is not technically a conditional clause, but its logic is still conditional: "Whoever [i.e., if anyone] says

---

these statements, it lies in a realm of theological nuances far subtler than Paul could have imagined." *Faith of Jesus Christ*, 134.

149 Yeung, *Faith in Jesus and Paul*, 294. She does, however, recognize different emphases in Jesus and Paul: "*Whereas Jesus offers salvation to those who place their faith in his ability to work miracles, Paul appeals for faith in Jesus' greatest miracle which is the basis of salvation.*" Yeung, 294; emphasis original. On the contrast in New Testament scholarship between Jesus's miracle faith and Paul's salvation faith, see Yeung, 16–17.

150 Scholars who hold this position include D. A. Carson, *Matthew*, EBC (Grand Rapids, MI: Zondervan, 1995), 446; R. T. France, *The Gospel of Mark*, NIGTC (Grand Rapids, MI: Eerdmans, 2002), 448.

151 Yeung, *Faith in Jesus and Paul*, 44; see 40–47 for her entire argument.

152 So ESV, NET, NIV 2011.

to this mountain, 'Be taken up and thrown into the sea,' and does not doubt in his heart, but believes that what he says will come to pass, [then] it will be done for him" (Mark 11:23).

Summary

In the previous two sections, I observed that these passages speak about our faith in God and even Christ. In this section, I have shown that some of them present this faith as a cause of justification or life (Gen. 15:6; Hab. 2:4), while others speak of faith as a condition of salvation (Isa. 8:14 LXX; 28:16; Jesus's teaching).

Conclusion

I have argued in this chapter that the sources Paul references in his teaching about faith describe our faith in God, and even in Christ, as a cause and condition of salvation and justification. The concept of faith in these texts is best described not as faithfulness to God but as faith in God. One piece of evidence I observed is the linguistic point that most of the Old Testament texts Paul quotes in his teaching about faith use the hiphil stem of אמן ("believe, trust") rather than its niphal stem ("be faithful"). This verb is translated by the Septuagint and Paul with the Greek verb πιστεύω ("believe"), a verb also used in Jesus's teaching about mountain-moving faith. This is not to say that there is no overlap between the concept of faith and faithfulness in Paul or in biblical theology (e.g., Neh. 9:8). Rather, it is to say that the word "faith" captures the overall concept much better than the word "faithfulness." "Faith" in these passages always moves from the human being (the subject) toward God and his word (the object). In none of these passages does Paul's interpretation clearly indicate that he sees Christ as the subject of faith, but in at least two, he clearly sees Christ as the object of faith (Isa. 28:16; 53:1).

These passages offer a rich historical background against which we may interpret Paul's teaching about Christ-oriented faith. Faith is trust in God's promise of life (Gen. 15:6), confidence in the goodness of the Lord (Ps. 116:10), reliance on his messianic plan of deliverance rather than one's own plan (Isa. 28:16), belief in the good news about justification through the suffering and exalted servant (Isa. 53:1), and waiting on the Lord to bring about his prophetic word (Hab. 2:4). Finally, in several of these texts, our faith plays a causal role (Gen. 15:6; Hab. 2:4) or a conditional role (Isa. 8:14 LXX; 28:16; Jesus's teaching) in justification and salvation. It should not be surprising, then, to see our faith play such a role in the apostle's theology as well.

2

Direct Statements of Christ-Oriented Faith in Paul's Letters

While Paul proclaims faith in God, he does not have in mind to overturn what he so often emphasizes concerning faith: namely, that all its stability rests in Christ.

JOHN CALVIN, *INSTITUTES OF THE CHRISTIAN RELIGION*

MARTIN LUTHER MIGHT SAY that this chapter is the one by which my book stands or falls. The thesis of this book is that Paul significantly emphasizes Christ-oriented faith in his theology. The previous chapter set the stage for this thesis by observing that the sources referred to in Paul's teaching about faith describe our faith in God, and even in Christ, as a cause and condition of salvation. Here I begin to argue for my thesis by means of a thorough exegesis of Paul's letters. Although Paul's theology is in continuity with the Old Testament passages to which he appeals, in the apostle's letters faith is more explicitly and fundamentally oriented toward Christ.[1]

---

1 I am not denying that Old Testament theology calls for faith in Jesus Christ in any sense. We have already seen that Isaiah speaks in a veiled way about Christ-oriented faith (Isa. 28:16; 53:1), and there is a broader sense in which all messianic prophecy calls for faith. Rather, I am arguing that we do not see explicit references to Christ-oriented faith until the time of the apostles (cf. Acts 3:16; 9:42; 10:43; 11:17; 14:23; 16:31; 19:4; 20:21; 24:24; 26:18).

My thesis, of course, is in conversation with the theological argument of the "faithfulness of Christ" translation of πίστις Χριστοῦ. It is crucial to see, however, that this chapter explores texts in Paul's letters that are *outside* the eight debated phrases. Advocates of the "faithfulness of Christ" translation have significantly de-emphasized the role of Christ-oriented faith not only in these phrases but in Paul's entire theology.[2] For example, Sam Williams suggests that "Paul was not accustomed to thinking of Christ as the 'object' of faith" and that "the person of Christ is not faith's object. *God* is."[3] And both Richard Hays and Douglas Campbell observe that Paul rarely speaks of Christ as the object of faith but rather speaks of faith in the gospel.[4] While this observation is technically correct, it can also be deeply misleading. Perhaps an analogy may be helpful. It is technically correct that Paul rarely calls Jesus Christ "God" (θεός) in his letters. But this observation is deeply misleading if it leads to the conclusion that Paul rarely speaks of Christ as God, for there are other ways in which he speaks of the divinity of Christ—such as with the title "Lord" (κύριος). In the same way, it is technically correct that Paul, unlike John, rarely uses the verb "believe" (πιστεύω) with Christ as the direct object.[5] But this observation should not obscure the fact that all Paul's faith language is oriented toward the person and work of Jesus Christ, as I demonstrate in this chapter.

I organize this chapter by the three ways in which Paul speaks about Christ-oriented faith. First, in some places he explicitly refers to Christ as the object of our faith. Second, in other places he speaks about God

---

2   This de-emphasis is in some cases an unintentional by-product of zeal to prove that, in the πίστις Χριστοῦ phrases, Christ is the subject of πίστις rather than its object. It is also, however, a product of the theological argument that we are not justified by our own faith but rather by the faithfulness of Jesus Christ (see the introduction).

3   Sam K. Williams, "Again *Pistis Christou*," *CBQ* 49, no. 3 (1987): 434.

4   Richard B. Hays, *The Faith of Jesus Christ: The Narrative Substructure of Galatians 3:1–4:11*, 2nd ed. (Grand Rapids, MI: Eerdmans, 2002), 276–77; D. A. Campbell, "False Presuppositions in the Πίστις Χριστου Debate: A Response to Brian Dodd," *JBL* 116, no. 4 (1997): 716.

5   For the many, many examples in John's Gospel and first epistle, see Paul A. Rainbow, *Johannine Theology: The Gospel, the Epistles, and the Apocalypse* (Downers Grove, IL: IVP Academic, 2014), 292.

himself as the object of our faith. It is striking that in these passages the apostle identifies God specifically as the one who raised Christ Jesus from the dead. In other words, our faith in God is by definition oriented toward the resurrection of Christ. Finally, Paul's most common way of speaking about the object of faith is to refer to faith in the gospel message, the good news "concerning [God's] Son" (Rom. 1:3). By examining these various passages, we see that Paul speaks often about belief and trust in the good news of Christ as a cause and condition of our salvation.[6]

Faith in Christ

In this section, we see that Paul's explicit statements about faith in the person of Christ are not as rare as it is sometimes said. Even outside the debated πίστις Χριστοῦ phrases, Paul speaks regularly about Christ-oriented faith. My argument here relies fundamentally on Paul's undisputed letters, but it is also supplemented by his disputed letters.[7] The most important statement of Christ-oriented faith in Paul's letters is probably Galatians 2:16b, because this verse is one of the most important statements of Pauline theology altogether. Thus, I begin with this verse and then examine statements with the verb "believe" (πιστεύω) and then statements with the noun "faith" (πίστις). The most questionable examples are discussed last—namely, those with the noun "faith" (πίστις) and the preposition "in" (ἐν).

Galatians 2:16b

Galatians 2:16 is arguably the most important text in which Paul speaks of Christ as the object of saving faith. The following citation changes

6   As I observed in the last chapter, I use the term *cause* in this chapter in a general way and not in a way that is intended to deny the imputation of Christ's righteousness. For a synthesis of causation and salvation in Pauline theology, see chap. 5, p. 259.

7   I think that it is much more likely that Paul wrote all thirteen of the letters in the New Testament ascribed to him than that the Pastoral Epistles, for example, were forgeries or written by someone else in the name of Paul. Nevertheless, I recognize that many scholars disagree with me, so I am attempting to rest my argument on the undisputed letters.

the ESV slightly by rendering the two πίστις Χριστοῦ phrases literally for the sake of argument:

> [a] We know that a person is not justified by works of the law but through faith of Jesus Christ [διὰ πίστεως ᾽Ιησοῦ Χριστοῦ], [b] so we also have believed in Christ Jesus, [c] in order to be justified by faith of Christ [ἐκ πίστεως Χριστοῦ] and not by works of the law, [d] because by works of the law no one will be justified.

This statement is not an isolated side comment in Galatians but part of a paragraph that many regard as a summary of the entire argument of this fiery little letter.[8] And if Paul's theology corresponds with the arguments of his letters, then we should expect this verse to guide us to a point of emphasis in his theology. Even if one translates the two debated πίστις Χριστοῦ phrases in 2:16a and 2:16c with "the faithfulness of Christ," it is still the case, as Richard Hays has conceded, that "Gal 2:16[b] speaks clearly and unambiguously of faith *in* Christ (εἰς Χριστὸν ᾽Ιησοῦν ἐπιστεύσαμεν), of an act of believing/trust directed toward Christ as 'object.'"[9]

The verb "we . . . have believed" (ἐπιστεύσαμεν) is better translated "we have come to believe" (ingressive aorist) because it describes the initial acceptance of the gospel by the first Jewish Christians who are here represented by Peter and Paul.[10] A similar use of this verb is seen in Romans 13:11: "Salvation is nearer to us now than when we first

---

8   Hays observes that "Betz's rhetorical analysis, which identifies 2:15–21 as the *propositio* [main proposition] of Paul's argument, has reconfirmed a point that has long been grasped intuitively by commentators on this letter: Gal 2:15–21 provides a highly condensed summary of the 'thesis' that Paul intends to argue in the subsequent chapters." *Faith of Jesus Christ*, 122.

9   Hays, *Faith of Jesus Christ*, 123.

10   So Karl Friedrich Ulrichs, *Christusglaube: Studien zum Syntagma πίστις Χριστοῦ und zum paulinischen Verständnis von Glaube und Rechtfertigung*, WUNT, 2nd ser., vol. 227 (Tübingen: Mohr Siebeck, 2007), 39; Martinus C. de Boer, *Galatians: A Commentary*, NTL (Louisville: Westminster John Knox, 2011), 142.

believed [ἐπιστεύσαμεν]."[11] Peter and Paul were "Jews by birth and not Gentile sinners" (Gal. 2:15), and yet they "also" had come to believe in Christ to be justified. Thus their faith here surely refers to their new belief that Jesus is the Christ, the Son of the living God (cf. Peter's confession recorded in Matt. 16:16 and Paul's Damascus experience recorded in Gal. 1:15–16). But it also refers to their trust in Christ rather than relying on works of the law for justification. It was their acknowledgment that no person can be justified by works of the law (including themselves), which led them to trust in Christ Jesus instead.[12]

Some have questioned whether the grammar of this verse actually presents the person of Christ as the object of human faith. These questions arise from Paul's use of a prepositional phrase (εἰς Χριστὸν Ἰησοῦν) rather than a dative direct object to indicate the object of "believe." Rudolf Bultmann argues that the use of πιστεύω εἰς was a distinctly Christian formulation that arose through Christian mission as an abbreviation of the idea of believing "that" (ὅτι) Jesus was the Christ or *that* he had died and been raised.[13] Karl Ulrichs similarly suggests a history-of-tradition relationship of believing εἰς Χριστὸν and believing "that" (ὅτι) Christ has died and risen. This relationship is spelled out in Romans 10, where believing "that God raised him from the dead" (Rom. 10:9) is summarized as believing in him (εἰς

---

11 Note that the word "first" is not in the Greek text as a stand-alone term but is rather the ESV's translation of the ingressive aorist verb ἐπιστεύσαμεν.

12 In his careful study of the rhetoric of this verse, Matlock observes that it moves from impersonal ("a person," ἄνθρωπος) to personal ("we," ἡμεῖς) to impersonal again ("no one," οὐ . . . πᾶσα σάρξ). He then pinpoints the "argumentative movement of the verse" as follows: "'In placing our trust in Christ, we Jews have implicitly acknowledged our place alongside, not above, the Gentiles where righteousness is concerned.' 'We Jews' take our place, literally . . . between ἄνθρωπος and πᾶσα σάρξ." R. Barry Matlock, "The Rhetoric of Πίστις in Paul: Galatians 2.16, 3.22, Romans 3.22, and Philippians 3.9," *JSNT* 30, no. 2 (2007): 199. Building on Matlock's analysis, Pifer concludes that "the antithesis [in Gal. 2:16] sets in contrast two alternative modes of dependence, one that displays dependence upon human effort in obeying the Law, the other displaying dependence upon the saving work of Christ." Jeanette Hagen Pifer, *Faith as Participation: An Exegetical Study of Some Key Pauline Texts*, WUNT, 2nd ser., vol. 486 (Tübingen: Mohr Siebeck, 2019), 152.

13 *TDNT*, s.v. "πιστεύω, κτλ.," 6:203–4.

ὄν, Rom. 10:14).[14] In other words, "the Christ title stands for the Christ event."[15] Or we could say that in this view, Galatians 2:16b refers not to faith in the person of Christ but to faith in the work of Christ. Williams also appeals to this line of thinking to support his view that "Paul is not accustomed to thinking of Christ as the object of faith." Rather, "'to believe in Christ' can better be understood as a Pauline way of saying 'to believe the gospel of God's redemptive work in and through Christ.'"[16] Further, he argues that εἰς Χριστὸν Ἰησοῦν in Galatians 2:16b refers to believing "into Christ," a concept similar to the idea of being baptized "into Christ" (εἰς Χριστὸν).[17] This argument is not unlike the one proposed by Gerhard Kittel a century earlier that the preposition εἰς in Galatians 2:16 need not indicate the "object . . . which faith grasps" (*Object . . . das der Glaube ergriest*) but the "direction . . . in which faith moves" (*Richtung . . . in welcher der Glaube sich bewegt*).[18]

The problem with these grammatical arguments is that they read too much into the preposition εἰς. It was common in Hellenistic Greek to indicate the object of the verb πιστεύω with various prepositions. In classical Greek this verb took its object in the dative, a use that continued in Hellenistic Greek and is seen in the New Testament.[19] But in the Hellenistic period, the dative was dropping out of use, and prepositions like ἐν, εἰς, and ἐπί began to be used to indicate the ob-

---

14 Ulrichs, *Christusglaube*, 114.

15 Ulrichs, *Christusglaube*, 116 (my trans.).

16 Williams, "Again *Pistis Christou*," 442.

17 Williams, "Again *Pistis Christou*," 443.

18 G. Kittel, "Πίστις Ἰησοῦ Χριστοῦ bei Paulus," *TSK* 79 (1906): 428. Both Kittel and Williams relate Paul's expression "into Christ" to the idea of being "in Christ" so that it refers to believers following Christ in his faith. Kittel, "Πίστις Ἰησοῦ Χριστοῦ," 428–29; Williams, "Again *Pistis Christou*," 443.

19 The dative is the predominant way that Josephus and Philo indicate the object of πιστεύω. Cf. Acts 18:8, which says that Crispus, a synagogue ruler in Corinth "believed in the Lord" (ἐπίστευσεν τῷ κυρίῳ, Acts 18:8). Paul uses the dative direct object with πιστεύω only a few times and usually when he is quoting from the Septuagint (Rom. 4:3 [cf. 4:17]; 10:16; Gal. 3:6; 2 Tim. 1:12; Titus 3:8).

ject of πιστεύω.[20] Further, there was apparently no clear distinction between πιστεύω εἰς and πιστεύω with the dative direct object. I say this because John, the New Testament author who uses πιστεύω εἰς most often, employs the two constructions interchangeably:[21]

> As he was saying these things, many believed in him [ἐπίστευσαν εἰς αὐτόν]. So Jesus said to the Jews who had believed him [τοὺς πεπιστευκότας αὐτῷ], "If you abide in my word, you are truly my disciples." (John 8:30–31)

> Though he had done so many signs before them, they still did not believe in him [οὐκ ἐπίστευον εἰς αὐτόν], so that the word spoken by the prophet Isaiah might be fulfilled:

> > "Lord, who has believed what he heard from us [ἐπίστευσεν τῇ ἀκοῇ ἡμῶν],
> > and to whom has the arm of the Lord been revealed?"
> > (John 12:37–38)

Thus, as C. F. D. Moule warned us long ago, we should be wary of reading too much into Paul's use of εἰς with the verb πιστεύω in Galatians 2:16, as if it were different from πιστεύω with the dative direct object.[22] The construction εἰς Χριστὸν Ἰησοῦν ἐπιστεύσαμεν was a natural way for Paul to speak about Christ as the object of faith.[23]

---

20   LSJ, s.v. "πίστ-." Bortone observes that in biblical Greek there is both "a visible increase in prepositional use" and "a reduction in the use of the dative." Pietro Bortone, *Greek Prepositions: From Antiquity to the Present* (New York: Oxford University Press, 2010), 179–83. He warns, however, against making a direct correlation between the loss of cases and the increase of prepositions. Bortone, 180.

21   Bortone observes a similar phenomenon with a different verb in John 8:25–26, where λαλῶ ὑμῖν and λαλῶ εἰς τὸν κόσμον are used with no difference in meaning. Bortone, *Greek Prepositions*, 181.

22   C. F. D. Moule, *An Idiom Book of New Testament Greek*, 2nd ed. (Cambridge: Cambridge University Press, 1959), 69.

23   This conclusion also means that we should not follow the many commentators who suggest that πιστεύω with εἰς in Gal. 2:16 has a deeper meaning than πιστεύω with the dative, signifying

Moreover, the argument that πιστεύω εἰς means believing *that* (ὅτι) rather than believing *in the person* of Christ wrongly opposes believing in a person and believing in the events surrounding that person. This point can be illustrated from a passage in the Shepherd of Hermas:

> First of all, believe that God is one [πίστευσον ὅτι εἷς ἐστιν ὁ θεός], who created all things and set them in order, and made out of what did not exist everything that is, and who contains all things but is himself alone uncontained. Believe in him, therefore [πίστευσον οὖν αὐτῷ], and fear him.[24]

Here there is no difference between the commandment to believe in God and the commandment to believe that he is the one God who created the world. Similarly, Paul explains Abraham's faith in God (τῷ θεῷ, Rom. 4:3) as belief "that [ὅτι] God was able to do what he had promised" (Rom. 4:21). Thus it seems unlikely that the apostle would have distinguished between believing in the person of Christ and believing that he died and was raised. Christ-oriented faith involves faith in both the person and work of Christ together. This supports my larger point that there is no reason to question whether Galatians 2:16 speaks about the person of Christ as the object of our faith, just as Hays conceded.

His concession, however, should have gone further. For Galatians 2:16 speaks not only about faith in Christ but about faith in Christ *as a cause of justification*: "We also have believed in Christ Jesus, in order to be justified." The term "in order that," or ἵνα, signals that justification

---

something like "believing in/into" or a deeper relationship of "acceptance and adherence" to Christ. Ernest De Witt Burton, *A Critical and Exegetical Commentary on the Epistle to the Galatians*, ICC 34 (Edinburgh: T&T Clark, 1921), 481; so Richard N. Longenecker, *Galatians*, WBC 41 (Dallas, TX: Word Books, 1990), 88; de Boer, *Galatians*, 142; Douglas J. Moo, *Galatians*, BECNT (Grand Rapids, MI: Baker Academic, 2013), 163.

24 Shepherd of Hermas, Mandate 26:1–2, in *The Apostolic Fathers in English*, trans. Michael W. Holmes, 3rd ed. (Grand Rapids, MI: Baker Academic, 2007), 505.

is a result of Christ-oriented faith, establishing a causal relationship between the two. Thus, although many aspects of Galatians 2:16 are debated, especially the translation of πίστις Χριστοῦ, the center of this important verse unambiguously establishes a causal relationship between Christ-oriented faith and justification. Even Sam Williams, an advocate of the "faithfulness of Christ" translation, observes that "above all, Hays overlooks the significance of Paul's ἵνα at 2.16."[25]

Scholars in the apocalyptic school have attempted to explain the ἵνα in various other ways. J. Louis Martyn argues that ἵνα does not link *our* faith causally with justification but rather indicates *God's* purpose:

> When *pistis Christou* is read as "faith *in* Christ," the conjunction "in order that" [ἵνα] falsely assumes a causative role, as though it had been Paul's intention to say, "We have believed in order to be *thereby* rectified, God's act of rectification being God's response to our deed of faith." As we have just noted, Paul's understanding of the primacy of God's rectifying act in Christ's faith and his consequent understanding of the genesis of our faith preclude such a view. By the conjunction "in order that" Paul means to speak of *God's purpose* that we be rectified by Christ's faith, and not by our observance of the Law.[26]

But Martyn seems to be ignoring Paul's words. The causative role of faith is not a conclusion from the decision to translate πίστις Χριστοῦ as "faith in Christ." Rather, it is clearly stated in the words "we also have believed in Christ Jesus, in order to be justified." The ἵνα in this verse indicates the purpose of a *human action*, namely, Peter and Paul coming to believe in Christ. Here Martyn's exegesis is clearly under

---

25 Sam K. Williams, "The Hearing of Faith: Ακοη Πιστεως in Galatians 3," *NTS* 35, no. 1 (1989): 89.

26 J. Louis Martyn, *Galatians: A New Translation with Introduction and Commentary*, AB 33A (New York: Doubleday, 1997), 276n182. Cf. de Boer: "The subordinating conjunction *hina* ('so that') probably does not point to Paul's own purpose or to that of other Christian Jews in coming to believe in Christ; the purpose is probably God's." *Galatians*, 154.

the control of his view of Pauline theology: the "primacy of God's rectifying act in Christ's faith" and the idea that justifying faith would be a "*deed* of faith" (emphasis mine). Douglas Campbell also sees the problem of the ἵνα in Galatians 2:16 and suggests that it does not mean "in order that" (a purpose) but rather "that" (an explanation), giving the content of what Paul believes about Christ.[27] It is true that many verbs are supplemented by an explanatory ἵνα in Greek, but I do not know of any place in which πιστεύω is followed by a ἵνα that indicates content.[28] This verb instead uses ὅτι to indicate content.[29] Like Martyn, Campbell's translation is really driven by his view of Pauline theology: his rejection of "justification theory" in favor of "an apocalyptic understanding of Paul."[30] A natural reading of the grammar in Galatians 2:16 links Peter and Paul's faith with justification in a causal relationship.

This is not to say that there is no causal link between Christ himself and justification in Galatians 2:16 and its context. There is already an implicit link between Christ and justification in that Peter and Paul now rely on Christ for justification. And Paul speaks more explicitly about Christ as a cause of justification in the following verses, mentioning "our endeavor to be justified by Christ" (Gal. 2:17)[31] and reasoning that "if righteousness were through the law, then Christ died for no purpose" (Gal. 2:21). Why would the death of Christ be in vain if righteousness came through the law? It is because Christ died to bring

---

27 Douglas A. Campbell, *The Deliverance of God: An Apocalyptic Rereading of Justification in Paul* (Grand Rapids, MI: Eerdmans, 2009), 840–41.

28 Campbell appeals to the second use of ἵνα listed in BDAG. Campbell, *Deliverance of God*, 840. But of the numerous verbs included in this category, πιστεύω is not one of them. BDAG, s.v. "ἵνα," 2.a.α–ζ.

29 BDAG, s.v. "πιστεύω," 1.a.β.

30 Campbell, *Deliverance of God*, 840.

31 Constantine Campbell argues that "in Christ" should be translated "by Christ" in Gal. 2:17 because the last clause in the verse ("Is Christ then a servant of sin?") speaks of Christ's agency in justification. Constantine R. Campbell, *Paul and Union with Christ: An Exegetical and Theological Study* (Grand Rapids, MI: Zondervan, 2012), 114–15. Thus I have changed the ESV's "in Christ" to "by Christ."

about the righteousness that the law could not (cf. Gal. 3:21–22). We see then that Paul speaks of *both* his faith *and* the death of Christ as causes of justification in Galatians 2:16–21.

It is also striking how Paul associates the grace of God with the death of Christ in Galatians 2:21: "I do not nullify the grace of God, for if righteousness were through the law, then Christ died for no purpose." This verse is significant for my thesis on two related points: First, Paul says that the object of our faith—Christ and his death—is an expression of God's grace. I suggest below that this is why the apostle so closely associates our faith with God's grace (Rom. 4:4–5, 16). Second, the fundamental opposition in Paul's theology, at least in this verse, is between God's grace in Christ and righteousness by the law, *not* between God's grace in Christ and righteousness by our faith.

Believe In . . .

There are several other texts in Paul's letters that, like Galatians 2:16b, use the verb "believe" (πιστεύω) with a preposition to present Christ as the object of our faith. Romans 10:14 begins a chain of questions spelling out the apostle's rationale for sending out preachers of the gospel: "How then will they call on him in whom they have not believed [εἰς ὃν οὐκ ἐπίστευσαν]?" By following his chain of questions in Romans 10:14–15, we can see that Paul views our faith as a response to the proclamation of the gospel, believing it to be true. The object of faith in 10:14 is the Lord Jesus, since the antecedent of "on him" (εἰς ὃν) is "the Lord" in the previous verse: "Everyone who calls on the name of the Lord will be saved" (Rom. 10:13, quoting Joel 2:32). While a few scholars have suggested that this Lord in whom one believes and on whom one calls may be God the Father,[32] most commentators rightly see a reference to Christ in Paul's citation,

32 Kittel, "Πίστις Ἰησοῦ Χριστοῦ," 421; Lloyd Gaston, *Paul and the Torah* (Vancouver: University of British Columbia Press, 1987), 131.

since he has just identified Jesus as the one whom Christians confess as the risen "Lord" (Rom. 10:9).[33]

This belief in the Lord Jesus plays a causal role in salvation, because the chain of questions is a chain of causation ending with salvation:

> For "everyone who calls on the name of the Lord will be saved."
>
> How then will they call on him in whom they have not believed? And how are they to believe in him of whom they have never heard? And how are they to hear without someone preaching? And how are they to preach unless they are sent? (Rom. 10:13–15)

Taking this in reverse order, the sending of gospel preachers leads to the preaching of the gospel, which leads to people hearing about the risen Lord, which leads to them believing in him, which leads to them calling on his name, which leads to salvation. Thus, in Romans 10:14, faith in the Lord Jesus is part of a chain of causation leading to salvation.

Philippians 1:29 speaks about the Christ-oriented faith of the Philippians in a side comment: "For it has been granted to you that for the sake of Christ you should not only believe in him [τὸ εἰς αὐτὸν πιστεύειν] but also suffer for his sake." Just a few verses earlier Paul describes the faith of the Philippians in terms of its gospel content, exhorting them to live worthy of the gospel so that he may hear that they are "striving side by side for the faith of the gospel [τῇ πίστει τοῦ εὐαγγελίου]" (Phil. 1:27). In this verse, πίστις most likely means the body of faith that unites these believers in a common front against opposition, and the genitive specifies the content of that faith as the good news itself ("the faith, which is the gospel").[34] It is unlikely that

---

33 E.g., Robert Jewett, *Romans*, Hermeneia (Minneapolis: Fortress, 2007), 663. See especially David B. Capes, *Old Testament Yahweh Texts in Paul's Christology*, WUNT, 2nd ser., vol. 47 (Tübingen: Mohr Siebeck, 1992), 116–23.

34 That is, an epexegetical, or appositional, genitive—so Gordon D. Fee, *Paul's Letter to the Philippians*, NICNT (Grand Rapids, MI: Eerdmans, 1995), 167. Alternately, "of the gospel" may be a subjective genitive meaning "the faith brought about by the gospel." Gerald F. Hawthorne, *Phi-*

πίστις in 1:27 means the Philippians' "faithfulness" or "loyalty" since Paul goes on to speak of their believing in 1:29 with the verb πιστεύω. Thus the focus seems to be on their belief and trust in the gospel.[35] As I observed in chapter 1, there is a close relationship between "the body of faith" that is believed (Phil. 1:27) and the faith by which one believes it (Phil. 1:29). In 1:29, the Philippians' gospel faith is specifically described in terms of believing "in him," referring to Christ as the object of their faith. Once again, Paul seems to see no real distinction between believing in the gospel content and believing in the person of Christ. Moreover, as Veronica Koperski observes, Paul distinguishes the Philippians' faith and their suffering in Philippians 1:29. This means that he thinks of their faith as something distinct from their faithfulness in suffering, two concepts that are often combined by advocates of the "faithfulness of Christ" translation.[36]

This statement is also significant for my thesis because Paul explicitly refers to God's gracious agency behind the Philippians' faith in Christ. As they face opposition, he encourages them that "not only" their coming to believe in Christ "but also" their suffering for his sake has been "granted" to them by God himself (Phil. 1:29).[37] None of this

---

lippians, WBC 43 (Waco, TX: Word Books, 1983), 57. Or some see "faith" as a reference to the Philippians' act of faith that is "in the gospel" (objective genitive). Rudolf Bultmann, *Theology of the New Testament*, trans. Kendrick Grobel (New York: Scribner, 1951), 1:318. But the emphasis on a united front ("striving side by side") makes it seem more likely to me that Paul refers to the common gospel content of the faith that unites believers.

35 Contra Gupta, who argues that πίστις in Phil. 1:27 means "faithfulness" or "loyalty" because of Paul's military imagery and context of opposition. Nijay K. Gupta, *Paul and the Language of Faith* (Grand Rapids, MI: Eerdmans, 2020), 87–88, 91, 94. The problem with this argument is that opposition can cause recantation of belief just as much as it can test one's faithfulness. Cf. Pifer on 1 Thessalonians in *Faith as Participation*, 48.

36 See Veronica Koperski, "The Meaning of *Pistis Christou* in Philippians 3:9," *LS* 18, no. 3 (1993): 205.

37 The verb "granted" is χαρίζομαι, which means "give graciously" (BDAG, use 1), and is related to the noun χάρις, which Paul uses to associate God's grace with both Christ and faith in places like Gal. 2:21 (see above discussion); Rom. 4:4–5, 16 (see following discussion); and Eph. 2:8–9. Ridderbos argues that in Phil. 1:29 it is not the Philippians' internal *faith* that is the gift but rather the external gospel that now allows the church to believe. Herman Ridderbos, *Paul: An Outline*

is an accident; it is all "from God" (Phil. 1:28).[38] For the purposes of this study, I must observe that Paul does not oppose the Philippians' faith to God's grace. Speaking broadly of this letter, Paul does seem to indicate an opposition between relying on or putting one's confidence in the Lord (Phil. 1:14; 2:24) and putting "confidence in the flesh" (Phil 3:3).[39] But he does not oppose human faith in Christ to God's gracious action in salvation. Rather, the apostle sees gracious divine agency behind the Philippians' faith and suffering. These things are God-given.

Paul's merged citation of Isaiah 8:14 and 28:16 in Romans 9:33 is another important example of Christ as the object of faith in Paul's letters:

> Behold, I am laying in Zion a stone of stumbling, and a rock of
>   offense;
> and whoever believes in him [ὁ πιστεύων ἐπ' αὐτῷ] will not be
>   put to shame.

In the last chapter, we observed that the prophet Isaiah called Israel to rely on the stone rather than to fear and rely on the other nations. Paul employs the prophet's words to explain why Israel rejected the preaching of the gospel, that they stumbled over the stone rather

---

of His Theology, trans. John Richard de Witt (Grand Rapids, MI: Eerdmans, 1966), 234n57. But the grammar of the verse seems to indicate that their act of believing is in fact the gift, since the infinitive "believe in him" (τὸ εἰς αὐτὸν πιστεύειν) is the subject that "has been granted" (ἐχαρίσθη).

38 The antecedent of the neuter "that from God" (τοῦτο ἀπὸ θεοῦ) in Phil. 1:28 is likely the entire experience of the Philippians, including their initial coming to faith and their current suffering, which was leading them toward salvation. Silva argues that it refers to "the whole complex of ideas: conflict, destruction, perseverance, and salvation. The true grounds for the Philippians' encouragement was the profound conviction that nothing in their experience took place outside God's superintendence." Moisés Silva, *Philippians*, 2nd ed., BECNT (Grand Rapids, MI: Baker Academic, 2005), 83.

39 These texts all use the second perfect form of the verb πείθω with the preposition ἐν. Cf. 2 Cor. 1:9, which is discussed below.

than believing in him. Once again, we see that faith refers to both belief (or unbelief) that Jesus is the Christ and trust or reliance on this stone.

We saw in the last chapter that the identity of the stone in Isaiah's prophecy is the Lord God himself (Isa. 8:14) and his plan for the deliverance of Jerusalem (Isa. 28:16). Although elusive, this latter stone reference is likely a reference to the establishment of the Davidic monarchy. This is surely the way Paul identifies the stone in Isaiah 28:16 since he cites this verse a second time in support of his discussion of confessing that Jesus is Lord and believing that God raised him from the dead:

> If you confess with your mouth that Jesus is Lord and believe in your heart that God raised him from the dead, you will be saved. For with the heart one believes and is justified, and with the mouth one confesses and is saved. For the Scripture says, "Everyone who believes in him [ὁ πιστεύων ἐπ' αὐτῷ] will not be put to shame." (Rom. 10:9–11)

In Romans 10:11, Paul uses Isaiah 28:16 to speak of the risen Lord as the object of faith. But in Romans 9:33, he merges Isaiah's stone texts together, allowing him to speak of Jesus, the object of our faith, as both Christ (Isa. 28:16) and God (Isa. 8:14).[40]

We also observed in the last chapter that the logic of Isaiah 28:16 is conditional: *if* one believes in this stone, *then* he or she will not be put to shame. Paul appeals to the logic of this verse in order to explain how Gentiles have attained righteousness—namely, "by faith"—whereas Israel has not (Rom. 9:30–31). Thus we see a conditional relationship between Christ-oriented faith and righteousness or justification in

---

40 It seems unlikely that Paul means for readers to see the stone in Rom. 9:32–33 as both the law *and* Christ, even though the two are related—*pace* N. T. Wright, *Paul and the Faithfulness of God*, COQG 4 (Minneapolis: Fortress, 2013), 1179. The law pointed to Christ (cf. Rom. 10:4) and was leading Israel to believe in him rather than stumble over him.

Romans 9:30–33. Finally, and perhaps most surprisingly, we see divine agency even in Israel's unbelief, because the point of Paul's citation is that God himself has laid this stone of stumbling in Jerusalem, hardening Israel in unbelief (cf. Rom. 11:7, 26).

The final two examples come from Paul's first letter to Timothy.[41] First, in a paragraph reflecting on the Lord's mercy to him, Paul states the reason why he was shown such mercy: "that in me, as the foremost [of sinners], Jesus Christ might display his perfect patience as an example to those who were to believe in him for eternal life" (1 Tim. 1:16). As with Galatians 2:16, Paul refers here to his initial coming to faith in contrast with his former life, in which he "had acted ignorantly in unbelief" (1 Tim. 1:13). In contrast with ignorance, his newfound faith refers to his coming to believe the truth about Christ "as an example to those who were [later] to believe in him [πιστεύειν ἐπ᾽ αὐτῷ]" (1 Tim. 1:16). The antecedent of "him" in 1 Timothy 1:16, the object of faith, is clearly "Jesus Christ."[42] And there is a causal relationship between Christ-oriented faith and salvation, for such faith leads to eternal life (εἰς ζωὴν αἰώνιον, 1 Tim. 1:16). Again, this is not to deny that Christ himself is the cause of salvation because Paul has just said that "the saying is trustworthy and deserving of full acceptance, that Christ Jesus came into the world to save sinners" (1 Tim. 1:15). The idea is that Christ saves sinners who believe.

This passage also supports the idea that faith is a gift of God. Paul's former life of blasphemy, persecution, and violence was overwhelmed by grace, faith, and love: "The grace of our Lord overflowed for me with the faith and love that are in Christ Jesus" (1 Tim. 1:14). Paul prioritizes the Lord's grace over his own faith and love by stating it first, but he also associates grace with faith and love as all abounding over

41   The authorship of this letter is disputed. My case does not rest on these two examples but simply refers to them as two more corroborating examples.

42   The textual tradition of 1 Tim. 1:16 is difficult in that some manuscripts say "Jesus Christ," some say "Christ Jesus," and others say "Jesus." But in any case Paul is referring to our faith in Christ.

his former life of blasphemy, persecution, and insolence (1 Tim. 1:13). His meaning is probably that the Lord's grace and his own faith and love are all a part of God's mercy, because 1 Timothy 1:14 explains the statement "I received mercy" in the preceding verse (1 Tim. 1:13).[43]

Finally, Paul also relates his newfound faith to his own faithful ministry by stating that God's mercy resulted in his being appointed as a faithful (πιστόν) minister of the gospel (1 Tim. 1:12). This word "faithful" means that Christ "entrusted" Paul with "the gospel of the glory of the blessed God" (1 Tim. 1:11). Paul's conversion (his faith) resulted in his faithful ministry. Thus his faith and faithfulness are related, though different.

Our last text is at the heart of the message of 1 Timothy, even though it probably reflects an earlier Christian confession or hymn about Christ.[44] This example is grammatically unique in this section in that it uses the verb "believe" in the passive voice with Christ as the subject:

> He was manifested in the flesh,
> > vindicated by the Spirit,
> > > seen by angels,
> > proclaimed among the nations,
> > > believed on [ἐπιστεύθη] in the world,
> > > > taken up in glory. (1 Tim. 3:16)

If we transform this passive use of πιστεύω into the active voice, we find that Christ himself, the great "mystery of godliness" (1 Tim. 3:16), is the object of our faith. As in Romans 10:14–15, our faith is a response to the proclamation of the gospel among the nations, and it embraces

---

43 On faith as a gift, faith as ours, and the priority of grace in 1 Tim. 1:14, see William D. Mounce, *Pastoral Epistles*, WBC 46 (Nashville: Thomas Nelson, 2000), 54.

44 Mounce notes, "It is now generally recognized that this paragraph is at the heart of the Pastoral corpus . . . which puts the instructions of the corpus into proper perspective." *Pastoral Epistles*, 214.

not only the person of Christ but also his incarnation, resurrection, appearance to angels, and ascension to glory.[45]

Faith In . . .

Now we come to several texts in which Paul uses the noun "faith" (πίστις) with a preposition to indicate Christ as the object of our faith. In chapter 1, I observed that πίστις typically means "faithfulness," "faith," or "body of faith" in the New Testament. I have argued in a previous article that whenever πίστις is followed by a preposition in Paul's letters, it should be translated as "faith" and not "faithfulness" because the preposition indicates the object of faith.[46] But this part of my argument was flawed because one can be "faithful" to an object as well. For example, the Greek construction πίστις πρὸς can mean either "faithfulness to" or "faith in." The former use can be seen in 3 Maccabees 3:3, which upholds the Jews' unswerving "loyalty toward the dynasty [πρὸς τοὺς βασιλεῖς . . . πίστιν]." The latter use is more likely in 4 Maccabees's encomium of the courageous mother of seven martyrs, whose enduring "faith in God [τὴν πρὸς θεὸν πίστιν]" (4 Macc. 15:24) is set in parallel with her "hope in God [τὴν ἐλπίδα . . . πρὸς τὸν θεόν]" (4 Macc. 17:4).[47] Though I no longer agree with this part of my previous argument, I argue in this section that in the context of Paul's letters, πίστις followed by a preposition typically refers to our "faith," specifically our faith in Christ.

---

45 The interpretation of this hymn is more difficult than one might think at first glance. My understanding of its six elements basically follows the interpretations of Mounce, *Pastoral Epistles*, 227–30; and Robert W. Yarbrough, *The Letters to Timothy and Titus*, PNTC (Grand Rapids, MI: Eerdmans, 2018), 221–25. For other options, see Mounce, *Pastoral Epistles*, 216–18, 225–26.

46 Kevin W. McFadden, "Does Πίστις Mean 'Faith(fulness)' in Paul?," *TynBul* 66, no. 2 (2015): 266–69.

47 Cf. 4 Macc. 16:22; 17:2. Note that 4 Maccabees also compares the mother's faith with Abraham's courageous faith in God, which led him to sacrifice Isaac (14:20; 16:20–23). This view of Gen. 15:6 seems to follow the line of Jewish interpretation that we saw in Philo and James in chap. 1, p. 63.

Three passages in Paul are similar to one another in that they offer thanksgiving for his readers' faith in Christ and love for all the saints. I am placing the passage from Philemon first because the authorship of Colossians and Ephesians is disputed by some scholars. But the similarities between these three thanksgiving sections are striking, supporting the theory that Paul wrote these three letters at the same time and sent them together with Tychicus:

> I thank my God always when I remember you in my prayers, because I hear of your love and of the *faith that you have toward the Lord Jesus* and for all the saints. (Philem. 4–5)

> We always thank God, the Father of our Lord Jesus Christ, when we pray for you, since we heard of your *faith in Christ Jesus* and of the love that you have for all the saints. (Col. 1:3–4)

> For this reason, because I have heard of your *faith in the Lord Jesus* and your love toward all the saints, I do not cease to give thanks for you, remembering you in my prayers. (Eph. 1:15–16)

Here Paul thanks God for the basic Christian virtues of "faith" (πίστις) and "love" (ἀγάπη). Colossians gives more detail by stating the reason for these virtues: "because of the hope laid up for you in heaven. Of this you have heard before in the word of the truth, the gospel" (Col. 1:5). Because their πίστις is a result of hearing about the hope of the gospel (from Epaphras, Col. 1:7), we should understand πίστις as a reference to their accepting the gospel message—that is, their "faith." Paul is probably thanking God for their initial conversion or coming to believe (cf. Rom. 10:14; Gal. 2:16), although perhaps he is also thanking God for their continuing faith. The fact that Paul thanks *God* for their faith in these passages supports further the idea that he views faith itself as a gift of God.

Christ is the object of faith in these similar statements. In each, the object of the recipients' love is the saints, marked by the preposition εἰς: "for/toward all the saints [εἰς πάντας τοὺς ἁγίους]." And in each, the object of the recipients' faith is Christ, marked by the prepositions πρὸς and ἐν:

"toward the Lord Jesus [πρὸς τὸν κύριον ᾽Ιησοῦν]" (Philem. 5)

"in Christ Jesus [ἐν Χριστῷ ᾽Ιησοῦ]" (Col. 1:4)

"in the Lord Jesus [ἐν τῷ κυρίῳ ᾽Ιησοῦ]" (Eph. 1:15)

The example in Philemon is slightly more complex because the syntax is debated. Literally, it reads, "hearing about your love and faith [faithfulness?] that you have toward the Lord Jesus and for all the saints." Some think Paul is speaking about Philemon's love and faithfulness toward both Jesus and the saints. This construal probably requires the translation "faithfulness" for πίστις since it is unlikely Paul would hear of Philemon's faith in the saints.[48] Because the thanksgiving sections in Colossians and Ephesians are so similar to Philemon, however, it seems more likely that Paul is thanking God for Philemon's love for the saints and faith in the Lord Jesus and that the syntax is written in a chiastic pattern:[49]

    a hearing about your love
      b and faith
      b that you have toward the Lord Jesus
    a and for all the saints

---

48 So CEB: "I've heard of your love and faithfulness, which you have both for the Lord Jesus and for all God's people." McKnight says that the oddity of speaking about faith in the saints is the ultimate problem with this construal. Scot McKnight, *The Letter to Philemon*, NICNT (Grand Rapids, MI: Eerdmans, 2017), 66.

49 This is the consensus position of commentators according to McKnight, *Philemon*, 66.

If this is correct, then the object of faith in each of these texts is the person of Christ. Just as their love is directed toward people (the saints), so their faith is directed toward a person (Christ).[50] On the other hand, as a response to the "word of truth, the gospel" (Col. 1:5–6), we can say that the object of their faith is the entire gospel message as well.

Paul's letter to the Colossians contains one other example of πίστις with a preposition to indicate Christ as the object of faith. This letter was probably written to confront false teachers who might persuade the Colossians to look beyond Christ, the one "in whom are hidden all the treasures of wisdom and knowledge" (Col. 2:3). But Paul is convinced that the Colossians themselves are standing firm: "For though I am absent in body, yet I am with you in spirit, rejoicing to see your good order and the firmness of your faith in Christ [τῆς εἰς Χριστὸν πίστεως ὑμῶν]" (Col. 2:5).[51] As in Colossians 1:4, πίστις is the response to what they "were taught" (Col. 2:7) by Epaphras and thus should be translated as the Colossians' response of "faith" in that teaching, believing it to be true. The object of this faith is Christ himself (εἰς Χριστὸν, Col. 2:5) about whose person ("the image of the invisible God," Col. 1:15) and work ("you . . . he has now reconciled . . . by his death," Col. 1:21–22) Paul has just spoken. But here Paul says that the Colossians' initial faith in Christ has continued and is characterized by "firmness" or perseverance in this belief (Col. 2:5).

Finally, we come to several texts in which it is possible but not entirely certain that Paul speaks about Christ as the object of our

---

50 Another parallel to these three passages can be seen in the thanksgiving section of 2 Thess. 1:3: "We ought always to give thanks to God for you, brothers, as is right, because your faith is growing abundantly, and the love of every one of you for one another is increasing." If we read this against Philem. 4–5; Col. 1:3–4; and Eph. 1:15, then the Thessalonians' faith for which Paul gives thanks is their faith in Christ, even though Paul does not explicitly state this.

51 Cf. the same Greek construction (πίστις + εἰς Χριστὸν) in Acts 24:24: "After some days Felix came with his wife Drusilla, who was Jewish, and he sent for Paul and heard him speak about faith in Christ Jesus [τῆς εἰς Χριστὸν Ἰησοῦν πίστεως]." This is the only place in the New Testament outside Paul's letters where we see "Christ Jesus" rather than "Jesus Christ" (although see the variant in 1 Pet. 5:10), showing the historical rootedness of this description of Paul's teaching.

faith. There are two texts in which the prepositional phrase "in Christ" or "in his blood" may modify the noun πίστις, indicating the object of faith, or it may modify another element in the sentence.[52] In Romans 3:25, the translations disagree over whether the phrase "by/in his blood" modifies "faith," referring to the object of our faith, or "propitiation," referring to the means by which atonement was made:

. . . a propitiation through faith in his blood. (KJV)

. . . a propitiation by his blood, to be received by faith. (ESV)

While the close relationship between atonement and blood favors the second translation (cf. Lev. 17:11), Paul's word order favors the first translation: ἱλαστήριον διὰ τῆς πίστεως ἐν τῷ αὐτοῦ αἵματι.[53]

This question is complicated by the well-known hypothesis that Paul is quoting an early Christian tradition in Romans 3:25. Those who hold this hypothesis normally suggest that Paul has inserted "by faith [διὰ τῆς πίστεως]" into the original formula "propitiation . . . by his blood [ἱλαστήριον . . . ἐν τῷ αὐτοῦ αἵματι]."[54] But Bruce Longenecker has rightly asked, "If Paul had intended to introduce a reference to the believer's faith into the formula, would he have done it in such a clumsy manner?"[55] Longenecker's solution is to view "by faith [διὰ τῆς πίστεως]" as part of the original formula but to

52 Interpreters often argue that πίστις ἐν in Rom. 3:25 and Gal. 3:26 cannot refer to Christ as the object of faith because Paul's undisputed letters do not use this construction; for example, R. Barry Matlock notes that this is a common argument and assumes it is correct. "ΠΙΣΤΙΣ in Galatians 3.26: Neglected Evidence for 'Faith in Christ'?," *NTS* 49, no. 3 (2003): 434, 436. But is not this line of argument begging the question?

53 Perhaps the omission of "through faith" (διὰ τῆς πίστεως) in manuscript A is due to the close relationship between propitiation (ἱλαστήριον) and blood (ἐν τῷ αὐτοῦ αἵματι).

54 E.g., Jewett, *Romans*, 287.

55 Bruce W. Longenecker, "Πίστις in Romans 3.25: Neglected Evidence for the 'Faithfulness of Christ'?" *NTS* 39, no. 3 (1993): 479.

interpret this word as a reference to Jesus's own "faithfulness" so that the three terms ("propitiation," "faithfulness," "blood") all refer to his death on the cross.[56] This simple solution is certainly possible. But would it not be as simple of a solution to the supposed awkwardness to say that "in his blood" comes after "faith" in order to present the death of Christ as the object of our faith (thus: "a propitiation through faith in his blood")?[57] A parallel to this way of speaking can be found in 1 Corinthians 15:3, where Paul says that the Corinthians had come to believe the tradition "that Christ died for our sins."[58] Perhaps Paul speaks of faith in the blood of Christ in Romans 3:25 because faith in the atoning death of Christ is the means by which people share in that atonement and thus experience the forgiveness of sins in justification.[59]

Galatians 3:26 presents a similar conundrum about whether the phrase "in Christ Jesus" modifies the noun "faith," signaling the object of faith, or whether it modifies the verb "are," referring to the Galatians' existence as sons of God in union with Christ. The difference can again be seen in the translations:

---

56 Downs and Lappenga now argue that "propitiation," "faithfulness," and "blood" in Rom. 3:25 refer not to Jesus's sacrificial death but to his resurrection life as an atonement (building on David Moffitt's innovative thesis about Hebrews). David J. Downs and Benjamin J. Lappenga, *The Faithfulness of the Risen Christ: Pistis and the Exalted Lord in the Pauline Letters* (Waco, TX: Baylor University Press, 2019), 117–25. But Paul speaks of Jesus's "blood" and his "death" synonymously in the argument in Rom. 5:9–10, making this new view unlikely.

57 So Mark A. Seifrid, *Christ, Our Righteousness: Paul's Theology of Justification*, NSBT 9 (Downers Grove, IL: InterVarsity Press, 2000), 134n13.

58 Cf. also Ignatius: "Even the heavenly beings and glory of angels and the rulers, both visible and invisible, are subject to judgment if they do not believe in the blood of Christ" (ἐὰν μὴ πιστεύσωσιν εἰς τὸ αἷμα Χριστοῦ). Ignatius, *To the Smyrnaeans*, 6.1, in Holmes, *Apostolic Fathers*, 253. Ignatius likely mentions the blood of Christ in response to those who did not truly believe that Jesus suffered and was raised (cf. 2.1).

59 John Calvin comments, "I think that his intention was to use a single idea to declare that God is reconciled to us as soon as we put our trust in the blood of Christ, because by faith we come to the possession of this benefit." *The Epistles of Paul the Apostle to the Romans and to the Thessalonians*, trans. Ross Mackenzie, ed. David W. Torrance and Thomas F. Torrance (Grand Rapids, MI: Eerdmans, 1979), 76.

For ye are all the children of God by faith in Christ Jesus. (KJV)

For in Christ Jesus you are all sons of God, through faith. (ESV)

Many commentators have been persuaded of the latter interpretation, because of the emphasis on participation with Christ in the context.[60] In fact, the same phrase, "in Christ Jesus," is used just two verses later to indicate union with Christ: "There is neither Jew nor Greek, there is neither slave nor free, there is no male and female, for you are all one in Christ Jesus" (Gal. 3:28). On the other hand, the phrase could be used in slightly different ways in Galatians 3:26 and 3:28, and the idea of faith in Christ and participation with Christ are closely related in Galatians.[61] Once again, Paul's word order in Galatians 3:26 suggests that the prepositional phrase modifies the noun "faith": διὰ τῆς πίστεως ἐν Χριστῷ Ἰησοῦ.[62] Hays says that the word order in Galatians 3:26 is insignificant, but he does not support this suggestion other than with the argument that most commentators now see ἐν Χριστῷ Ἰησοῦ as a reference to union with Christ.[63] But commentators can be wrong, of course, and word order is not entirely insignificant in ancient Greek.[64] Perhaps, then, Galatians 3:26 is making a statement about Christ-oriented faith

60 For example, Schreiner takes "in Christ Jesus" as a reference to participation in Christ because Gal. 3:27 speaks about baptism into Christ, Gal. 3:28 says believers are "one in Christ Jesus," and Gal. 3:29 says believers belong to Christ. Thomas R. Schreiner, *Galatians*, ZECNT (Grand Rapids, MI: Zondervan, 2010), 256. He notes that J. B. Lightfoot, Hans Dieter Betz, F. F. Bruce, and Gordon Fee hold this view. Schreiner, 256n6.

61 Wolter notes that one category of the "in Christ" phrase is Christ as the object of faith and boasting, although he does not see such a use in Gal. 3:26. Michael Wolter, *Paul: An Outline of His Theology*, trans. Robert L. Brawley (Waco, TX: Baylor University Press, 2015), 230, 234n68.

62 In contrast, in Gal. 3:28, the phrase "in Christ Jesus" immediately follows the verb "you are."

63 Hays, *Faith of Jesus Christ*, 155–56. A better argument is given by Fee, who thinks that ἐν Χριστῷ Ἰησοῦ means union with Christ and that Paul has placed it at the end of the sentence for emphasis. Gordon D. Fee, "Paul's Use of Locative ἐν in Galatians: On Text and Meaning in Galatians 1.6; 1.1; 2.20; 3.11–12, and 3.26," in *The Impartial God: Essays in Biblical Studies in Honor of Jouette M. Bassler*, ed. Calvin J. Roetzel and Robert L. Foster, NTMon 22 (Sheffield: Sheffield Phoenix, 2007), 182–83.

64 It is common for Greek grammars to discuss word order—e.g., BDF, §§472–78.

as the means by which the Gentiles have become the children of God. Again, this is not to deny that the Gentiles are the children of Abraham because of their union with Christ as well (see Gal. 3:29).

The disputed Pastoral Epistles also have a few examples in which ἐν Χριστῷ Ἰησοῦ could refer to Christ as the object of our faith or speak more generally about union with Christ:

> Those who serve well as deacons gain a good standing for themselves and also great confidence in the faith that is in Christ Jesus [ἐν πίστει τῇ ἐν Χριστῷ Ἰησοῦ]. (1 Tim. 3:13)

> From childhood you have been acquainted with the sacred writings, which are able to make you wise for salvation through faith in Christ Jesus [διὰ πίστεως τῆς ἐν Χριστῷ Ἰησοῦ]. (2 Tim. 3:15)[65]

This same grammatical construction (article + ἐν Χριστῷ Ἰησοῦ) occurs in the Pastorals with "life" (2 Tim. 1:1), "grace" (2 Tim. 1:9; cf. 1 Cor. 1:4), and "salvation" (2 Tim. 2:10). So perhaps it is simply a way of designating how faith relates to union with Christ. On the other hand, perhaps when the construction is paired with πίστις, it specifically designates the object of faith.[66] The example in 2 Timothy 3:15 is also significant for my thesis because it speaks about such faith as a means or cause of "salvation." But it has also been recently argued that this verse speaks about salvation "through the faith(fulness) that is in Christ Jesus," so it cannot be a decisive piece of evidence for the argument of this chapter, which is attempting to address texts outside the πίστις Χριστοῦ debate.[67]

---

65 Cf. also "faith and love that are in Christ Jesus" in 1 Tim. 1:14 and 2 Tim. 1:13, although in these verses it may be that ἐν Χριστῷ Ἰησοῦ modifies only "love" and not "faith."

66 Mounce sees both as possible. *Pastoral Epistles*, 55.

67 Downs argues for this translation based on the larger context of 2 Timothy, in which the phrase would evoke "two themes developed earlier in the letter: first, participatory union for those 'in Christ,' and second, Christ's own faithfulness in 2:8–13 (cf. 1:12; 4:18)." David J. Downs,

Summary

We have seen many texts outside the debated πίστις Χριστοῦ phrases in which Paul speaks explicitly about our faith in Christ. One of these texts lies at the heart of the Pauline theology (Gal. 2:16b), and several others occur in his undisputed letters (Rom. 3:25[?]; 9:33 and 10:11, both quoting Isa. 28:16; Rom. 10:14; Gal. 3:26[?]; Phil. 1:29; Philem. 4–5). His disputed letters give additional evidence for those who think they were written by Paul, as I do (Eph. 1:15–16; Col. 1:3–4; 2:5; 1 Tim. 1:16; 3:13[?]; 3:16; 2 Tim. 3:14[?]). In these texts, faith is both belief in the truth that Jesus is the Christ *and* trust in him rather than relying on the law for justification (Gal. 2:16b). The object of our faith in these texts is the person of Christ, although I have observed at several points that the apostle does not neatly distinguish between faith in the person of Christ and faith in the events of the gospel. Finally, Christ-oriented faith is clearly presented as a cause of our justification (Rom. 9:30–33; Gal. 2:16b) and salvation (Rom. 10:13–15). Paul has no qualms about saying that faith justifies, as long as it is faith in the Christ who justifies. Just as the death of Christ is an expression of God's grace, so even our faith in Christ is a part of God's gift of salvation to us (Phil. 1:29; cf. 1 Tim. 1:13–14 and the thanksgiving passages).

We begin to see, then, that Paul significantly emphasizes Christ-oriented faith in his theology. In the next two sections, I establish this thesis further by showing that when Paul speaks about faith in God, such faith is typically oriented toward the resurrection of Christ, and when Paul speaks about faith in the gospel, it is nothing less than the gospel of God's Son.

Faith in the God Who Raised Christ from the Dead

Scholars who hold to the "faithfulness of Christ" translation of πίστις Χριστοῦ sometimes observe that Paul often speaks about faith in God

---

"Faith(fulness) in Christ Jesus in 2 Timothy 3:15," *JBL* 131, no. 1 (2012): 158. For interaction with Downs on Christ's faithfulness, see chap. 5, p. 246.

rather than faith in Christ. For example, Hays opens his treatment of Romans 3:21–26 with this statement:

> Romans is from start to finish thoroughly theocentric. Nowhere is there any statement comparable to Gal 2:16 that unambiguously presents Christ as an object of faith. In Romans, righteousness is reckoned "to those who believe in *the One who raised Jesus our Lord from the dead.*"[68]

This statement is incorrect. We have already seen unambiguous references to Christ as the object of faith in Romans 9:33; 10:11; and 10:14.[69] But it is also misleading at a deeper level, because it sets the apostle's theocentrism in Romans against his Christology and implies that faith in God is by definition *not* faith in Christ. But even in the verse Hays cites (Rom. 4:24), the object of faith is the God "who raised from the dead *Jesus our Lord.*" In this section, I observe that this is the typical way Paul speaks about our faith in God. Faith in God includes the belief that God has raised Christ from the dead and thus is by definition oriented toward Christ.

Romans 4

Paul's longest and most important reflection about faith in God is found in Romans 4. In this chapter, the apostle quotes Genesis 15:6 and demonstrates on the basis of this verse that even the patriarch Abraham was not justified by works but was justified by faith: "Abraham believed God, and it was counted to him as righteousness" (Rom. 4:3).[70] Another concern in this chapter is Abraham's fatherhood of the Gentiles (especially Rom. 4:9–12, 16–17), but my discussion focuses on Abraham's faith and justification since this is the subject of our study.

---

68 Hays, *Faith of Jesus Christ*, 156.
69 Ulrichs also observes that these texts are a reason *not* to play "theocentrism" off Christology as Hays does. *Christusglaube*, 152.
70 See chap. 1, p. 60, for a discussion of Gen. 15:6 in its original context and in Paul's quotation.

Romans 4:18–21 is a commentary on Genesis 15:6a, opening with the verb "he believed," explaining this clause, and immediately being followed by a quotation of Genesis 15:6b: "That is why his faith was 'counted to him as righteousness'" (Rom. 4:22). Thus, these verses illuminate Paul's understanding of faith in God perhaps more than any other passage in the apostle's letters:

> In hope he believed against hope, that he should become the father of many nations, as he had been told, "So shall your offspring be." He did not weaken in faith when he considered his own body, which was as good as dead (since he was about a hundred years old), or when he considered the barrenness [lit. "deadness," νέκρωσιν] of Sarah's womb. No unbelief made him waver concerning the promise of God, but he grew strong in his faith as he gave glory to God, fully convinced that God was able to do what he had promised. (Rom. 4:18–21)

Here faith involves both belief and trust for Abraham. He believed in the truth of God's promise that his offspring would be like the stars, just as God had said: "So shall your offspring be" (Rom. 4:18, quoting Gen. 15:5).[71] And he trusted in God's ability to fulfill that promise, being "fully convinced that God was able to do what he had promised" (Rom. 4:21). Paul may initially be describing Abraham's coming to believe the promise in Genesis 15:6.[72] But the focus of Paul's commentary is on Abraham's persevering faith over time because there are several allusions to Genesis 17, including Abraham's age ("about a hundred years old,"

---

71 Cf. Rom. 4:20: "No unbelief made him waver concerning the promise of God." Schliesser has now argued at length that the verb διακρίνω in this verse should be translated not "waver" or "doubt" God's promise but rather "dispute" or "argue" with God's promise. Benjamin Schliesser, "'Abraham Did Not "Doubt" in Unbelief' (Rom. 4:20): Faith, Doubt, and Dispute in Paul's Letter to the Romans," *JTS* 63, no. 2 (2012): 492–522. In either case, Paul's point is that Abraham believed God's promise.

72 If this is the case, we can translate the verb "believed" (ἐπίστευσεν) in Rom. 4:18 with an ingressive aorist, "he came to believe." So Schliesser, "Rom. 4:20," 513; cf. Gal. 2:16.

Rom. 4:19; cf. Gen. 17:1, 17) and the promise that he would be "the father of many nations" (Rom. 4:18; cf. Gen. 17:5). Over the course of the many years between the promise and fulfillment, Abraham "did not weaken in faith" (Rom. 4:19) but "grew strong in his faith as he gave glory to God" (Rom. 4:20).[73]

What stands out in Paul's description of Abraham's faith in these verses is the *paradoxical nature of Abraham's faith*. Paul's opening words express this paradox, which, translated, literally says, "Who, against hope on the basis of hope, believed." Abraham believed "against hope" because God's promise of a living child was contrary to all natural human expectations. Paul says that Abraham gave full consideration to what the apostle calls the reality of death: "He considered his own body, which was as good as dead," and "the deadness of Sarah's womb" (Rom. 4:19, my trans.).[74] There was no real hope that Abraham and Sarah could have children. And yet, Abraham still believed "on the basis of hope" (Rom. 4:18, my trans.) that he would have children because he was "fully convinced that God was able to do what he had promised" (Rom. 4:21). Thus, the basis of Abraham's hope was the promise of God, which contradicted the hopeless reality of the circumstances. There is a paradoxical element in Abraham's faith that trusts in God's promise of life despite the contrary circumstances of death.

---

73 As many have observed, the idea that Abraham's faith "gave glory to God" indicates that faith is an act of worship, which is the opposite of Gentile idolaters, who do not glorify God (Rom. 1:18–32). Perhaps Paul assumes the Jewish tradition rooted in Josh. 24:2–3 that Abraham rejected his family's idolatry; on this tradition, see Edward Adams, "Abraham's Faith and Gentile Disobedience: Textual Links between Romans 1 and 4," *JSNT* 19, no. 65 (1997): 55–59.

74 Gathercole observes that "here Pauline faith involves not only believing what is not visible; it involves also staring facts in the face." S. J. Gathercole, "Justified by Faith, Justified by His Blood: The Evidence of Romans 3:21–4:25," in *Justification and Variegated Nomism*, vol. 2, *The Paradoxes of Paul*, ed. D. A. Carson, Peter T. O'Brien, and Mark A. Seifrid, WUNT, 2nd ser., vol. 181 (Grand Rapids, MI: Baker, 2004), 162. Note that some manuscripts add the word "not" (οὐ) to the verb "considered" (see the KJV translation), which was perhaps a scribal attempt to smooth out the paradox.

The reason Abraham's faith is paradoxical is because the object of his faith is the God who raises the dead—that is, the one who acts in ways that are contrary to normal human circumstances. Paul describes the object of faith three times in Romans 4. First, he describes the object of Abraham's faith as "him who justifies the ungodly" (Rom. 4:5). This description highlights what John Barclay calls the "incongruous" grace of God, the justification of ungodly people contrary to what they deserve.[75] Second, Paul describes the object of Abraham's faith as the one "who gives life to the dead and calls into existence the things that do not exist" (Rom. 4:17). This description highlights God's power to raise the dead and create "*ex nihilo*, or rather *ex contrario*."[76] In other words, it highlights the supernatural power of God that can do what is humanly impossible. Third, in the end of the passage, Paul describes Christian faith in God similarly as belief "in him who raised from the dead Jesus our Lord" (Rom. 4:24). This description is more specific in that it says God has already concretely demonstrated his supernatural power by raising Jesus our Lord. Thus, the reason that Abraham's faith is a paradox is because the object of his faith is the God who miraculously contradicts natural human circumstances.[77] God, the object of our faith, justifies the ungodly and creates life out of death, and he has now done both of these things by raising our Lord Jesus from the dead.

---

75 John Barclay, *Paul and the Gift* (Grand Rapids, MI: Eerdmans, 2015), 486–87. We can contrast Paul's interpretation of Gen. 15:6 with Philo, who argues that Abraham's faith was simply an act of righteousness or justice, "for nothing is so just or righteous as to put in God alone a trust which is pure and unalloyed." Philo, *Who Is the Heir of Divine Things?*, trans. F. H. Colson, LCL 261 (Cambridge, MA: Harvard University Press, 1932), §§94–95.

76 Karl Barth, *Church Dogmatics*, ed. G. W. Bromiley and T. F. Torrance, trans. G. W. Bromiley, G. T. Thomson, and Harold Knight (London: T&T Clark, 2009), 4.1:574. For this reference I am indebted to Gathercole, "Justified by Faith," 166.

77 Schliesser observes that "Paul's use of δυνατός [in Rom. 4:21] (and ἐνεδυναμώθη [in Rom. 4:20]) recalls the keyword δύναμις from his *propositio* [in Rom. 1:16]. . . . Both terms belong to the miracle-terminology." Benjamin Schliesser, *Abraham's Faith in Romans 4: Paul's Concept of Faith in Light of the History of Reception of Genesis 15:6*, WUNT, 2nd ser., vol. 224 (Tübingen: Mohr Siebeck, 2007), 386n1193.

Paul presents Abraham's faith as a model for Christian faith in that we all believe in the same God who raises the dead.[78] He does not say that Abraham believed in Christ beforehand.[79] Nor does he, strictly speaking, say that Abraham believed in the God who raised Christ.[80] Rather, he says that Abraham believed in the God "who justifies the ungodly" (Rom. 4:5) and "who gives life to the dead" (Rom. 4:17). This is why his faith is a model, or type, of our faith, which believes in the God who has raised our Lord Jesus from the dead for our justification (Rom. 4:24–25). We can say, then, that our faith in God is clearly oriented toward the resurrection of Christ and that Abraham's faith in God is a type of our Christ-oriented faith, which was to come later.[81]

Paul speaks of this faith as a cause of our justification. I observed in the last chapter that the logic of Genesis 15:6 presents Abraham's faith as a cause of his righteousness: "Abraham believed God, and [the result was that] it was counted to him as righteousness" (Rom. 4:3, quoting Gen. 15:6). Ian Wallis, defending the theological argument of the "faithfulness of Christ" view, says that Paul here "understands the relationship between faith and righteousness to be one of coincidence rather than consequence."[82] He paraphrases his understanding of Paul this way: "In response to God's free-election and promise to make him the father of all nations, Abraham believed in God, who justifies the ungodly independently of their initiatives."[83] The problem with this

---

78 On the question whether Paul views Abraham's faith as a model for Jesus's faith, see chap. 1, p. 81. At the very least, it is clear that Abraham is presented as a paradigm for the Christian's faith in Rom. 4:12, 23–25.

79 Cf. John 8:56, where Jesus tells the Jewish leaders, "Your father Abraham rejoiced that he would see my day. He saw it and was glad."

80 *Pace* Hill's argument that "God *was* for Abraham the God who would raise Jesus." Wesley Hill, *Paul and the Trinity: Persons, Relations, and the Pauline Letters* (Grand Rapids, MI: Eerdmans, 2015), 61. Strictly speaking, Paul does not quite say this in Rom. 4.

81 On Abraham's faith as a type of Christian faith, see Schliesser, *Abraham's Faith*, 404–16.

82 Ian G. Wallis, *The Faith of Jesus Christ in Early Christian Traditions*, SNTSMS 84 (Cambridge: Cambridge University Press, 1995), 94.

83 Wallis, *Faith of Jesus Christ*, 95.

argument is that Paul makes the logic of Genesis 15:6 explicit in his commentary on the verse. First he explains the clause "Abraham believed God" (Rom. 4:3; cf. Gen. 15:6a) in Romans 4:18–21. Then he draws an inference that shows the consequence of the patriarch's faith: "That is why [διὸ] his faith was 'counted to him as righteousness'" (Rom. 4:22, quoting Gen. 15:6b). Thus Paul understands Abraham's faith as a cause that resulted in his justification.[84]

This is not to set Paul's anthropology against his Christology, for in the final sentence of Romans 4, Paul describes Christ himself as a cause leading to our justification: "who was delivered up for our trespasses and raised for our justification" (Rom. 4:25). The preposition "for" (διά) in the second half of this verse is most likely prospective, indicating the purpose for which Christ was raised: our justification.[85] Taken as a whole, this pithy sentence refers to both the death and resurrection of Christ resulting in the Christian's justification, for the death of Christ is the basis of the forgiveness of trespasses on which the reckoning of righteousness stands (cf. Rom. 5:9). This means that Paul speaks of both our faith *and* the work of Christ as causes of justification in Romans 4. Or, as he puts it in the next chapter, we are both "justified by faith" (Rom. 5:1) *and* "justified by his blood" (Rom. 5:9). Thus, we should not exclude either human faith or the death and resurrection of Christ as causes of justification in Pauline theology.

Finally, Romans 4 contains some of Paul's most important reflection on the relationship between faith, works, and grace. Here we see that Paul does not set our faith and God's grace in opposition but rather associates faith with grace, setting both in opposition to works and the law. In his first discussion of Genesis 15:6, Paul draws a contrast

---

84 Ulrichs observes that the causal role of faith is also seen in Paul's language about the "righteousness of faith" (Rom. 4:13; cf. 4:11, in which the ESV's translation "righteousness that he had by faith" is literally "the righteousness of faith"), which refers to faith as the ground of righteousness. *Christusglaube*, 154.

85 So, e.g., Thomas R. Schreiner, *Romans*, 2nd ed. BECNT (Grand Rapids, MI: Baker Academic, 2018), 251–52. See discussion in Moule, *Idiom Book*, 55.

between the worker and the believer: "Now to the one who works, his wages are not counted as a gift but as his due. And to the one who does not work but believes in him who justifies the ungodly, his faith is counted as righteousness" (Rom. 4:4–5).[86] Paul's description of the worker is of one who receives his "due," or the pay that is owed him. This manner of reception is by definition for Paul not counted "as a gift" (κατὰ χάριν). His description of the believer, however, is of one who "does not work but believes in him who justifies the ungodly." Paul's point is that the believer believes in the God of grace who justifies those who do not deserve to be justified. Thus we see the implication that, for Paul, receiving righteousness by faith is by definition counted "as a gift," or according to grace (κατὰ χάριν).[87] He associates faith with grace in opposition to works.

Paul says much the same thing a few verses later when he argues that the Abrahamic inheritance could not come by the law but only by faith: "For if it is the adherents of the law who are to be the heirs, faith is null and the promise is void. For the law brings wrath. . . . That is why it depends on faith, in order that the promise may rest on grace [κατὰ χάριν]" (Rom. 4:14–16). Once again, the apostle associates faith with grace, here in opposition to the law. In fact, he says that receiving the promise by faith results in it resting "on grace" (κατὰ χάριν).

Why does Paul associate our faith so closely with God's grace in Romans 4? I suggest that he does so because the object of our faith (and Abraham's faith) is the God who is gracious, who "justifies the

---

86 Martyn has argued that Paul does not focus his attention on two lines of human action for justification but rather opposes human action with divine action (see the introduction, p. 36). But as Ulrichs has observed, Rom. 4:4–5 clearly opposes two lines of human action: the worker and the believer. *Christusglaube*, 155.

87 For Paul, this is specifically an *undeserved* gift. Barclay observes that in antiquity even gifts were generally given according to the worth of the recipient. Thus Paul could have contrasted pay-for-work with Abraham's faith being nobly rewarded with the gift of righteousness. But instead, "Paul 'perfects' the notion of gift in what we have come to see as his typical fashion. The term χάρις is perfected as an *incongruous gift*, so that the opposite to pay-for-work is here not gift-to-the-worthy but a startling expression of non-correspondence." *Paul and the Gift*, 485.

ungodly" (Rom. 4:4).[88] Therefore, in Pauline theology, not only is our faith itself a part of God's grace (Phil. 1:29), but the object of our faith is the God of grace who has forgiven our trespasses and justified us by the death and resurrection of his Son (Rom. 4:24–25; cf. 8:32).

2 Corinthians 1:9; 4:13–14

In his second letter to the Corinthians, the suffering apostle speaks twice of his faith in the God who raised Christ from the dead. The first example comes in a disclosure to the Corinthians of the purpose for his suffering in Asia:

> For we do not want you to be unaware, brothers, of the affliction we experienced in Asia. For we were so utterly burdened beyond our strength that we despaired of life itself. Indeed, we felt that we had received the sentence of death. But that was to make us rely not on ourselves but on God who raises the dead. (2 Cor. 1:8–9)

Paul almost always uses the verb πιστεύω or the noun πίστις in his teaching about faith. But here we find an exception, in which he uses the second perfect form of the verb πείθω, which means "to be so convinced that one puts confidence in" someone.[89] This verb depicts Paul's faith as reliant or confident trust in God. But this trust also involves belief in certain truths about God—namely, that he is the "God who raises the dead."

The object of Paul's confidence is spelled out in a negative and positive fashion: God led him through such extreme suffering in Asia so

88 The idea that God is a God who forgives his people's sin and gives them what they do not deserve has deep roots in Old Testament theology. (For example, Gathercole follows Otfried Hofius in noting especially Hosea, Jeremiah, and Isa. 40–55. "Justified by Faith," 166.) But it has a sharper edge for the apostle who proclaims that "Christ died for the ungodly" (Rom. 5:6).

89 BDAG, s.v. "πείθω," use 2. Perhaps he uses this verb because it is the one he tends to employ when speaking specifically about trusting in oneself, as he does in this passage (cf. Rom. 2:19; Phil. 3:3).

that he would rely *not* on himself ("on ourselves"[90]) *but* "on God who raises the dead." One might argue that Paul is speaking about faith in God with no reference to Christ in this passage.[91] But he has just argued that his suffering is a sharing in the sufferings of Christ (2 Cor. 1:5), so it is more likely that the reason he identifies God as the one "who raises the dead" is because God had raised the suffering Christ from the dead. My theory is confirmed by a second passage in which Paul speaks about his faith in God in this letter. This passage occurs a few chapters later but in the same major section of the letter: "Since we have the same spirit of faith according to what has been written, 'I believed, and so I spoke,' we also believe, and so we also speak, knowing that he who raised the Lord Jesus will raise us also with Jesus and bring us with you into his presence" (2 Cor. 4:13–14). Here Paul appeals to the psalmist's faith (cf. Ps. 116:10), which led him to speak in the midst of suffering, as a pattern for his own speaking of the gospel in the midst of suffering.[92]

In his larger argument Paul is giving a rationale for why he does not lose heart in his ministry of the gospel even though he is suffering for it (2 Cor. 4:1, 16): because he walks by faith and not by sight (cf. 2 Cor. 5:7). Our passage is a kind of microcosm of that argument, giving a rationale for why Paul continues to speak in the midst of suffering. Just like the psalmist, it is because of his faith: "We also believe, and so we also speak" (2 Cor. 4:13). This rationale is then further explained in the next verse with a causal participle that describes the content of

---

90 Paul uses the first person plural throughout the opening chapters of 2 Corinthians to refer to himself and his apostolic ministry.

91 Some have suggested that Paul is using a traditional description of God seen also in the second petition and final benediction of the Jewish prayers known as the "Eighteen Benedictions." E.g., Victor Paul Furnish, *II Corinthians: A New Translation with Introduction and Commentary*, AB 32A (New York: Doubleday, 1984), 114. Surely Paul's description of God is in continuity with Jewish tradition, but it seems more likely that his fundamental influence was the resurrection of Christ (cf. 2 Cor. 4:13–14).

92 Many "faithfulness of Christ" advocates have argued that Paul reads Ps. 116 as a messianic psalm and patterns his faith after Jesus's faith. For an evaluation of this view, see chap. 1, p. 82.

Paul's faith: "knowing that he who raised the Lord Jesus will raise us also with Jesus" (2 Cor. 4:14). Thus, the content or object of Paul's faith in 2 Corinthians 4:13–14 is that the God who raised Jesus will also raise him and the Corinthians with Jesus.

The similarity of 2 Corinthians 4:13–14 with 2 Corinthians 1:9 shows that when Paul writes in the earlier passage about relying on the "God who raises the dead," he means that he can rely on God because God has raised Jesus from the dead. Moreover, as in 2 Corinthians 4:13–14, there is a correlation between confidence that God has raised Jesus and confidence that God will raise us: Paul is convinced that the God who raised the suffering Christ will deliver him from suffering as well: "He delivered us from such a deadly peril, and he will deliver us. On him we have set our hope that he will deliver us again" (2 Cor. 1:10; cf. 2 Tim. 4:17–18).[93]

In conclusion, in 2 Corinthians Paul recounts how he had learned through suffering to rely on God. His trust in God was bound up with certain beliefs about God—namely, that God had delivered Jesus from his suffering through resurrection and thus would deliver Paul and the Corinthians through resurrection as well. He is the God who raises the dead. Thus we see that Paul's faith in God is fundamentally oriented toward the resurrection of Christ.[94]

1 Thessalonians 1:2–10; 4:14

Paul's earliest statement about faith in God appears in the thanksgiving section of his first letter to the Thessalonians, in which he tells them that news of their faith had spread around the world: "Your faith in God has gone forth everywhere, so that we need not say anything"

---

93 We also see in 2 Cor. 1:10 the future orientation of faith in Paul's letters, which I discuss under the theme of "hope" in chap. 3, p. 170.

94 Lambrecht notes that Paul speaks of the resurrection because he "believes in God *as revealed by Jesus.*" Jan Lambrecht, "A Matter of Method (II): 2 Cor 4,13 and the Recent Studies of Schenck and Campbell," *ETL* 86, no. 4 (2010): 447; emphasis mine.

(1 Thess. 1:8).[95] Here Paul describes the Thessalonians' initial coming to faith: Paul, Silas, and Timothy brought the gospel to them, and they "received the word in much affliction, with the joy of the Holy Spirit, so that [they] became an example to all the believers in Macedonia and in Achaia" (1 Thess. 1:6–7). Thus we see that faith in this passage is a reception of the gospel and its preachers (cf. 1 Thess. 1:9), even in the face of opposition.

The gospel preached by Paul is a message about God, because he says that God himself is the object of the Thessalonians' well-known faith: "Your faith in God [ἡ πίστις ὑμῶν ἡ πρὸς τὸν θεὸν] has gone forth everywhere" (1 Thess. 1:8). He then describes this faith in God as a conversion, turning "to God from idols," and he gives two purposes for this turning: "to serve the living and true God, and to wait for his Son from heaven, whom he [God] raised from the dead, Jesus who delivers us from the wrath to come" (1 Thess. 1:9–10).[96] These two purposes for their conversion give us a definition of the God who is the object of the Thessalonians' faith. He is the "living and true God," in contrast with the dead and false idols they had previously served. And he has a Son whom he raised from the dead and who will come from heaven to deliver us from the final judgment (cf. Rom. 5:9). Thus, the faith of the Thessalonians was not only oriented toward the gospel and God but toward the resurrection of Christ and the promise of his coming. Michael Wolter observes of these verses that "'faith in God' and 'faith in Christ' do not denote two different orientations of faith but have to do with one and the same faith."[97] And Charles Wanamaker

---

95 Morris comments, "This may be a hyperbole; but it may also reflect the fact that Aquila and Priscilla had come to Corinth from Rome just before Paul wrote this letter (Acts 18:2), and what was known at Rome could be presumed to be known everywhere." Leon Morris, *1 and 2 Thessalonians*, TNTC (Downers Grove, IL: InterVarsity Press, 1984), 46.

96 Some have argued that these words are a pre-Pauline formula about missionary preaching to the Gentiles. See Wanamaker for several reasons to question this hypothesis. Charles A. Wanamaker, *The Epistle to the Thessalonians*, NIGTC (Grand Rapids, MI: Eerdmans, 1990), 84–89. Even if Paul has adopted an earlier formula, he has incorporated it into his own argument and theology.

97 Wolter, *Paul*, 75.

concludes that "the parousia expectation lay at the very heart of the Thessalonians' faith."[98]

I include here a brief discussion of 1 Thessalonians 4:14: "For since we believe that Jesus died and rose again, even so, God will bring with him those who have fallen asleep through Jesus" (1 Thess. 4:14).[99] This statement could be examined in the next section about faith in the gospel, because the object of our faith in this verse is the fact "*that* Jesus died and rose again," a gospel summary that is very similar to the traditional formulation of 1 Corinthians 15:3–4. But the conclusion Paul draws from this belief in 1 Thessalonians 4:14 is a confident trust that "even so, *God* will bring with him those who have fallen asleep through Jesus."[100] Thus Paul's focus is on *God's* work in raising Christ from the dead, not unlike 1 Thessalonians 1:10. Addressing the Thessalonians' grief over fellow believers "who are asleep," Paul reminds them that the fundamental confession of their faith ("Jesus died and rose again") should give them confidence that God will raise these sleeping believers as well and bring them with Christ to heaven (1 Thess. 4:13, 16–17). Thus the object of the Thessalonians' faith in this verse is Jesus's death and resurrection, but implicit in this belief is the idea that *God* is the one who raised Jesus and will raise us as

---

98 Wanamaker, *Thessalonians*, 88. I should observe that Morgan is clearly wrong in her thesis that Paul did not call for faith in Christ in his earlier letters to the Thessalonians and Corinthians but only in his later letters to the Galatians, Romans, and Philippians. Teresa Morgan, *Roman Faith and Christian Faith:* Pistis *and* Fides *in the Early Roman Empire and Early Churches* (New York: Oxford University Press, 2015), 215, 231, 305, et al. This developmental thesis makes too much of the distinction between faith in the person of Christ and faith in his work (e.g., 231). And it also falters on the fact that Galatians may have been written before the Thessalonian and Corinthian correspondence.

99 I have slightly changed the ESV here because it seems more likely to me that "through Jesus" modifies not "God will bring" but "those who have fallen asleep," speaking specifically about Christians in union with Christ. So Morris, *1 and 2 Thessalonians*, 90–91; Wanamaker, *Thessalonians*, 169. Cf. "the dead in Christ" in 1 Thess. 4:16.

100 Pifer helpfully observes that in 1 Thess. 4:14, "Paul is not making a conditional statement; the future of those who are dead is not based on the belief of the living Christians. Rather, Paul is explaining the logical extension of their belief in Christ's death and resurrection." *Faith as Participation*, 57.

well (cf. 2 Cor. 4:14). We see, then, that the Thessalonians' faith in the gospel, in God, and in the death and resurrection of Jesus are all of a piece, since the good news is that God has raised his Son, who will deliver us from the wrath to come. This is the living and true God in whom they had come to believe.

Titus 3:8

Paul mentions faith in God one more time in the Pastoral Epistles: "The saying is trustworthy, and I want you to insist on these things, so that those who have believed in God may be careful to devote themselves to good works" (Titus 3:8).[101] In this brief statement, he refers to the Cretans who have come to faith after hearing the gospel. This is the one text in this section that does not explicitly describe God, the object of faith, as the one who raised Christ from the dead. In that sense it is the exception that proves the rule. Even in this text, however, we see that faith in God includes faith in the entire gospel. Paul tells Titus to insist that the Cretans pursue good works because, as Mounce observes, "it is essential that they live out the practical implications of their theology as expressed by the creed."[102] This creed is the saying Paul has just recounted and described as "trustworthy" (πιστὸς), or worthy of the Cretans' faith (Titus 3:8):

> But when the goodness and loving kindness of God our Savior ap-
> peared, he saved us, not because of works done by us in righteousness,
> but according to his own mercy, by the washing of regeneration and
> renewal of the Holy Spirit, whom he poured out on us richly through
> Jesus Christ our Savior, so that being justified by his grace we might
> become heirs according to the hope of eternal life. (Titus 3:4–7)

---

101 Cf. also his personal comment in 2 Tim. 1:12: "I am not ashamed, for I know whom I have believed." In context the antecedent of "whom" (ᾧ) could be either God or Christ. Perhaps it is even purposely ambiguous.

102 Mounce, *Pastoral Epistles*, 452.

At the very least, we again see that the God who is the object of our faith is the one who saves us according to his mercy through the Holy Spirit and Jesus Christ. Paul does not oppose the Cretans' faith with God's mercy but rather says that the God who is the object of their faith is the one who has saved them apart from their works.

Summary

In this section, I have attempted to further support my thesis that Paul significantly emphasizes Christ-oriented faith in his theology by observing that in Paul's letters, faith in God is fundamentally oriented toward the resurrection of Christ. We have seen that faith in God involves both belief and trust, as we saw in the previous section. One unique element of faith that we saw in this section is its paradoxical nature since it is oriented toward the God who raises the dead (Rom. 4:18–21). Faith in this God entails believing in his work of raising Christ from the dead as well as having confidence that he will raise us and bring us with his Son at his coming to deliver us from the final judgment (Rom. 4:24; 2 Cor. 1:10; 4:14; 1 Thess. 1:10; 4:14; cf. also Rom. 6:8; 8:11). Therefore, we should not oppose faith in God to faith in Christ as if Paul speaks about believing in God *rather than* believing in Christ.[103] For Paul, to believe in the true God *is by definition* to believe that he has raised Christ from the dead, for his identity is now bound up with this event. As Wolter observes about Pauline theology more generally, "Every statement about God in the gospel is a statement about Jesus Christ—and vice versa."[104] Finally, Paul views our faith in God as a cause of justification, the reason that Abraham was justified (Rom. 4:22). This is not to say that faith is a work, because Paul clearly opposes the

---

103 Coming from the opposite direction, Bultmann rightly observes that faith in Christ may seem to push "the relation to God into the background. Nevertheless, the faith which is oriented to Christ believes precisely in God's act in Christ. . . . God and Christ are not set before the believer as two different objects of faith which are either co-ordinated or subordinated." *TDNT*, s.v. "πιστεύω, κτλ.," 6:217.

104 Wolter, *Paul*, 59.

worker and the believer (Rom. 4:4–5). Rather, our faith is associated fundamentally with God's grace because we believe in the God of grace who justifies the ungodly (Rom. 4:4–5, 16). Further, to say that faith is a cause of justification is not to deny that Christ himself is a cause of justification (Rom. 4:25). In the next section, we begin to see a hint of how these two causes of justification relate, although a full synthesis is not given until chapter 5.

Faith in the Gospel

One of Paul's most common ways of specifying the object of our faith is to speak about faith in the gospel or the message proclaimed (the kerygma). In the first section, I observed that even when Paul speaks about faith in the person of Christ, he does not neatly distinguish between faith in his person and faith in the events of the gospel. Now I suggest that the opposite is true as well: Paul does not make a neat conceptual distinction between faith in the gospel and faith in the person of Christ. Wolter has observed that "the phrases 'to proclaim the gospel' (Gal 2:2; 1 Thess 2:9), 'to proclaim Christ' (1 Cor 1:23; 2 Cor 1:19; 4:5; Phil 1:15), and 'to proclaim the word of faith' (Rom 10:8) denote one and the same content of Paul's missionary preaching."[105] Similarly, Paul says both that he proclaims the Son of God (Gal. 1:16) and that he proclaims "the faith"—that is, the body of faith, or the gospel (Gal. 1:23).[106] These observations prepare us to see in this section that believing the gospel and believing in Christ are really the same thing for Paul.[107] Finally, one element that emerges from these texts is the *conditionality* of Christ-oriented faith in Paul's soteriology. Just as faith does not save apart from Christ, so Christ does not save

---

105 Wolter, *Paul*, 54 (cf. 60–62). It is not clear to me, therefore, why he later argues that πίστις Χριστοῦ is not an objective genitive, because "Christ" stands for the gospel content. Wolter, 75.

106 For this observation I am indebted to Ulrichs, *Christusglaube*, 97.

107 By way of analogy, if I say that "I love my marriage," it is not conceptually different from saying that "I love my wife." Similarly, when Paul speaks about believing in the gospel, it is not conceptually different from believing in Christ.

apart from faith according to Paul. The apostle speaks of the gospel as a cause of salvation *as it is believed.*

1 Corinthians 1:18–2:5

In our first passage, Paul speaks about the message of Christ crucified that was proclaimed to the Corinthians (the kerygma) as the power of God to save those who believe it to be true. Here he focuses on the foolishness of the cross to address the pride of the Corinthians. This passage is one of the most important statements in all Paul's letters. After years of writing about Paul, Joseph Fitzmyer views "the heart of the Apostle's theological teaching" as best summed up by 1 Corinthians 1:21–24 and its message of Christ crucified.[108] He states, "This formulation, 'Christ crucified,' supplies the key to Pauline theology, because from it Paul develops all his other doctrinal and ethical teaching, for Christ crucified is for Paul the criterion and norm of all Christian thought and conduct."[109] Thus, faith oriented toward the crucified Christ is not a minor theme in Paul's soteriology but a central emphasis: "It pleased God through the folly of what we preach to save *those who believe*" (1 Cor. 1:21).

The object of faith in this passage is the message proclaimed, the crucified Christ. Even though 1 Corinthians 1:21 does not explicitly state an object of faith, the first half of the verse makes it clear that Paul is referring to those who believe his proclamation (κηρύγματος; cf. 1 Cor. 3:5). That is, Paul refers to those who believe in Christ crucified: "We preach [κηρύσσομεν] Christ crucified" (1 Cor. 1:23). In this passage, faith is not simply an affirmation of the event of the crucifixion but a right perception of its saving significance, that the cross is the wisdom and power of God. Paul observes how unbelievers and believers perceive the significance of the cross in opposite ways: "For the word of the

---

108 Joseph A. Fitzmyer, *First Corinthians: A New Translation with Introduction and Commentary*, AB 32 (New Haven, CT: Yale University Press, 2008), 69–70.

109 Fitzmyer, *First Corinthians*, 160.

cross is folly to those who are perishing, but to us who are being saved it is the power of God" (1 Cor. 1:18). Christ crucified is "a stumbling block to Jews and folly to Gentiles, but to those who are called, both Jews and Greeks, Christ the power of God and the wisdom of God" (1 Cor. 1:23–24). Unbelief is viewing the cross as a stumbling block or foolishness, whereas faith is perceiving it correctly as the power of God for salvation (cf. Rom. 1:16). This is why in the end of the passage, Paul says that he conducted his ministry in such a way "so that your faith might not rest in the wisdom of men [ἐν σοφίᾳ ἀνθρώπων] but in the power of God [ἐν δυνάμει θεοῦ]" (1 Cor. 2:5). The phrase "power of God" refers immediately to the powerful Spirit through which Paul demonstrated the truth of the gospel (1 Cor. 2:4).[110] But it is also a way of referring to the message of the cross (1 Cor. 1:18) and even to the crucified one himself (1 Cor. 1:24). Paul argues that human wisdom will not help or deliver the Corinthians. Thus, he preaches in such a way that their faith will be not in human wisdom but in God's power to save. Here we see that their faith is oriented not only toward God's saving power in the message of the cross but also toward his powerful work through the Spirit in their lives testifying to this message. Thus, the object of faith in 1 Corinthians 1:18–2:5 is the power of God in Christ and the Spirit.

The cause of salvation in this passage is the believed kerygma. Paul speaks of the foolish message itself as a cause of salvation: "It pleased God through the folly of what we preach [διὰ τῆς μωρίας τοῦ κη-ρύγματος] to save those who believe" (1 Cor. 1:21). Another way to say this is that in 1 Corinthians 1:18–2:5, Christ himself is a cause of salvation. There is truth in the theological argument of the "faithfulness

---

110 Paul is likely alluding to the miracles he performed by the Spirit when he proclaimed the gospel in Corinth as well as to their own reception of the Spirit and the Spirit's powerful work in their lives. Romans gives a nice parallel in which Paul recalls how Christ had worked through him in his mission "by the power of signs and wonders, by the power of the Spirit of God" (Rom. 15:19), and Galatians reminds Paul's converts of their initial reception of the Spirit along with miracles (Gal. 3:2–5; cf. also 1 Thess. 1:5).

of Christ" view that for Paul salvation is by means of the death of Christ. Paul, however, does not use the noun πίστις or the verb πιστεύω to refer to the death of Christ in this soteriological statement. Rather, he uses these words to refer to our faith: "those who believe [τοὺς πιστεύοντας]" in 1 Corinthians 1:21 and "your faith [ἡ πίστις ὑμῶν]" in 1 Corinthians 2:5. Moreover, Paul presents this faith as a condition for salvation when he specifies the direct object of God's saving work as "those who believe" (1 Cor. 1:21). This grammatical construction limits the extent of God's saving action through Christ to a specified object, to believers. Thus one can rightly say that for Paul, the message of the cross is God's power for salvation *only if one believes that message.* If one regards it as foolishness, then it remains just that.

A final element of Paul's soteriology in this passage that touches on our theological debate is the agency of God in both belief *and* unbelief in the message of Christ crucified. One of Paul's major arguments in this passage is that God has *designed* the cross to be perceived as foolishness by some: "Has not God made foolish the wisdom of the world?" (1 Cor. 1:20). Paul was not surprised that Greeks who sought wisdom perceived the message of the crucified Christ as folly. One of God's designs in the cross was that it would be misperceived and rejected in order to turn the world's wisdom into foolishness. The prophet Isaiah informs Paul's thinking about God's purpose in unbelief in this passage. God designed the message of the cross to be perceived as foolish by the wise:

For it is written,

"I will destroy the wisdom of the wise,
    and the discernment of the discerning I will thwart."
        (1 Cor.1:19, quoting Isa. 29:14)

The same idea is present in the perception of Christ as a "stumbling block" for the Jews (1 Cor. 1:23), for this way of referring to Israel's unbelief is rooted in God's purpose in Christ (cf. Rom. 9:32–33, quoting Isa. 8:14; 28:16). On the other hand, Paul also argues that God designed the crucified Christ to be perceived as God's power and wisdom "to those who are called" (1 Cor. 1:24). "Calling" in this passage is another way of referring to God's choice of believers, for Paul describes their "calling" (1 Cor. 1:26) in this way:

> God chose what is foolish in the world to shame the wise; God chose what is weak in the world to shame the strong; God chose what is low and despised in the world, even things that are not, to bring to nothing things that are, so that no human being might boast in the presence of God. (1 Cor. 1:27–29)

Thus, while the conditional role of faith cannot be excluded from Paul's soteriology, human faith can never be a reason for boasting in Paul's understanding, because faith is rooted in God's prior call of the undeserving.

1 Corinthians 15:1–19

In this passage we move from a focus on the cross to a focus on the resurrection, because the church was apparently being swayed to reject the bodily resurrection: "Now if Christ is proclaimed as raised from the dead, how can some of you say there is no resurrection of the dead?" (1 Cor. 15:12). Most likely these Greek Christians found it more plausible to believe in the immortality of the soul rather than the resurrection of the body.[111] Paul responds by saying that the resurrection of Christ is central to the gospel they had "come to believe" (1 Cor. 15:2, my trans.).[112] He argues that if their position were correct, then Christ himself would not be raised (1 Cor.

---

111 So Fitzmyer, *First Corinthians*, 559–61. See his discussion for other options.

112 As in Gal. 2:16b (and possibly Rom. 4:18), here Paul uses the aorist "believed" (ἐπιστεύσατε) to describe the initial faith of the Corinthians (ingressive aorist).

15:13, 16).[113] We see, then, that faith in this passage is believing in the truth of the gospel, specifically the truth of Christ's resurrection. As with the previous passage, Paul's argument here represents a central emphasis in his understanding of the gospel and theology. For he says he had delivered this message "as of first importance" (1 Cor. 15:3).[114]

First Corinthians 15:11–12 demonstrates how Paul thinks of the kerygma and the person of Christ together as the object of the Corinthians' faith. The first verse explains that the apostolic preaching (the kerygma) is the object of the Corinthians' faith: "Whether then it was I or they [the other apostles], so we preach [κηρύσσομεν] and so you believed [ἐπιστεύσατε]" (1 Cor. 15:11). The next verse then uses the passive form of the same verb [κηρύσσεται] with Christ as the subject, presenting Christ himself as the content of the apostolic kerygma and thus the object of the Corinthians' faith. Finally, Paul specifies what exactly it means to "preach" and believe in Christ: it means "that he has been raised from the dead" (1 Cor. 15:12, my trans.).[115] Thus, believing in Christ and believing "that" (ὅτι) he has been raised are the same thing for Paul. The Corinthians' faith in this passage is clearly oriented toward Christ, with a decided focus on the historical reality of his resurrection. But although he focuses on the resurrection, Paul also mentions Christ's death, burial, and appearances as part of the gospel that the Corinthians had "come to believe" (1 Cor. 15:2, my trans.).

Paul speaks of this gospel itself as a cause of salvation: "Now I would remind you, brothers, of the gospel I preached to you, . . . *by which*

---

113 German scholars have debated intensely the logic of 1 Cor. 15:12–19. See Fee and Fitzmyer's commentaries for discussions. In my view, Paul's parallel conditional statements in 1 Cor. 15:13 and 16 both state that if their position is correct, it inevitably leads to the conclusion that "Christ has not been raised."

114 The phrase "as of first importance" (ἐν πρώτοις) could be translated temporally ("at first"), but most commentators take it as a reference to the important nature of the gospel Paul had initially taught them. E.g., Anthony C. Thiselton, *The First Epistle to the Corinthians*, NIGTC (Grand Rapids, MI: Eerdmans, 2000), 1186; see BDAG, s.v. "πρῶτος," use 2.a.

115 My translation here is more literal than the ESV's "as raised from the dead" (1 Cor. 15:12).

you are being saved" (1 Cor. 15:1–2; cf. 1:18). Similarly, he later speaks of Christ himself as a cause of salvation: "But thanks be to God, who gives us the victory *through our Lord Jesus Christ*" (1 Cor. 15:57). Once again, however, we see that this salvation that comes through Christ is conditioned on human faith: "You are being saved, *if* you hold fast to the word I preached to you—*unless* you believed in vain" (1 Cor. 15:2).[116] The first condition speaks of the need for the Corinthians to continue to "hold fast" the gospel they had initially "received" (1 Cor. 15:1–2). Receiving the gospel is another way of speaking about coming to believe it (cf. 1 Thess. 2:13). Holding it firmly is another way of speaking about continuing to believe it. Thus Paul says that the Corinthians' salvation is contingent on their continuing or persevering faith. The second condition speaks of the possibility that their initial faith had been "in vain" (1 Cor. 15:2). Perhaps Paul is again referring to the sincerity and perseverance of the Corinthians' faith, "implying that at least some Corinthian Christians are confused and may not have been clinging to the gospel as it was preached to them."[117] But in light of the following verses, this second condition is more likely referring to the *object* of the Corinthians' faith: "If Christ has not been raised, then our preaching is in vain and your faith is in vain" (1 Cor. 15:14); "If Christ has not been raised, your faith is futile and you are still in your sins" (1 Cor. 15:17).[118] Thus, this vanity of faith refers to

---

116 The syntax of this verse is difficult, but most commentators see these conditional clauses as modifying the verb "you are being saved" (σῴζεσθε). For example, Fitzmyer comments that the "continuing of the Corinthian Christians to be among the *hoi sōzomenio*, 'those who are being saved' (1:18), is thus doubly conditional." *First Corinthians*, 545.

117 Fitzmyer, *First Corinthians*, 545. Fitzmyer is probably following BDAG's suggested gloss of "without careful thought, *without due consideration, in a haphazard manner*" (use 4), because he says that "the credence they have put in the gospel as 'good news' may have been heedless, not well considered." Fitzmyer, 545. Cf. 2 Cor. 6:1, where Paul warns the Corinthians "not to receive the grace of God in vain," probably referring to their perseverance in receiving Paul as a gospel messenger.

118 Fee also observes the connection between the vanity of faith in 1 Corinthians 15:2 and 14. *First Corinthians*, 800n39. Paul uses three different synonyms to refer to the vanity of faith in these verses: εἰκῇ (15:2), κενός (15:14), and ματαία (15:17).

the possibility that the Corinthians had believed in something that didn't actually happen. We see, then, an intimate relationship between our faith and its Christological object in Paul's soteriology: salvation is contingent both on the continuance of our faith and on the historical reality of Christ's resurrection.

Romans 1:1–17

Paul's letter to the Romans probably represents his theology more clearly than any of his other letters.[119] The opening sections of Paul's letters often introduce the letter's most important topics, and it is notable that the long introduction in Romans focuses on the *faith* of the saints in Rome. Here Paul informs them that the risen Son of God has granted him "grace and apostleship to bring about the obedience of faith for the sake of his name among all the nations" (Rom. 1:5). In the next chapter, I discuss the exact meaning of the phrase "obedience of faith," but for now I want to observe that it refers to the proper response to the preaching of the gospel that brings honor to the name of God's Son. Paul says that the Romans are among those who have believed in the gospel among the nations. In fact, this is the primary reason why he gives thanks to God for them: "I thank my God through Jesus Christ for all of you, because your faith is proclaimed in all the world" (Rom. 1:8).[120] Paul has never visited the believers in Rome, but he longs to visit them to strengthen them, "that is, that we may be mutually encouraged by each other's faith, both yours and mine" (Rom. 1:12). Here we see the role of encouraging one another in order to grow stronger in our initial faith.

---

119 Dunn structures his Pauline theology around the argument of Romans, observing that the letter is "far removed from a dogmatic or systematic treatise on theology, but it nevertheless is the most sustained and reflective statement of Paul's own theology by Paul himself." James D. G. Dunn, *The Theology of Paul the Apostle* (Grand Rapids, MI: Eerdmans, 1998), 25.

120 Note again that Paul's thanksgiving for faith indicates that this faith has its origin in the prior work of God, specifically when he "called" them "to belong to Jesus Christ" (Rom. 1:6) and "to be saints" (Rom. 1:7).

All this faith language prepares us for one of the most important statements about faith in Paul's letters: Romans 1:16–17. This text is widely regarded as a kind of thesis statement for the structured argument of Romans, and thus is one of the most important statements of his theology. In Romans 1:16, Paul speaks of his confidence in the gospel because "it is the power of God for salvation to everyone who believes, to the Jew first and also to the Greek." He then explains this statement in Romans 1:17: "For in it the righteousness of God is revealed from faith for faith [ἐκ πίστεως εἰς πίστιν], as it is written, 'The righteous shall live by faith [ἐκ πίστεως].'" Whereas "everyone who believes" in 1:16 is clearly a reference to the faith of everyone who believes the gospel (whether Jew or Gentile), the meaning and referent of Paul's three uses of πίστις in 1:17 are highly debated. In the last chapter, I examined the third use of πίστις in 1:17, the citation of Habakkuk 2:4, and concluded that Paul understands it as a reference to the justification of the believer by faith, just as he does in his citation of Habakkuk 2:4 in Galatians 3:11. It is unlikely that he cites this verse as a reference to the justification of Christ by faith since he gives no indication of this notion in the context. On the other hand, Paul does clearly speak about the gospel as God's power to save everyone who believes it in Romans 1:16. This contextual argument should also influence the interpretation of ἐκ πίστεως εἰς πίστιν in Romans 1:17. Between Romans 1:16 and Paul's citation of Habakkuk 2:4, we would expect another reference to faith as a response to the gospel. Several recent interpreters, however, have argued strongly that the first ἐκ πίστεως in Romans 1:17 refers to the faithfulness of God or Christ.[121] Because these arguments are so bound up with the πίστις Χριστοῦ debate, I concede this as a possibility and wait to address

---

121 For the interpretation "by God's faithfulness," see James D. G. Dunn, *Romans 1–8*, WBC 38A (Nashville: Thomas Nelson, 1988), 44. For the interpretation "by Christ's faithfulness," see Douglas A. Campbell, "Romans 1:17—A *Crux Interpretum* for the Πιστις Χριστου Debate," *JBL* 113, no. 2 (1994): 265–85.

the issue until chapter 4. For the argument of this chapter, I observe only that most interpreters agree that εἰς πίστιν in Romans 1:17 is a reference to our faith in the gospel.

But we can be more specific about the object of faith in Romans 1:16–17, because Paul explains the content of the gospel in Romans 1:3–4: "concerning his Son, who was descended from David according to the flesh and was declared to be the Son of God in power according to the Spirit of holiness by his resurrection from the dead, Jesus Christ our Lord." Like the faith of the Thessalonians, so the faith of the Romans is oriented fundamentally toward God's Son. Specifically, Paul highlights his Davidic descent and his messianic enthronement in power at the resurrection.[122] There is an interesting textual variant in Romans 1:16 that became a part of the majority of manuscripts and thus is seen in the King James Version: "I am not ashamed of the gospel *of Christ*." But even though this variant was surely added by a later scribe, it reflects the context of Romans 1:16. The gospel that Paul was not ashamed to proclaim and that the Romans had come to believe is the good news about the messianic Son of God (Rom. 1:3–4).

Finally, Paul speaks of this gospel as a cause of salvation *as it is believed*. Romans 1:16 is reminiscent of 1 Corinthians 1:18–2:5. In both passages Paul speaks of the message about Christ as the power of God (cf. 1 Cor. 1:18), and in both he speaks of Jews and Greeks (cf. 1 Cor. 1:24). But the closest point of comparison is the wording of 1 Corinthians 1:21:

It pleased God through the folly of what we preach to save those who believe. (1 Cor. 1:21)

---

122 Bates suggests the interesting thesis that the participle "descended" (γενομένου) means "came to be" and thus implies the Son's incarnation. Matthew W. Bates, "A Christology of Incarnation and Enthronement: Romans 1:3–4 as Unified, Nonadoptionist, and Nonconciliatory," *CBQ* 77, no. 1 (2015): 115–17. Perhaps, though, he is reading too much into the verb since it is used elsewhere to refer to Abraham's coming to be born (John 8:58). Note also that the second participle, "declared" (ὁρισθέντος), is better translated "appointed" and refers to the Son's enthronement as the messianic King (cf. Ps. 2:7). Schreiner, *Romans*, 46.

It [the gospel] is the power of God for salvation to everyone who
believes. (Rom. 1:16)

As in 1 Corinthians 1:21, so in Romans 1:16, it is the message about
Christ that leads to salvation: "It is the power of God for salvation."[123]
Paul, however, again limits this saving power to specific recipients,
here with a dative of advantage, "to everyone who believes [παντὶ τῷ
πιστεύοντι]" (Rom. 1:16). Thus he presents faith in the good news
about God's Son as a condition for salvation.

Romans 10:6–13

I conclude with Romans 10:6–13 because this passage speaks in the
same context about faith in the gospel, faith in God, and faith in Christ.
Thus it supports my larger point that these are simply different ways in
Pauline theology to refer to the same reality of Christ-oriented faith.
In this passage Paul uses Moses's description of the nearness of the law
to Israel typologically to describe the nearness of the gospel to us. He
glosses various aspects of Moses's words to explain the fulfillment of the
foreshadowing, and his third gloss refers to our faith: "But what does it
say? 'The word is near you, in your mouth and in your heart' (that is, the
word of faith that we proclaim)" (Rom. 10:8). This "word of faith" that
Paul proclaims most likely refers to the message of the gospel, which calls
for faith as a response (cf. Rom. 10:9–11).[124] Paul's point is that Christ
has already come and the word has already been proclaimed. It is near!
All that must be done now is to believe it, to receive it as true, or, in Paul's
words in the following verse, to "confess" it to be true.[125]

---

123 We can probably say as well that the risen Christ himself is God's power for salvation in Rom.
   1:16 because this verse specifies the nature of the Son's "power" (Rom. 1:4) as the power to save.
124 So C. E. B. Cranfield, *The Epistle to the Romans*, ICC (Edinburgh: T&T Clark, 1979), 2:526.
   Cranfield notes Theodor Zahn's comparison with "law of faith" (νόμος πίστεως) in Rom. 3:27.
   Cranfield, 2:526.
125 Kim observes that Rom. 10:6–13 "makes it clear that faith is essentially a response to the preached
   word." Seyoon Kim, *The Origin of Paul's Gospel* (Grand Rapids, MI: Eerdmans, 1981), 299.

This proclaimed word, the object of our faith, is profoundly oriented toward the work of Christ. Paul's first two glosses of Deuteronomy 30:12–14 explain the word in terms of Christ's coming down and going up: "Do not say in your heart, 'Who will ascend into heaven?' (that is, to bring Christ down) or 'Who will descend into the abyss?' (that is, to bring Christ up from the dead)" (Rom. 10:6–7). Bringing Christ down from heaven refers to his incarnation.[126] And bringing him up from the dead clearly refers to his resurrection. Paul's point is that these things have both happened and now are being proclaimed in the world. Here we can observe how close Christ and the gospel are in Paul's thinking: Christ has come near both in his work *and* in the word about his work. All that is needed now is to confess and believe it as Paul says in Romans 10:9. In this verse we see that the object of our confession includes the person of Christ: "Jesus is Lord." It also includes the work of God in raising him from the dead. Finally, we come full circle in this chapter as Paul cites Isaiah 28:16 a second time to present Christ, the Rock, as the object of saving faith: "For the Scripture says, 'Everyone who believes in him will not be put to shame'" (Rom. 10:11). According to the logic of Romans 10:9–11, in which 10:11 is the ground of 10:9–10, believing "in him" (Rom. 10:11) involves the confession that Jesus is Lord as well as the belief that God raised him from the dead (Rom. 10:9). Thus, in this passage we see clearly that Paul makes no distinction between believing in the word, believing in the incarnation and resurrection of Christ, believing in God's work of raising Christ, and believing in the person of Christ himself. These are all a part of the object of saving, justifying faith for the apostle.

Paul seems to see very little difference in his understanding of justification and salvation in this passage. He explains his statement about

---

126 Fitzmyer observes that "to bring Christ down" in Rom. 10:6 is an "indirect allusion to the incarnation of Christ" and "the closest one comes in the Pauline letters to such an idea." Joseph A. Fitzmyer, *Romans: A New Translation with Introduction and Commentary*, AB 33 (New Haven, CT: Yale University Press, 1993), 590.

being "saved" in Romans 10:9 with a statement about both righteousness and salvation: "For with the heart one believes and is justified,
and with the mouth one confesses and is saved" (Rom. 10:10). There
is no reason to see a difference between heart believing and mouth
confessing in this verse, as if justification were the result of believing
but salvation the result of confession. Paul is simply borrowing the
language of "heart" and "mouth" from Deuteronomy 30:14 (see Rom.
10:8). Instead, Paul uses variation in his language to speak of the same
reality. This variation follows a larger pattern in Romans that we can
see by comparing Romans 1:16 with Romans 10:4:

> It [the gospel] is the power of God for salvation [εἰς σωτηρίαν] to
> everyone who believes. (Rom. 1:16)

> Christ is the end of the law for righteousness [εἰς δικαιοσύνην] to
> everyone who believes. (Rom. 10:4)

Both these statements speak of a soteriological result from the gospel or
Christ, except that Paul speaks of "salvation" in 1:16 and "righteousness"
in 10:4. And both speak of Christ as the cause of salvation/justification,
except that in 1:16 he speaks of the gospel of Christ and in 10:4 of
Christ himself. Both these verses also limit this salvation/justification
to everyone who believes, presenting faith as a condition for salvation.
But it is fascinating to then compare Romans 10:10 with these verses,
for in 10:10 Paul uses the same grammatical construction but places
faith in the role of cause for both justification and salvation:

> For with the heart one believes and is justified [εἰς δικαιοσύνην],
> and with the mouth one confesses and is saved [εἰς σωτηρίαν].

Clearly, Paul speaks of both Christ himself *and* our response of faith
as causes of salvation. The question is how these two causes relate to

one another. I discuss this question in chapter 5, but we have already observed in this chapter that Paul often says in these passages that the cause of salvation is the gospel *as it is believed*. This means that our faith plays a conditional role in Paul's soteriology, as he states perhaps most clearly in Romans 10:9: "If you confess with your mouth that Jesus is Lord and believe in your heart that God raised him from the dead, you will be saved."

Summary

In this section, we have examined some of the most central passages in Paul's letters and theology, passages in which Paul speaks about faith as a response to the message of the gospel or the message that is proclaimed (the kerygma).[127] The way Paul explains the content of this gospel varies depending on the situation he is addressing, but in each case he centers on the work of Christ: his crucifixion (1 Cor. 1:18, 23), his resurrection (1 Cor. 15:12), his Davidic descent and messianic enthronement (Rom. 1:3–4), and his incarnation and resurrection (Rom. 10:6). I also observed that in Romans 10:6–13, Paul speaks in the same context about the word, the work of Christ, God's work, and the person of Christ as the object of our faith. Thus, there is no neat distinction between faith in Christ, faith in God, and faith in the gospel in Paul's theology. They are all part of the good news that Christians have come to believe. This gospel is the cause of justification and salvation for Paul *as it is believed*. We found it to be a consistent pattern that faith plays a conditional role to salvation in each of these passages. It is conditional both in the sense that one must come to believe it (Rom. 10:9) and in the sense that one must continue to believe it (1 Cor. 15:2). This does not mean that salvation is fundamentally contingent on us because

---

127 Cf. also the early letter of 2 Thessalonians, in which Paul says that they had believed the "testimony" that was proclaimed by Paul, Silas, and Timothy (2 Thess. 1:10) and later speaks of the condemnation of those "who did not believe the truth" of the gospel (2 Thess. 2:12).

Paul also says that our faith is the result of God's prior initiating call or choice (Rom. 1:6–7; 1 Cor. 1:27–29). In one passage we also saw that faith itself is presented as a cause of justification and salvation (Rom. 10:10). Once again, we see that Paul speaks of both Christ and faith as causes of salvation. The two are closely related to each other in Paul's theology, so much so that Paul says that our faith would be in vain if Christ has not been raised from the dead (1 Cor. 15:2, 14, 17).

Conclusion

What then shall we say to these things? I have argued in this chapter that Paul significantly emphasizes Christ-oriented faith in his theology. The apostle speaks often about faith in Christ—and does so in one of the most important statements of his theology (Gal. 2:16). When he speaks about faith in God, he typically says it is a faith in the God who raised Christ from the dead. And Paul most commonly refers to the gospel as the object of our faith, including in passages that lie at the very heart of his theology (Rom. 1:1–17; 1 Cor. 1:18–2:5). This gospel proclaimed by the apostles is the message of the incarnate, crucified, risen, and enthroned Son of God, who will deliver us from the wrath to come. Therefore, we can say that faith is fundamentally oriented toward Christ in the apostle's theology and that Paul significantly emphasizes Christ-oriented faith in his theology.[128] Moreover, Paul presents such faith as a cause of justification and as a condition of salvation. Does this mean that he rests our salvation entirely on our faith and not on the grace of God in Christ? May it never be! Rather, he speaks of both our faith and the object of our faith (Christ) as a part of God's gift of salvation to us. How exactly he relates faith and Christ is synthesized in chapter 5.

---

128 Wolter similarly observes that there is a "fundamental christological orientation of Paul's understanding of faith." *Paul*, 74.

In the next chapter, I examine conceptual parallels to Christ-oriented faith in Paul's letters in order to strengthen my thesis. But permit me one final observation: In this chapter, I have examined only texts outside the πίστις Χριστοῦ debate. Is it not striking that in all these many texts, the noun πίστις and the verb πιστεύω consistently refer to human faith oriented toward Christ?

3

Conceptual Parallels to Christ-Oriented Faith in Paul's Letters

*Lord, I would seek you, calling upon you—and
calling upon you is an act of believing in you. . . . My
faith, Lord, calls upon you. It is your gift to me.*
AUGUSTINE, CONFESSIONS

AUGUSTINE SPOKE MEMORABLY in his *Confessions* of calling on the
Lord as an act of faith, but centuries before he did so, the apostle Paul
wrote of calling on the Lord as a conceptual parallel to faith in Christ
in his letter to the Romans. In this chapter, I examine this parallel
along with several others to establish more deeply my thesis that Paul
significantly emphasizes Christ-oriented faith in his theology. In the last
chapter, I argued for this thesis from texts in Paul's letters that use the
verb "believe" (πιστεύω) or the corresponding noun "faith" (πίστις),
with the exception of 1 Corinthians 1:9. But there are several other
ways in which the apostle speaks about Christ as the object of our faith
in his letters. To understand his theology of Christ-oriented faith more
fully, we must explore these conceptual parallels.

How can we determine what is and is not a parallel to Christ-
oriented faith in Paul's letters? Surely no criterion would satisfy every

reader, but I have attempted to refine my study by looking at conceptual parallels that come within the immediate context of Paul's direct statements of Christ-oriented faith (i.e., the statements we examined in the last chapter). This approach enables me to prove that each parallel genuinely overlaps with Paul's direct statements. It also enables me to show *how* these different concepts overlap with Paul's teaching about faith. Finally, this approach enables me to deepen our understanding of faith in the very passages we examined in the last chapter.

Using this criterion, I have isolated four conceptual parallels to Christ-oriented faith in Paul's letters, which I discuss in canonical order: obedience to the gospel (Rom. 1:5; 10:16), calling on the name of the Lord (Rom. 10:12–13), hoping in Christ (1 Cor. 15:19), and seeing the glory of the Lord (2 Cor. 3:18; 4:4–6). Each of these parallels is found in a passage outside the debated πίστις Χριστοῦ phrases. By taking the same approach as the last chapter, I hope to show again, and in more depth, that Paul significantly emphasizes Christ-oriented faith in his theology, no matter which position one takes in the πίστις Χριστοῦ debate. In my discussion of each parallel, I first show how these concepts overlap with Paul's direct statements about faith in Christ. Then I reflect on how they deepen our understanding of the apostle's theology of Christ-oriented faith.

Obedience to the Gospel

Paul speaks about obedience as a conceptual parallel to faith in the gospel within Romans 1:1–17 (Rom. 1:5) and immediately following Romans 10:6–13 (Rom. 10:16). The latter reference is a concession to the apostle's chain of cause and effect about sending, preaching, hearing, believing, and calling on the Lord (Rom. 10:14–15). His conclusion from this line of reasoning is that "faith comes from hearing, and hearing through the word of Christ" (Rom. 10:17). He first concedes, however, that faith in Christ does not inevitably follow from "hearing" (ἀκοή) the gospel:[1] "But they have not all obeyed the gospel. For Isaiah says, 'Lord, who has believed what he has heard from us?'" (Rom. 10:16, citing Isa. 53:1). In this verse we can clearly see Paul's parallel between obedience to the gospel and belief in what has been heard. In fact, the verb "obey" (ὑπακούω) is a wordplay on the verb "hear" (ἀκούω) in this passage. One can hear the gospel without *really* hearing/obeying it. Paul is probably thinking specifically about the fact that many of the Jewish people had not believed in the gospel, since this is the presenting issue in Romans 9–11 (and Isa. 53:1).[2] They have heard the gospel but have not obeyed it. In contrast, Paul speaks several times in this letter about the "obedience" of the Gentiles (Rom. 1:5; 6:17; 15:18; 16:19, 26). The most important of these statements for my study is "the obedience of faith" in Romans 1:5, because it comes within the apostle's discussion about faith in the gospel in Romans 1:1–17. Unfortunately, interpreters disagree about how exactly faith is associated with obedience in this phrase.

Many commentators argue that we should understand "the obedience of faith" in Romans 1:5 as a reference to the obedience that comes from faith (genitive of source) or is produced by faith (subjective genitive).[3] The main argument in support of this view is the fact that in Romans and in Pauline theology more generally, faith always results in a life of

---

1   The word ἀκοή can be translated here in Rom. 10:17 as either the "act of hearing" or by extension as the "message that is heard" (BDAG, uses 2, 4.b). BDAG suggests the latter definition for Rom. 10:17 because this is the way it is used in the apostle's citation of Isa. 53:1 (Rom. 10:16). While Paul is certainly dependent on the language of Isa. 53:1, it is more likely that ἀκοή means "hearing" in Rom. 10:17 (see my discussion in chap. 1, p. 68).

2   So Thomas R. Schreiner, *Romans*, 2nd ed. BECNT (Grand Rapids, MI: Baker Academic, 2018), 556.

3   E.g., Richard N. Longenecker, *The Epistle to the Romans*, NIGTC (Grand Rapids, MI: Eerdmans, 2016), 80; Schreiner, *Romans*, 40. Garlington argues that the phrase is ambiguous and communicates both "the obedience which consists in faith [epexegetical genitive], and the obedience which is the product of faith [genitive of source]." Don Garlington, *Faith, Obedience, and Perseverance: Aspects of Paul's Letter to the Romans*, WUNT 79 (Tübingen: Mohr Siebeck, 1994), 30. Garlington thinks that the category of adjectival genitive ("faith's obedience") best communicates this ambiguity. *Faith, Obedience, and Perseverance*, 30.

obedience (e.g., Rom. 6:1–7:6; 8:1–13; 12:1–13:14; cf. Gal. 5:6). It is certainly true that faith cannot be separated from a life of obedience in Paul's theology. But a problem with this view of the grammar is that it puts the focus on this resulting obedience and not on faith itself. Paul, however, presents "the obedience of faith" as the purpose of his apostolic proclamation of the gospel (Rom. 1:5; cf. 16:26). If the phrase means "the obedience that comes from faith," then Paul is presenting the goal of his preaching fundamentally as this life of obedience. While this is certainly possible, I suggest that it does not follow the pattern we saw in the last chapter, in which faith itself is the intended result of gospel preaching (e.g., Rom. 10:14–17; 1 Thess. 1:2–10).[4]

Thus, I hold what is probably the view of the majority of commentators, that the phrase in Romans 1:5 means "the obedience that is faith" (epexegetical genitive).[5] The main argument in support of this view is the hard linguistic evidence that Paul speaks about faith in the gospel and obedience to the gospel as equivalent concepts in the letter. The clearest example is Romans 10:16, which I have discussed above. Other examples include the parallel statements found in the introduction and conclusion of the letter: "Your faith is proclaimed in all the world" (Rom. 1:8), and "Your obedience is known to all" (Rom. 16:19). This last statement comes in the context of a warning against false teachers who would contradict "the doctrine that you have been

---

4   Cf. also 1 Thess. 3:5, where the goal of Paul's apostolic "labor" is "your faith."

5   E.g., C. E. B. Cranfield, *The Epistle to the Romans*, ICC (Edinburgh: T&T Clark, 1975), 66–67; Joseph A. Fitzmyer, *Romans: A New Translation with Introduction and Commentary*, AB 33 (New Haven, CT: Yale University Press, 1993), 237; N. T. Wright, *The Letter to the Romans*, in vol. 10 of *The New Interpreter's Bible* (Nashville: Abingdon, 2002), 420. This is also the position of Calvin: "Faith is properly that by which we obey the gospel." John Calvin, *The Epistles of Paul to the Romans and Thessalonians*, trans. Ross Mackenzie, vol. 8 of *Calvin's New Testament Commentary*, ed. David W. Torrance and Thomas F. Torrance (Grand Rapids, MI: Eerdmans, 1960), 18. Ulrichs argues for the epexegetical genitive in Rom. 1:5 but then says that it is also an objective genitive meaning "obedience to the [body of] faith." Karl Friedrich Ulrichs, *Christusglaube: Studien zum Syntagma πίστις Χριστοῦ und zum paulinischen Verständnis von Glaube und Rechtfertigung*, WUNT, 2nd ser., vol. 227 (Tübingen: Mohr Siebeck, 2007), 154. This seems unlikely because, in context, Paul is focused on the Gentiles' act of faith in response to the gospel (Rom. 1:6–8).

taught" (Rom. 16:17). Such a warning is probably talking not about peripheral teachings but about the heart of what the Romans had been taught: the gospel itself.[6] Thus it seems likely that the Romans' "obedience" refers specifically to their obedience to this gospel.

I conclude that the phrase "obedience of faith" is an epexegetical genitive meaning "the obedience that is faith" and explaining the specific kind of obedience that the gospel calls for: faith. In this grammatical construction, faith is a smaller category that defines and clarifies the larger category of obedience.[7] Paul speaks about many kinds of obedience in his letters, but the specific kind of obedience called for by his apostolic preaching of the gospel is faith (Rom. 1:6; 16:26), as shown in figure 4.1.

Figure 4.1 The Obedience of Faith

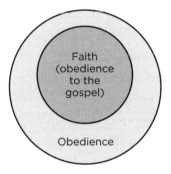

What does this parallel teach us about the concept of Christ-oriented faith in Paul? It teaches that Paul views faith as *submission* to the proclamation of the gospel of Christ. The noun "obedience" (ὑπακοή) means "a state of being in compliance," and the verb "obey" (ὑπακούω) means "to follow instructions, *obey, follow, be subject to*."[8] On the one hand, this means

---

6 Schreiner, *Romans*, 777.

7 For a discussion of the epexegetical genitive, see Daniel B. Wallace, *Greek Grammar beyond the Basics: An Exegetical Syntax of the New Testament* (Grand Rapids, MI: Zondervan, 1996), 95–97.

8 BDAG, s.v. "ὑπακοή," use 1; and s.v. "ὑπακούω," use 1. Cf. "To obey . . . in faith is to submit freely to the word that has been heard, because its truth is guaranteed by God, who is Truth itself." *Catechism of the Catholic Church*, rev. ed. (London: Geoffrey Chapman, 1999), 36.

that faith is not merely intellectual for Paul but involves subjection to the lordship of Christ.[9] Unbelief, conversely, is not merely an intellectual defect but a refusal to "submit to God's righteousness" (Rom. 10:3; cf. 2 Thess. 1:8). On the other hand, obedience to the gospel, according to Paul, is a profoundly intellectual submission. He emphasizes this intellectual aspect of obedience in the defense of his gospel ministry in 2 Corinthians 10:4–6:

> For the weapons of our warfare are not of the flesh but have divine power to destroy strongholds. We destroy arguments and every lofty opinion raised against the knowledge of God, and take every thought captive to obey Christ, being ready to punish every disobedience, when your obedience is complete.

Here Paul uses a military metaphor to describe his ministry. His proclamation of the gospel is a warfare waged by divine power in destroying strongholds and taking thoughts captive to obey Christ.[10] Perhaps the "arguments" or thoughts (λογισμοὺς) Paul has in view are specifically the thoughts of those who "suspect" or think (τοὺς λογιζομένους) that he is walking according to the flesh in his ministry (2 Cor. 10:2). But he also broadens the scope of these thoughts to include "every thought" that must be taken captive to obey Christ, perhaps thinking of how his proclamation of the crucified Christ is a "stumbling block" to Jews and

---

9   Schreiner comments on Rom. 10:16 that the parallel between obedience and faith "demonstrates that the Pauline concept of faith always involves commitment and submission to the lordship of Jesus (cf. 10:9). For Paul, faith is not merely verbal assent but also entails a wholehearted commitment to God." *Romans*, 557. Fitzmyer similarly translates the phrase "obedience of faith" in Rom. 1:5 as "a commitment of faith." *Romans*, 237.

10   The phrase "to obey Christ [εἰς τὴν ὑπακοὴν τοῦ Χριστοῦ]" is surely an objective genitive—so Michael Wolter, *Paul: An Outline of His Theology*, trans. Robert L. Brawley (Waco, TX: Baylor University Press, 2015), 57–58n19; *pace* Seifrid, who suggests that the genitive is more semantically rich, so that Paul speaks of both obedience *to Christ* and "more fundamentally of the obedience that *comes from Christ* and his saving work." Mark A. Seifrid, *The Second Letter to the Corinthians*, PNTC (Grand Rapids, MI: Eerdmans, 2014), 383. This statement, though correct theologically, is probably not what Paul meant to communicate with the phrase.

"folly" to Gentiles (cf. 1 Cor. 1:23).[11] Thus his proclamation of the gospel aims to establish an intellectual submission, to bring low things that are raised "against the knowledge of God" and to take "every thought captive to obey Christ" (2 Cor. 10:5).[12] It should be observed that the object of this obedience is Christ himself. Thus, the obedience of faith is not fundamentally a surrender of one's previous understanding of oneself or one's own righteousness, as Bultmann described it.[13] Rather, it is a humble submission to the truth of the apostolic gospel of Christ.

Paul says that he proclaimed this gospel to bring about such humble submission to Christ among the Gentiles: "In Christ Jesus, then, I have reason to be proud of my work for God. For I will not venture to speak of anything except what Christ has accomplished through me to bring the Gentiles to obedience" (Rom. 15:17). Schreiner comments, "The obedience of the Gentiles is nothing less than the conversion of the Gentiles. It is equivalent to 'the obedience of faith' (1:5; 16:26), which is the goal of the Pauline mission among the Gentiles."[14]

Finally, in two passages Paul says that thanks and praise should be given to *God* for this obedience. In Romans 6:17, he calls the Romans to join him in thanking God for their own obedience: "But thanks be to God, that you who were once slaves of sin have become obedient from the heart to the standard of teaching to which you were committed." This verse probably describes the conversion of the Romans as their obedience to Christian

---

11 For this observation I am indebted to Paul Barnett, *The Second Epistle to the Corinthians*, NICNT (Grand Rapids, MI: Eerdmans, 1997), 466.

12 Wolter observes that "Paul puts the 'knowledge of God' and the 'obedience to Christ' on the same level with each other with a complementary *parallelismus membrorum*, because there is no difference between the two." *Paul*, 60. Note that the obedience Paul speaks about in 2 Cor. 10:6 is probably broader than the Corinthians' faith but not less than it (see figure 4.1).

13 Rudolf Bultmann, *Theology of the New Testament*, trans. Kendrick Grobel (New York: Scribner, 1951), 1:315, 317, 323, 324. There is some truth to Bultmann's view in that Paul says that unbelieving Jews did not submit to God's righteousness because they were seeking to establish their own righteousness (Rom. 10:3; cf. Phil. 3:9). Nevertheless, surrendering self-righteousness is not the object, focus, or fundamental orientation of faith for Paul: it is Christ himself.

14 Schreiner, *Romans*, 742. As in 2 Cor. 10:6, the "obedience" of the Gentiles in Rom. 15:17 may be broader than faith, but it is not less than faith (see again figure 4.1).

teaching.[15] God's agency in this obedience is seen in Paul's thanksgiving as well as in the unusual statement about being committed or handed over (παρεδόθητε) to Christian teaching.[16] Since it was common to speak of tradition being handed over to people (cf. 1 Cor. 15:3), Robert Gagnon suggests that Paul may be engaging in deliberate wordplay: it is not so much that the teaching is handed over to them as that they are handed over to the teaching.[17] The point is that their deliverance from sin and their obedience to the teaching are God's work.[18] Similarly, in 2 Corinthians 9:13, Paul says that the saints in Jerusalem, who receive the love offering of the Corinthians, will give thanks to God and glorify him "because of the submission of your confession of the gospel of Christ, and the generosity of your contribution for them and for all others."[19] Some take the "submission of your confession" as a reference to the Corinthians' submission in giving the offering.[20] But since Paul mentions the offering in the following words ("and the generosity of your contribution"), it seems more likely that their submission *is* their confession of the gospel.[21] If this is correct, then Paul says

15 Schreiner comments, "Paul is probably thinking of the conversion of the Roman Christians, in which they exercised 'the obedience of faith' (1:5; 16:26)." *Romans*, 333. The phrase "standard of teaching [τύπον διδαχῆς]" is difficult, but most interpreters at least agree that it is a reference to Christian teaching. For the various interpretations, see Robert A. J. Gagnon, "Heart of Wax and a Teaching That Stamps: Τυπος Διδαχης (Rom 6:17b) Once More," *JBL* 112, no. 4 (1993): 675–87. As in 2 Cor. 10:6 and Rom. 15:17, this obedience in Rom. 6:17 may be broader than the Romans' faith, but it also includes their faith since it refers to their conversion (see once more figure 4.1).

16 Note that the same verb (παραδίδωμι) is used in Rom. 1:24, 26, and 28 to refer to God handing over the wicked to their sin.

17 Gagnon, "Heart of Wax," 671. Cf. Gal. 4:9: "You have come to know God, or rather to be known by God."

18 So Schreiner, *Romans*, 335. He also follows Gagnon in seeing a reference to the new covenant in their obedience "from the heart." Schreiner, 335. Cf. Deut. 30:6; Jer. 31:33; Ezek. 36:26–27.

19 I have replaced the ESV's interpretive "because of your submission that comes from your confession" with the more literal "because of the submission of your confession [ἐπὶ τῇ ὑποταγῇ τῆς ὁμολογίας ὑμῶν]."

20 So Barnett, because Paul discusses the offering in the context. *Second Corinthians*, 446. The genitive "of your confession of the gospel" is then taken as a genitive of source: "submission that comes from your confession."

21 That is, an epexegetical genitive—so Seifrid: "Paul describes this confession of the Gospel as a subjection to it, just as he does in Rom 10:3." *Second Corinthians*, 364–65. Wolter suggests that

that the Jerusalem saints will thank and glorify God for the Corinthians' submission to the gospel (i.e., their faith) and for the generosity of their offering (i.e., their love).[22] Thus, in these two passages, Paul indicates that even human obedience to the gospel is ultimately God's work.

Calling on the Name of the Lord

In the context of Romans 10:6–13, Paul speaks of another conceptual parallel to faith in Christ, one that manifests itself in two related ideas: confessing that Jesus is Lord (Rom. 10:9–10) and calling on the name of the Lord (Rom. 10:12–13). These two ideas sandwich Paul's citation of Isaiah 28:16 in Romans 10:11, showing how closely related they are to believing in Christ. Both seem to refer to the same outward expression of faith that is conveyed with human lips.[23]

Theologically, there seems to be no difference in Paul's argument between believing in Christ and either confessing him to be Lord or calling on him. Both confessing and believing are held together as a condition of salvation: "If you confess with your mouth that Jesus is Lord and believe in your heart that God raised him from the dead, you will be saved" (Rom. 10:9; cf. Acts 22:16). Similarly, Paul cites Isaiah 28:16 and Joel 3:5 in parallel, limiting the riches of salvation to "everyone who believes in him" (Rom. 10:11) or "everyone who calls on the name of the Lord" (Rom. 10:13).[24] Paul's focus in Romans 10:11–13 is not on the limitation of salvation to believers but rather on the inclusiveness of salvation for both Jewish and Gentile believers:

---

the phrase "submission of your confession" is "semantically isotopic" with "obedience of faith" (Rom. 1:5) and "obedience of Christ" (2 Cor. 10:5, my literal trans.). *Paul*, 28n39.

22 This is not unlike the opening thanksgiving passages in Paul's Thessalonian correspondence and Prison Epistles, in which he thanks God for his readers' faith and love.

23 Hurtado observes from the context of Rom. 10:9–13 that Paul understands "calling on the name of the Lord" to mean the "ritual act" of confessing Jesus as Lord. Larry W. Hurtado, *Lord Jesus Christ: Devotion to Jesus in Earliest Christianity* (Grand Rapids, MI: Eerdmans, 2003), 198.

24 J. Ross Wagner observes that "Paul has crafted this citation of Isaiah 28:16 to create a close parallel with the quotation of Joel 2:32 LXX in Romans 10:13." *Heralds of the Good News: Isaiah and Paul "In Concert" in the Letter to the Romans* (Leiden: Brill, 2003), 156.

"everyone" (πᾶς).[25] He even adds the word "everyone" to his citation of Isaiah 28:16 to emphasize this inclusiveness. Nevertheless, within this inclusiveness there is also a condition: "The same Lord is Lord of all, bestowing his riches on all *who call on him*" (Rom. 10:12). Thus we see that calling on the Lord plays the same conditional role in salvation as believing in him did in the last chapter. Paul does seem to indicate a temporal distinction between believing in Christ and calling on him when he asks, "How then will they call on him in whom they have not believed?" (Rom. 10:14). Here believing in him must come before calling on him. But theologically, there seems to be no distinction between this inward belief and its outward expression in calling. Just as the righteousness of God is "for all who believe [εἰς πάντας τοὺς πιστεύοντας]" (Rom. 3:22; cf. 1:16), so God bestows the riches of his salvation "on all who call on him [εἰς πάντας τοὺς ἐπικαλουμένους αὐτόν]" (Rom. 10:12).[26]

What does it mean to use one's lips to confess Jesus and call on him as Lord? To confess Jesus as Lord is to make a public acknowledgment of his lordship and to profess allegiance to him.[27] It is likely also a confession of his divinity—that is, worship. In Philippians 2:11, Paul uses language that is very similar to Romans 10:9: "Every tongue [will] confess that Jesus Christ is Lord, to the glory of God the Father." This verse is an allusion to the Greek translation of Isaiah 45:23, which prophesies that "every tongue" will make confession to God. Thus, a confession of Jesus as Lord is likely a confession that he is the one true God who saves (cf. Isa. 45:22–25).[28]

---

25 Note that the word πᾶς is used four times in Rom. 10:11–13.

26 I am indebted to Ulrichs's observation of these parallel statements. *Christusglaube*, 176–77. It is interesting to note as well that Paul occasionally describes Christians as "those who . . . call upon the name of our Lord Jesus Christ" (1 Cor. 1:2; cf. 2 Tim. 2:22). Fee comments that for the early Christians, "the phrase became a near synonym for 'believers'" (cf. Acts 9:14). Gordon D. Fee, *The First Epistle to the Corinthians*, rev. ed., NICNT (Grand Rapids, MI: Eerdmans, 2014), 30n24.

27 BDAG, s.v. "ὁμολογέω," use 4.b.

28 Cf. Capes on Phil. 2:10–11: "Jewish believers would have recognized the core phrases as Old Testament language reserved for Yahweh and now, as a result of the exaltation, applied to the Lord Jesus. Furthermore, they would certainly be aware that these phrases have been applied to the Risen Lord *along with the divine name* (κύριος). They would probably assume that Jesus reigns, not as

Calling on the name of the Lord is also a Jewish idiom for worship. Abraham in particular is often said to have called on the name of the Lord in worship (Gen. 12:8; 13:4; 21:33; cf. 26:25).[29] But this idiom is used more often for prayer. There is a strong theme in Jewish theology that calling on the Lord in prayer results in salvation, especially in the Psalter:

> I call upon the LORD, who is worthy to be praised,
> and I am saved from my enemies. (Ps. 18:3 // 2 Sam. 22:4)

> O LORD, save the king!
> May he answer us when we call. (Ps. 20:9)

> O LORD, let me not be put to shame,
> for I call upon you. (Ps. 31:17)

> Call upon me in the day of trouble;
> I will deliver you, and you shall glorify me. (Ps. 50:15)

> In distress you called, and I delivered you. (Ps. 81:7)

> Then I called on the name of the LORD:
> "O LORD, I pray, deliver my soul!" (Ps. 116:4)

An interesting example is found in the pseudonymous Psalms of Solomon, because it is probably alluding to Joel 2:32, the text Paul cites in Romans 10:13: "Happy is the man whose heart is ready to call on the name of the Lord [ἐπικαλέσασθαι τὸ ὄνομα κυρίου]; when he remembers the name of the Lord [τὸ ὄνομα κυρίου], he will be saved

---

a second God but as One who shares full equality and divinity with God. Jesus would thereby be viewed as an object of worship and veneration." David B. Capes, *Old Testament Yahweh Texts in Paul's Christology*, WUNT, 2nd ser., vol. 47 (Tübingen: Mohr Siebeck, 1992), 159; emphasis original.

29 Cf. Jdt. 3:8, where "calling upon him" is an idiom for worshiping Nebuchadnezzar alone as God.

[σωθήσεται]" (Ps. Sol. 6:1).[30] And in a final example, Ben Sira sees a parallel, as does Paul, between calling on the name of the Lord and trusting in the Lord: "Consider the ancient generations and see: who trusted in the Lord [ἐνεπίστευσεν κυρίῳ] and was put to shame? Or who persevered in the fear of the Lord and was forsaken? Or who called upon him [ἐπεκαλέσατο αὐτόν] and was overlooked?" (Sir. 2:10).

The main difference between Paul and these Old Testament and intertestamental examples is the identity of "the Lord." Paul quotes from the Greek translation of Joel 2:32:[31] "Everyone who calls on the name of the Lord [κυρίου] will be saved" (Rom. 10:13). This is an exact translation of the Hebrew, in which "Lord" (κύριος) translates "Yahweh" (יְהוָה), the name of Israel's God. But in the context of Paul's argument, the "Lord" is the Lord Jesus, whom God has raised from the dead (Rom. 10:9, 12).[32] Thus, according to Paul, our faith is expressed outwardly by using our lips to confess *Jesus* as Lord and to call on him for salvation. It is profoundly oriented toward the person and work of Christ. And the main contribution that this conceptual parallel makes to our understanding of Christ-oriented faith in Pauline theology is that such faith is expressed outwardly in worship and prayer.

Hoping in Christ

There is a close relationship between faith and hope in Paul's theology, as many have observed.[33] In several texts about Christ-oriented faith,

---

30 The English translation is that of R. B. Wright, in *The Old Testament Pseudepigrapha*, vol. 2, ed. James H. Charlesworth (New York: Doubleday, 1985), 657. Although the Psalms of Solomon was probably originally written in Hebrew, the primary extant witnesses are in Greek.

31 According to the versification of the Septuagint and Masoretic Text, this is Joel 3:5.

32 So Capes, *Old Testament Yahweh Texts*, 121–23; N. T. Wright, *Paul and the Faithfulness of God*, COQG 4 (Minneapolis: Fortress, 2013), 703.

33 For example, Schreiner describes the relationship of faith and hope in Pauline theology like this: "One of the marks of authentic faith is perseverance, and faith perseveres because it is sustained by hope." Thomas R. Schreiner, *Paul, Apostle of God's Glory in Christ: A Pauline Theology* (Downers Grove, IL: IVP Academic, 2001), 271. See especially Col. 1:4–5, 23.

Paul draws a close parallel with hoping in Christ. Most important is 1 Corinthians 15:1–19, where Paul explains the Corinthians' "faith" (1 Cor. 15:17) as their "hope in Christ" (1 Cor. 15:19):[34] "If we have put our hope in Christ for this life only, we should be pitied more than anyone" (1 Cor. 15:19 CSB).[35] In context, this faith and hope are in the gospel, the Christ proclaimed by the apostles (cf. 1 Cor. 15:2, 11–12, 14, 17, 19). Paul makes a similar explanatory move in 2 Corinthians 1:9–10, where he speaks of the God who raises the dead as the object of his own trust (2 Cor. 1:9) and hope (2 Cor. 1:10) in the midst of suffering. And in 1 Thessalonians 4:13–14, Paul draws a contrast between those "who have no hope" (1 Thess. 4:13) and the Thessalonians who "believe that Jesus died and rose again" (1 Thess. 4:14).[36]

Thus, there is clearly a conceptual overlap for Paul between believing in Christ and hoping in Christ.[37] The apostle, however, also famously draws a theological distinction between faith and hope (and especially love): "So now faith, hope, and love abide, these three; but the greatest of these is love" (1 Cor. 13:13).[38] In light of this distinction, I suggest that believing in Christ and hoping in Christ are theologically distinct yet overlapping concepts in Paul's theology (see figure 4.2).

---

34 Ulrichs similarly observes that hope in 1 Cor. 15:19 is an expression of faith (1 Cor. 15:14, 17). *Christusglaube*, 83.

35 I have quoted from the CSB because it indicates more clearly than the ESV that "in Christ" (ἐν Χριστῷ) is the object of "we have put our hope"—so BDAG, s.v. "ἐλπίζω," use 1.c.

36 Note also the close relationship in Rom. 15:12–13 between the "hope" of the Gentiles in the root of Jesse (Isa. 11:10 LXX) and their "believing." And in Eph. 1:12–13, Paul speaks of the Jewish Christians, who were "the first to hope in Christ" (Eph. 1:12), and then Gentile Christians, who also "believed" (Eph. 1:13).

37 Ridderbos observes that "hope is indissolubly bound up with faith . . . by virtue of faith's focus on Christ." Herman Ridderbos, *Paul: An Outline of His Theology*, trans. John Richard de Witt (Grand Rapids, MI: Eerdmans, 1975), 248.

38 An argument could be made that loving the Lord overlaps with believing in him (see 1 Cor. 16:22; Eph. 6:24; 2 Tim. 4:8). But the only text in which Paul clearly draws this parallel is 2 Thess. 2:10–12, where he describes those who "refused to love the truth" as those who "did not believe the truth."

Figure 4.2   **Believing and Hoping in Christ**

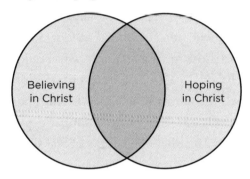

With this conceptual parallel, we see that Christ-oriented faith has a future orientation and especially an eschatological orientation. Hope is by its nature oriented toward the unseen future for Paul: "Now hope that is seen is not hope. For who hopes for what he sees? But if we hope for what we do not see, we wait for it with patience" (Rom. 8:24–25). Elsewhere, Paul says the same of faith: "We walk by faith, not by sight" (2 Cor. 5:7).[39] Thus, believers are like Abraham, who "believed on the basis of hope" (Rom. 4:18, my trans.; cf. Col. 1:4–5). But more specifically, our hope in Christ is oriented toward the *eschatological* future for Paul. He says to the Corinthians, "If we have put our hope in Christ for this life only, we should be pitied more than anyone" (1 Cor. 15:19 CSB). Here he assumes the Jewish theological distinction between "this life" and the eschatological life of the resurrection. This view of the future looks forward to a decisive, culminating fulfillment of God's oracles, "a permanent and radical break with the preceding historical epoch."[40] This is not to deny that Paul also views Christ as offering hope for this life but rather to say

39 Wolter concludes from these two parallel statements that "hope is given along with Christian faith and not something that must be added on to it later." *Paul*, 180.

40 G. K. Beale, *A New Testament Biblical Theology: The Unfolding of the Old Testament in the New* (Grand Rapids, MI: Baker Academic, 2011), 114. Beale is describing the eschatological storyline of the Old Testament as expressed in the phrase "the latter days." Beale, 88–116.

that faith in Christ is fundamentally oriented toward the resurrection life to come. Paul trusted in the "God who raises the dead" to deliver him from the burden of his afflictions in Asia and to deliver him "again," whether that be in this life or in the one to come (2 Cor. 1:8–11; cf. 2 Tim. 4:17–18).[41]

Hope is also closely associated with "waiting" for Paul: "If we hope for what we do not see, we wait for it with patience" (Rom. 8:25). He speaks in several of his letters about Christ-oriented hope as "waiting for" Jesus to save us.[42] The eschatological orientation of this hope is clear since it awaits ultimate salvation from the final judgment through God's Son:

> You turned to God from idols . . . to wait for his Son from heaven, whom he raised from the dead, Jesus who delivers us from the wrath to come. (1 Thess. 1:9–10)

> You are not lacking in any gift, as you wait for the revealing of our Lord Jesus Christ. (1 Cor. 1:7)

> But our citizenship is in heaven, and from it we await a Savior, the Lord Jesus Christ. (Phil. 3:20)

> . . . waiting for our blessed hope, the appearing of the glory of our great God and Savior Jesus Christ. (Titus 2:13)[43]

---

41 Seifrid comments on this passage that Paul's "intentional ambiguity leaves the present outcome of Paul's trouble open. Even if God should not deliver him from death *now*, God shall do so *finally*, without question. Whatever may come, his deliverance is certain and assured." Seifrid dubs this the "ambiguity of faith." *Second Corinthians*, 44.

42 He uses different verbs for "wait for" in these passages, but they are synonymous.

43 On this text, Yarbrough comments, "It is clear that 'wait' can describe a posture, not of passivity in the face of a fickle future (cf. *Waiting for Godot* in Samuel Beckett's absurdist play), but of dogged confidence in God and his sure promises, however remote they may seem at times." Robert W. Yarbrough, *The Letters to Timothy and Titus*, PNTC (Grand Rapids, MI: Eerdmans, 2018), 529.

Similarly, Paul speaks in 1 Thessalonians 5:8 about the "hope of salvation," which probably means our hope *for* salvation.[44] He gives this reason: "For God has not destined us for wrath, but to obtain salvation through our Lord Jesus Christ, who died for us so that whether we are awake or asleep we might live with him" (1 Thess. 5:9–10; cf. Rom. 5:9). Finally, Paul tells the Galatians that we await the hope of final justification: "Through the Spirit, [n.b.] by faith, we ourselves eagerly wait for the hope of righteousness" (Gal. 5:5).[45] Thus, Christ-oriented faith or hope awaits the eschatological future, when Jesus delivers believers from the final judgment.

Seeing the Lord's Glory

I observed in chapter 2 that 2 Corinthians 4:13–14 is a kind of microcosm of the larger argument of 2 Corinthians 4–5. In these chapters, Paul explains why he does not lose heart as he suffers for speaking the gospel (2 Cor. 4:1, 16): it is because he pays attention not to temporary things, which are seen, but to eternal things, which are unseen (2 Cor. 4:16–5:10). In other words, he speaks because he believes that God will raise him and the Corinthians from the dead (2 Cor. 4:13–14).[46] Or as Paul states in 2 Corinthians 5:7, which is also a microcosm of the larger argument, "We walk by faith, not by sight." In this section, I explore how Paul uses the physical sense of sight as a conceptual parallel with Christ-oriented faith in 2 Corinthians 3–5. The interesting thing is that he uses sight both as

---

44 That is, an objective genitive—so Charles A. Wanamaker, *The Epistle to the Thessalonians*, NIGTC (Grand Rapids, MI: Eerdmans, 1990), 186.

45 Moo argues that "hope of righteousness" means the "hope which is righteousness" (epexegetical genitive), referring to final justification. He reasons that in context the Galatians have begun by faith but are "in danger of being convinced that they can maintain their status of righteousness only by adding torah obedience to their faith in Christ. . . . The situation requires that Paul emphasize how the Galatians are to *maintain* their status of righteousness and how they can expect to be found to be in the 'right' in the judgment." Douglas J. Moo, *Galatians*, BECNT (Grand Rapids, MI: Baker Academic, 2013), 328.

46 Note again the eschatological orientation of Paul's faith.

the antonym of faith (2 Cor. 4:18; 5:7) and as a metaphor for faith (2 Cor. 3:18; 4:4–6).

First, in 2 Corinthians 3:12–4:6, Paul speaks of sight as a concrete metaphor for the abstract virtue of faith in Christ. This metaphor appears within a defense of the apostle's ministry of the new covenant. Paul says that the hope of eternal glory bound up with the new covenant leads him to proceed with much frankness in his proclamation of the gospel (2 Cor. 3:12).[47] He contrasts this frankness with the story of Moses, who, after he met with the Lord, put a veil over his face to hide the glory of the Lord from the Israelites (Ex. 34:29–35). He also contrasts it with what are apparently accusations some have made about his ministry being shifty in some way: "We have renounced disgraceful, underhanded ways. We refuse to practice cunning or to tamper with God's word, but by the open statement of the truth we would commend ourselves to everyone's conscience in the sight of God" (2 Cor. 4:2). This leads to a question: If Paul proclaims the gospel with such frankness, why does it seem hidden to so many? In other words, why do so many not believe the gospel?

Paul first reflects on this question in his telling of the story of Moses and the veil, reading the story as an allegory for Israel's inability to understand and keep the old covenant—that is, their unbelief:

We are . . . not like Moses, who would put a veil over his face so that the Israelites might not gaze at the outcome [τέλος] of what was being brought to an end. But their minds were hardened. For to this day, when they read the old covenant, that same veil remains unlifted, because only through Christ is it taken away.

---

47 Most English versions translate παρρησία in 2 Cor. 3:12 as "boldness." But Paul contrasts his παρρησία with "Moses, who would put a veil over his face" (2 Cor. 3:13). Thus it seems better to translate the word as "a use of speech that conceals nothing and passes over nothing, *outspokenness, frankness, plainness.*" BDAG, s.v. "παρρησία," use 2; so Barnett, *Second Corinthians*, 191. The KJV has "we use great plainness of speech."

Yes, to this day whenever Moses is read a veil lies over their hearts.
(2 Cor. 3:12–15)

This is the beginning of Paul's metaphor of sight for faith. What
could the Israelites not see when they looked at Moses or the old
covenant? They could not see the "outcome," or literally the "end"
(τέλος), of the glory that was passing away. Since he elsewhere calls
Christ the "end" (τέλος) of the law, perhaps Paul is saying that they
could not see the new covenant glory of Christ to which the glory of
the law was pointing.[48] Rather, their minds were hardened against
seeing Christ and are in fact hardened to this very day when the
law is read in the synagogue. In contrast, Paul describes the faith of
Christians ("we all") as "beholding the glory of the Lord":

But when one turns to the Lord, the veil is removed. Now the Lord is
the Spirit, and where the Spirit of the Lord is, there is freedom. And
we all, with unveiled face, beholding the glory of the Lord, are being
transformed into the same image from one degree of glory to another.
For this comes from the Lord who is the Spirit. (2 Cor. 3:16–18)

Having the veil of unbelief removed, those with the Spirit can now
"behold," or "contemplate," the new covenant glory of the Lord
Jesus Christ in the reading of the law and be changed into his im-

---

48 Similarly, Wright suggests that "the end of what was being abolished" is "a cryptic way of referring
to both the . . . glory of Moses' face . . . and to the ultimate 'end' or 'goal,' the final future glory
of which Moses' glory was a foretaste." *Paul and the Faithfulness of God*, 1225. *Pace* Hafemann,
who forcefully argues that the "end" in 2 Cor. 3:13 is not Christ but rather the judgment of God's
glory against sinful Israel, from which Moses's veil mercifully spared Israel (cf. 2 Cor. 3:7). Scott J.
Hafemann, *Paul, Moses, and the History of Israel: The Letter/Spirit Contrast and the Argument from
Scripture in 2 Corinthians 3*, WUNT 81 (Tübingen: Mohr Siebeck, 1995), 347–62. Theologically, Hafemann's interpretation is related to mine: "It is precisely because Moses had to veil the
purpose (τέλος) of the glory of the old covenant from Israel [i.e., judgment] due to their hard
hearts (2 Cor. 3:13b) that Christ must become the τέλος of the Law (Rom. 10:4)." Hafemann,
358.

age.[49] In the next paragraph, Paul extends this veil metaphor to all unbelievers (ἀπίστων) in the present day: "And even if our gospel is veiled, it is veiled to those who are perishing. In their case the god of this world has blinded the minds of the unbelievers, to keep them from seeing the light of the gospel of the glory of Christ, who is the image of God" (2 Cor. 4:3–4).

Why then does Paul's gospel seem veiled and hidden? Not because Paul is wearing a veil as Moses did but rather because Satan has blinded the minds of unbelievers so that they do not see it. Thus Paul clearly uses blindness and sight as a metaphor for unbelief and faith in this passage. The object of unbelief or faith is "the light of the gospel of the glory of Christ, who is the image of God" (2 Cor. 4:4). As we saw in the last chapter, there is a close relationship for Paul between the gospel (the message about Christ) and Christ himself. These phrases probably mean that the gospel is the good news about Christ's glory, so that the gospel itself can be said to have a light. Unbelievers cannot see this light because Satan has blinded their minds, not because Paul has veiled it for some selfish reason. Paul speaks the gospel of Christ openly, and the reason he does so is that he knows that the Creator God will enlighten hearts to believe it: "For what we proclaim is not ourselves, but Jesus Christ as Lord, with ourselves as your servants for Jesus's sake. For God, who said, 'Let light shine out of darkness,' has shone in our hearts to give the light of the knowledge of the glory of God in the face of Jesus Christ" (2 Cor. 4:5–6). Here the "light of the knowledge of the glory of God" probably means that the light that God shines into our dark hearts *is* the knowledge of God's glory. That is, just as God created the world by speaking light into darkness (cf. Gen. 1:3), so he now speaks through the gospel that Paul proclaims to cause us to know truly (that is, to believe) God's glory in the face of Jesus

---

49 The Greek verb "behold" (κατοπτρίζω) probably means "to look at something as in a mirror," that is, to "contemplate" it carefully. BDAG, s.v. "κατοπτρίζω."

Christ. Christ is the "image of God" (2 Cor. 4:4), which means that beholding his glory (2 Cor. 3:18) or seeing the light of the gospel of his glory (2 Cor. 4:4) is really seeing, in his face, the very glory of God (2 Cor. 4:6).[50] Thus, the object of faith to which unbelievers are blind and believers are enlightened in 2 Corinthians 3:12–4:6 is the person of Christ and specifically the glory or radiance of his divine nature.

We move now from Paul's use of sight as a metaphor for faith to his use of sight as the antonym of Christ-oriented faith in 2 Corinthians 4:16–5:10. This negative parallel occurs within an explanation of his suffering and why he does not lose heart in the midst of it (2 Cor. 4:16; 5:6). The reason Paul does not lose heart in the midst of suffering is his confidence in the "eternal weight of glory" being prepared for him by God (cf. 2 Cor. 5:5):

> So we do not lose heart. Though our outer self is wasting away, our inner self is being renewed day by day. For this light momentary affliction is preparing for us an eternal weight of glory beyond all comparison, so[51] we look not to the things that are seen but to the things that are unseen. For the things that are seen are transient, but the things that are unseen are eternal. (2 Cor. 4:16–18)

In these verses Paul continues to use sight as a metaphor for faith: "We *look* not to the things that are seen but to the things that are unseen" (2 Cor. 4:18). But he also uses sight as the antonym of faith because the object of his attention is not what is "seen" but what is "unseen." This use of sight as an antonym for faith is then spelled out more clearly in his later conclusion about his courage in the midst of suffering: "So

---

50 Schreiner observes that "image of God" alludes to Gen. 1:27, where humanity is created "in the image of God," but that there is a difference in that Paul says Jesus *is* the image of God: "Christ as the image of God surpasses Adam because the word *image* suggests that he shares the very nature of God." *Paul*, 155.

51 I have replaced "as" in the ESV with "so" because I think the participle σκοπούντων indicates a result (so CSB, NIV).

we are always of good courage. We know that while we are at home in the body we are away from the Lord, for we walk by faith, not by sight. Yes, we are of good courage, and we would rather be away from the body and at home with the Lord" (2 Cor. 5:6–8).

The reason Paul uses sight as an antonym for faith is his eschatology, his distinction between the present age of "momentary affliction" and the age to come of eternal glory. He seems to be thinking specifically of the resurrection body. His faith does not look at his present body, which is wasting away, but to the eternal, glorious body. His faith is in the Lord himself, whom he does not see right now in the present age but with whom he will one day be home (notice how faith and sight in 2 Cor. 5:7 are oriented toward the Lord). Paul, however, also sees the future age of glory operating in the present age in "our inner self," which "is being renewed day by day" (2 Cor. 4:15). Thus, there is a distinction not only between present and future in this passage but also between internal (already) and external (not yet). As Paul suffers in his body, his inner self is daily being renewed, being transformed into the image of the glory of the Lord by the Spirit (2 Cor. 3:18; 4:16; 5:5). And he is confident that this internal glory will one day become an external "weight of glory beyond all comparison" (2 Cor. 4:17). Thus his faith is fixed on the things he cannot see: the glory of the Lord and his future participation in that glory at the resurrection. He walks "by faith, not by sight" (2 Cor. 5:7).[52]

How, then, does the parallel of physical sight help us understand Christ-oriented faith in Paul's theology? First, it explains more fully what I called in the last chapter the paradoxical nature of faith in Paul. Christ-oriented faith sees what cannot be seen.[53] Paul, like Abraham,

---

52 In contrast with the act of "faith," εἴδους probably means the act of seeing, or "sight," rather than what is seen, or "form." So BDAG, s.v. "εἶδος"; *pace* Nijay K. Gupta, *Paul and the Language of Faith* (Grand Rapids, MI: Eerdmans, 2020), 130.

53 Gupta memorably speaks of this paradox in the Corinthian correspondence as believing the unbelievable; e.g., *Language of Faith*, 133.

sees death with his eyes, but he is confident in God's promise of life. Faith sees the glory of the risen Lord, but it does not yet see the Lord with the eyes. The reason Paul speaks of his faith as a paradox in 2 Corinthians, as he does in describing Abraham's faith, is that Paul believes in the God who raises the dead. But here we can define this reason even more clearly: Paul speaks of faith as a paradox because his eschatology is oriented toward Christ—he sees the glory of the Lord already, but his eyes are firmly fixed on the glory that has not yet come. Second, the parallel of physical sight significantly reinforces the idea that Paul views our faith in Christ as a product of divine agency. Unbelievers have had their minds blinded by the god of this world (2 Cor. 4:4). But believers have experienced Isaiah's promised new creation: God has caused light to shine in our dark hearts so that we can see the glory of Jesus Christ (2 Cor. 4:6; cf. 5:16–17).[54]

Conclusion

In this chapter, I have explored four conceptual parallels that occur within the immediate context of Paul's direct statements about Christ-oriented faith: obedience to the gospel, calling on the name of the Lord, hoping in Christ, and seeing the Lord's glory. This exploration has found that Christ-oriented faith in Paul's letters involves submission to the truth of the gospel of Christ (obedience), is expressed outwardly with the lips in worship and prayer to Christ (calling on), is oriented toward his coming to deliver us from the final judgment (hoping), and for this reason paradoxically sees what cannot (yet) be seen with the eyes: the glory of God in the face of Jesus Christ (seeing). This chapter has also reinforced the idea that Paul does not oppose our faith and divine agency but rather sees God as the source of our obedience to the gospel and our new creation

---

54 Beale shows how 2 Cor. 5:17 alludes to both Isa. 43:18–19 and 65:17. *New Testament Biblical Theology*, 299–300.

vision of Christ. In summary, we see again that Paul significantly emphasizes Christ-oriented faith in his letters, even outside the debated πίστις Χριστοῦ phrases. But in the next chapter, I argue that these phrases show even further the fundamental Christological orientation of our faith in Paul's theology.

4

Ἐκ Πίστεως Χριστοῦ as a Pauline Idiom for Christ-Oriented Faith

As I have said, faith grasps and embraces Christ, the Son of God, who was given for us, as Paul teaches here. When He has been grasped by faith, we have righteousness and life.

MARTIN LUTHER, *LECTURES ON GALATIANS*

A READER COULD DISAGREE with the argument of this chapter while agreeing with the thesis of my book. In the last three chapters, I have argued that Paul significantly emphasizes Christ-oriented faith in his theology. I first showed that Paul's teaching about faith refers to sources that speak about our faith in God, and occasionally in Christ, as a cause and condition of our salvation. Next, I demonstrated that Paul speaks often, albeit in different ways, about Christ-oriented faith as a cause and condition of our justification. Finally, I explored four conceptual parallels to faith in Christ in Paul's letters to establish more deeply my thesis about the importance of Christ-oriented faith in the apostle's theology. In each of these chapters, I have purposely examined texts outside the debated πίστις Χριστοῦ phrases so that my thesis would not "stand or fall" with the πίστις Χριστοῦ debate. Thus, readers could technically agree with my overall thesis while disagreeing with my view of πίστις Χριστοῦ in Paul's letters—namely, that these phrases mean "faith in Christ."

Advocates of the "faithfulness of Christ" translation, however, have rightly seen that these eight debated phrases are closely related to Paul's entire theology of salvation. In fact, it is unfortunate that this debate has been labeled the "πίστις Χριστοῦ debate," because the phrase πίστις Χριστοῦ never actually occurs in Paul's letters. Instead, the construction always occurs within a prepositional phrase:[1]

δια πίστεως 'Ιησοῦ Χριστοῦ (Rom. 3:22)
ἐκ πίστεως 'Ιησοῦ (Rom. 3:26)
διὰ πίστεως 'Ιησοῦ Χριστοῦ (Gal. 2:16a)
ἐκ πίστεως Χριστοῦ (Gal. 2:16c)
ἐν πίστει . . . τῇ τοῦ υἱοῦ τοῦ θεοῦ (Gal. 2:20)
ἐκ πίστεως 'Ιησοῦ Χριστοῦ (Gal. 3:22)
διὰ τῆς πίστεως αὐτοῦ (Eph. 3:12)[2]
διὰ πίστεως Χριστοῦ (Phil. 3:9)

These phrases are lengthened forms of the phrase "by faith," which is common in the Pauline corpus and often contrasted with salvation "by works of the law," "by the law," or "by works."[3] Thus, a better label for this debate would be the "ἐκ πίστεως Χριστοῦ debate," because this label shows how these phrases speak about the role that πίστις plays in Paul's soteriology.[4] Moreover, six of these eight phrases occur

---

1   Ulrichs, a careful observer of the text, has noted this phenomenon. Karl Friedrich Ulrichs, *Christusglaube: Studien zum Syntagma πίστις Χριστοῦ und zum paulinischen Verständnis von Glaube und Rechtfertigung*, WUNT, 2nd ser., vol. 227 (Tübingen: Mohr Siebeck, 2007), 6.

2   Because the authorship of Ephesians is disputed, my argument does not rest on Eph. 3:12—though I do treat it as Pauline. One reason for addressing this text is that Hays also considers it significant to the debate.

3   See Douglas A. Campbell, "The Meaning of Πιστις and Νομος in Paul: A Linguistic and Structural Perspective," *JBL* 111, no. 1 (1992): 98–99.

4   Two examples of this construction that are not found within an instrumental prepositional phrase have been suggested in Paul's letters: "to the unity of the faith and of the knowledge of the Son

in some of the apostle's most important statements about justification (Rom. 3:21–26; Gal. 2:15–21; Phil. 3:2–11). All this means that the translation of these phrases really makes a difference in one's view of Pauline theology. In other words, even though my thesis does not stand or fall with the argument of this chapter, the πίστις Χριστοῦ debate still matters for my overall thesis.

The goal of this chapter, then, is to engage in the πίστις Χριστοῦ debate. First, I sketch a history of the translation and interpretation of these phrases, showing that the debate is a product of modern exegesis. Next, I evaluate Richard Hays's Christological view of πίστις, walking through each of the eight phrases in Paul. Finally, I argue that the phrase "by faith" is a consistent Pauline idiom for Christ-oriented faith. Surely my argument will not satisfy all readers, because so much has been written on this debate. But for those with ears to hear, it will help us see just how central the theme of Christ-oriented faith is in Pauline theology.

A History of Translation and Interpretation

This section briefly surveys how Paul's phrase ἐκ πίστεως Χριστοῦ has been translated and interpreted in the two thousand years since he wrote his letters.[5] I attempt to demonstrate that the πίστις Χριστοῦ debate is a product of modern exegesis and especially the influential dissertation of Richard Hays. This is not to say that premodern theologians never considered the topic of Jesus's own faith or faithfulness. For example, medieval theologians reflected on the question whether Jesus had faith.[6] Rather, it is to say that there was apparently no real question among interpreters of

---

of God" (Eph. 4:13); "your work of faith and labor of love and steadfastness of hope in our Lord Jesus Christ" (1 Thess. 1:3). (On this latter example, see especially Ulrichs, *Christusglaube*, 89–91.) In neither of these examples, however, is it likely that the genitive "of the Son of God" or "of our Lord Jesus Christ" qualifies πίστις.

5 Note that I am using the phrase ἐκ πίστεως Χριστοῦ as a shorthand for the eight phrases that have more variation in actual usage (see above, p. 184).

6 Peter Lombard and Thomas Aquinas discussed this question. Benjamin Schliesser, *Abraham's Faith in Romans 4: Paul's Concept of Faith in Light of the History of Reception of Genesis 15:6*, WUNT, 2nd ser., vol. 224 (Tübingen: Mohr Siebeck, 2007), 260.

Paul about the meaning of the phrase ἐκ πίστεως Χριστοῦ in his letters. There have been several studies of the church fathers in the course of this debate.[7] But one problem dogging this line of investigation is a focus on the theology of the fathers themselves rather than on how they interpret Paul. While this line of inquiry is fascinating in itself, it does not really illuminate or clarify the πίστις Χριστοῦ debate, especially because the interpretation of the fathers is as debated as the interpretation of Paul.[8] Thus, we must focus our attention in this survey on the history of the translation and interpretation of these eight phrases in *Paul's* letters.

One grammatical point should be established before we begin: the word πίστις followed by the genitive of person in ancient Greek can refer to either that person's own faith or faithfulness (subjective genitive) or to faith in that person (objective genitive).[9] Some advocates of the "faithfulness of Christ" translation have argued that the objective genitive is "bad Greek."[10] But Roy Harrisville has shown clear examples of the objective genitive with πίστις

7 In favor of the subjective genitive ("faithfulness of Christ"), see especially Ian G. Wallis, *The Faith of Jesus Christ in Early Christian Traditions*, SNTSMS 84 (Cambridge: Cambridge University Press, 1995), chap. 6. In favor of the objective genitive ("faith in Christ"), see especially Roy A. Harrisville III, "Πίστις Χριστου: Witness of the Fathers," *NovT* 36, no. 3 (1994): 233–41.

8 Schliesser rightly observes that "modern interpretations of the Fathers' comments contradict each other diametrically, which is not least due to the fact that the statements of the Fathers seem as ambiguous as Paul's own." Benjamin Schliesser, "'Exegetical Amnesia' and Πίστις Χριστου: The 'Faith *of* Christ' in Nineteenth-Century Pauline Scholarship," *JTS* 66, no. 1 (2015): 63n7. For example, both Yong and Whitenton have marshaled the witness of the apostolic fathers and come to almost opposite conclusions on the debate. See Kukwah Philemon Yong, "The Faith of Jesus Christ: An Analysis of Paul's Use of Πίστις Χριστου" (PhD diss., Southern Baptist Theological Seminary, 2003); Michael R. Whitenton, "After Πίστις Χριστου: Neglected Evidence from the Apostolic Fathers," *JTS* 61, no. 1 (2010): 82–109. Note also the recent exchange over Hippolytus's *De Christo et Antichristo* between Bird/Whitenton and Cirafesi/Peterman. Michael F. Bird and Michael R. Whitenton, "The Faithfulness of Jesus Christ in Hippolytus's *De Christo et Antichristo*: Overlooked Patristic Evidence in the Πίστις Χριστοῦ Debate," *NTS* 55, no. 4 (2009): 552–62; Wally V. Cirafesi and Gerald W. Peterman, "Πίστις and Christ in Hippolytus's *De Christo et Antichristo*: A Response to Michael F. Bird and Michael R. Whitenton," *NTS* 57, no. 4 (2011): 594–603.

9 That is, "faith of Christ" in ancient Greek is like "love of God" in modern English, which could refer to either our love for God or God's love for us, depending on the context.

10 For example, Howard suggests that "it was inappropriate to the Hellenistic Jewish mentality to express the object of faith by means of the objective genitive." George Howard, "Faith of Christ," in *Anchor Bible Dictionary*, ed. David Noel Freedman (New York: Doubleday, 1992), 2:758.

in ancient Greek.[11] And even Hays has observed that Mark 11:22 is a clear example of πίστις with an objective genitive in the New Testament: "Have faith in God [πίστιν θεοῦ]."[12] Arguments against the objective genitive from statistics or "predominant usage" are really meaningless.[13] For as Moisés Silva memorably puts it, "The vast majority of occurrences of English *sale* in juxtaposition with other nouns are 'objective' (*car sale, shoe sale, book sale*), but that hardly means that *garage sale* indicates that someone is selling a garage."[14] On the other hand, the common grammatical argument against the subjective genitive based on the absence of the article before πίστις in most of these phrases is not compelling either.[15] Thus, Paul's phrase ἐκ πίστεως Χριστοῦ can hypothetically be translated as "by faith in Christ" or "by the faithfulness of Christ." The question is which translation best fits the historical and literary context.

Ancient Versions

The ancient versions translate Paul's eight phrases literally, which unfortunately means that they reflect the same ambiguity as the original. The Syriac Peshitta was probably made around the beginning of the

11 See Roy A. Harrisville III, "Before Πιστις Χριστου: The Objective Genitive as Good Greek," *NovT* 48, no. 4 (2006): 353–58. Morgan also discusses an interesting example of an objective genitive in Plutarch's *Moralia* (165b), who writes that a defining feature of atheism is ἀπιστία τοῦ θεοῦ, which Morgan translates as "disbelief in the divine." Teresa Morgan, *Roman Faith and Christian Faith: Pistis and Fides in the Early Roman Empire and Early Churches* (New York: Oxford University Press, 2015), 143.

12 Richard B. Hays, *The Faith of Jesus Christ: The Narrative Substructure of Galatians 3:1–4:11*, 2nd ed. (Grand Rapids, MI: Eerdmans, 2002), 149.

13 For example, Wallace argues that "the predominant usage in the NT is with a subjective gen[itive]." Daniel B. Wallace, *Greek Grammar beyond the Basics: An Exegetical Syntax of the New Testament* (Grand Rapids, MI: Zondervan, 1996), 116.

14 Moisés Silva, "Faith versus Works of Law in Galatians," in *Justification and Variegated Nomism*, vol. 2, *The Paradoxes of Paul*, ed. D. A. Carson, Peter T. O'Brien, and Mark A. Seifrid, WUNT, 2nd ser., vol. 181 (Grand Rapids, MI: Baker Academic, 2004), 229n32.

15 For example, in his debate with Hays, Dunn argues that the article must be present to indicate a subjective genitive. In Hays, *Faith of Jesus Christ*, 252–54. But the problem with this grammatical "rule" is that Rom. 4:16 is a clear exception, which leads Dunn to special pleading in order to excuse it. See *Faith of Jesus Christ*, 254. Wallace also observes that prepositional phrases tend to omit the article. *Greek Grammar*, 115.

fifth century as a revision of the Old Syriac translation.[16] In seven of the eight phrases, it translates the Greek genitive with the particle *d-* ("of"), the most common way to indicate a genitive relationship in Syriac.[17] In Ephesians 3:12, "faith of him" (τῆς πίστεως αὐτοῦ) is translated with the Syriac word for "faith" or "faithfulness" in the construct (genitive) state and the third-person masculine singular pronominal suffix. It is interesting to observe that modern English translators of the Syriac disagree about whether to translate these phrases as "faith in Christ" or "faithfulness of Christ." James Murdock's translation from the nineteenth century renders each of these phrases with "faith in" (objective genitive).[18] The more recent translations published by Gorgias Press have one translator for Romans–Corinthians (Daniel King) and another for Galatians–Philemon (J. Edward Walters). King uses the translation "faith in" (objective genitive) in Romans 3:22 and 26,[19] whereas Walters uses the translation "faithfulness of" (subjective genitive) for all but one (Phil. 3:9) of the other six phrases under consideration.[20] Thus we can see that the same ambiguity exists in the Syriac Peshitta as in the Greek.

16 The Peshitta is "the earliest surviving Syriac version of Paul's letters." Daniel King, trans., *The Syriac Peshitta Bible with English Translations: Romans–Corinthians* (Piscataway, NJ: Gorgias, 2013), xiii.

17 J. F. Coakley, *Robinson's Paradigms and Exercises in Syriac Grammar*, 6th ed. (Oxford: Oxford University Press, 2013), 21. Technically, one of these examples (Gal. 2:16c) translates πίστεως Χριστοῦ with both the third-person masculine pronominal suffix *and* the particle *d-* ("of") with "Messiah" (literally, "faith of him, of the Messiah"). This is a "very common" way to indicate the genitive relationship in Syriac. Coakley, 28. Howard argues that the anticipatory "of him" indicates more explicitly that the phrase refers to Christ's own faith. "Faith of Christ," 759. But this is not necessarily the case, as can be seen in Murdock's nineteenth-century English translation of the Peshitta, which renders Gal. 2:16c with "faith in the Messiah." James Murdock, *The New Testament, Translated into English from the Syriac Peshitto Version* (Piscataway, NJ: Gorgias, 2001), 345.

18 Technically, Murdock translates Eph. 3:12 with "his faith," but he has this footnote: "i.e., faith in him." *New Testament*, 354.

19 King, *Syriac Peshitta: Romans–Corinthians*, 17.

20 J. Edward Walters, trans., *The Syriac Peshitta Bible with English Translations: Galatians–Philemon* (Piscataway, NJ: Gorgias, 2013). It is unclear to me why Walters renders Phil. 3:9 as "faith in the Messiah" when it follows the same basic construction as the five other examples, which he translates "faithfulness of." See Walters, 72–73.

The other ancient versions are similar. In the early centuries of Christianity, the Bible was translated into both the northern (Bohairic) and southern (Sahidic) dialects of Coptic, the ancient Egyptian language written with Greek characters.[21] In both these dialects, seven of Paul's genitive constructions are translated with the genitive particle $\bar{N}$ (or $\bar{M}$).[22] Each of these is translated into English literally as "faith of."[23] The Sahidic of Ephesians 3:12 does not translate the Greek genitive "of him" (αὐτοῦ) for some reason but simply has "the faith."[24] The Bohairic translates it with a third-person masculine prefixed possessive article, which functions "exactly like the mark of relationship $\bar{N}$."[25]

The Latin Vulgate was a revision of the Old Latin version made by Jerome in the late fourth century.[26] It became the Bible of the Western church until the time of the Reformation, when modern Bible translations were made. In this version, all eight Pauline phrases are translated with the genitive case in Latin. This is brought literally into English by the Douay-Rheims Bible with the translation "faith of." Thus we see that the ancient versions translate Paul's construction literally and do not interpret the phrase or disambiguate the meaning of the genitive for us.[27] For interpretation, we must go to the commentaries of the church fathers.

---

21 These translations were probably made by the fourth century AD. See Bruce M. Metzger, *The Early Versions of the New Testament: Their Origin, Transmission, and Limitations* (New York: Oxford University Press, 1977), 125–27.

22 $\bar{M}$ is an allomorph of $\bar{N}$ used in some cases. See Bentley Layton, *A Coptic Grammar*, 2nd ed. (Wiesbaden: Harrassowitz, 2004), §21.

23 The one exception is Rom. 3:26 in the northern dialect (Bohairic), which the translator renders "faith in Jesus Christ." His reasoning is not clear since the Coptic uses the genitive particle here.

24 *The Coptic Version of the New Testament in the Southern Dialect*, vol. 5, *The Epistles of S. Paul (Continued), Register of Fragments, Etc.* (Oxford: Clarendon, 1911), 220–21.

25 Layton, *Coptic Grammar*, §54.

26 It is doubtful that Jerome is actually the one responsible for revising Paul's letters in the Vulgate. For discussion, see Metzger, *Early Versions*, 356–59.

27 Thus, it is a remarkable claim that "the early versions of the NT (the Syriac, Latin, and Coptic) make it clear that the early Church understood *pistis Christou* to mean 'faith(fulness) of Christ.'"

Ancient Commentary

The evidence of the patristic commentaries is somewhat sparse, but we do have a few comments in which the fathers interpret ἐκ πίστεως Χριστοῦ as a reference to our faith in Christ. In the third century, Origen comments that Romans 3:26 refers to

> the one who believes in Jesus [εἰς Ἰησοῦν] and through Jesus in God and it is not at all strange to say beforehand, "justifying the one of faith of Jesus" [ἐκ πίστεως Ἰησοῦ] because just as "Abraham believed God and it was reckoned to him as righteousness" thus those who believe in Jesus [εἰς τὸν Ἰησοῦν] or God through Jesus, God reckons that faith for righteousness and thus he justifies the one of faith of Jesus [ἐκ πίστεως Ἰησοῦ].[28]

It is clear from this comment that Origen sees the phrase "by faith of Jesus" (ἐκ πίστεως Ἰησοῦ) as a reference to our faith in Jesus (εἰς Ἰησοῦν), which he compares to Abraham's faith in God.

In the following century, the great preacher John Chrysostom makes this homiletic comment on Romans 3:22, emphasizing the importance of our faith while making no mention of Christ's faithfulness:

> But that no one should say, How are we to be saved without contributing anything at all to the object in view? He shews that we also offer no small matter toward this, I mean our faith. Therefore after saying, *the righteousness of God,* he adds straightway, *by faith unto all and upon all them that believe.*[29]

Howard, "Faith of Christ," 759. Only if one assumes that every use of the genitive in these versions is intended to be taken as subjective could one make this claim.

28 *Le Commentaire d'Origène sur Rom III 5–V 7,* ed. Jean Scherer (Cairo: L'Institut Français d'Archéologie Orientale, 1957), 162. This English translation is that of Harrisville, to whom I am indebted for this reference. "Witness of the Fathers," 238.

29 *The Homilies of S. John Chrysostom,* vol. 7, *The Apostle of St. Paul to the Romans,* Library of Fathers (Oxford: John Henry Parker, 1841), 92; the italics indicate Scripture quotations.

Even more illuminating is Jerome's comment on the phrase διὰ πίστεως ’Ιησοῦ Χριστοῦ in Galatians 2:16a:

> The saints who lived long ago . . . were justified by faith in Christ. Abraham foresaw the day of Christ and rejoiced. "Moses regarded disgrace for the sake of Christ as of greater value than the treasures of Egypt, because he was looking ahead to his reward." Isaiah beheld the glory of Christ, as John the Evangelist notes. Jude speaks generally about all [the saints of old]: "Although you already know all this, I want to remind you that Jesus delivered his people out of Egypt but later destroyed those who did not believe."[30]

This comment presents the faith of the Old Testament saints as oriented toward Christ: Abraham foreseeing the day of Christ (John 8:56), Moses being willing to face disgrace for Christ (Heb. 11:26), and Isaiah beholding the glory of Christ (John 12:41). Thus it is clear that Jerome views the phrase διὰ πίστεως ’Ιησοῦ Χριστοῦ in Galatians 2:16a as a reference to our faith in Christ.

In addition, Augustine, commenting on Galatians 2:20, says that Paul means that "*Christ lives* in the believer by dwelling in the 'inner self' through faith so that afterwards he may satisfy him through sight."[31] Augustine's allusion to 2 Corinthians 5:7 shows that he understands "by faith of the Son of God" as a reference to our faith, which will one day be turned to sight, not to Christ's faith or faithfulness.[32]

Another significant comment from Augustine is actually found not in a commentary but in Augustine's explanation of "through faith of

---

30 St. Jerome, *Commentary on Galatians*, trans. Andrew Cain, vol. 121 of *The Fathers of the Church* (Washington, DC: Catholic University of America Press, 2010), 112.

31 *Augustine's Commentary on Galatians: Introduction, Text, Translation, and Notes*, trans. Eric Plumer, OECS (New York: Oxford University Press, 2003), 151; the italics indicate Scripture quotations.

32 Augustine is commenting on the Latin translation, but recall that the Latin translates the Greek literally, maintaining its ambiguity. Thus, Augustine's comment clarifies how he interprets the genitive.

Jesus Christ" (Rom. 3:22) in *On the Spirit and the Letter*. The reason this comment is important is because it explicitly addresses the genitive relationship:

> [Paul] advances a step further, and adds "But righteousness of God by faith of Jesus Christ," that is, by the faith wherewith one believes in Christ; for just as there is not meant the faith with which Christ Himself believes, so also there is not meant the righteousness whereby God Himself is righteous. Both no doubt are ours, but they are called God's and Christ's, because it is by their bounty that these gifts are bestowed upon us.[33]

Here Augustine considers the possibility that the genitive could refer to Christ's own faith. But he thinks it is so clear that the genitive refers to our faith in Christ that this becomes the basis for his conclusion that "the righteousness of God" does not mean God's own righteousness. His discussion is slightly more complex, because he also seems to suggest that the genitive indicates possession: our faith is called "Christ's" because he gives it to us as a gift. But whether or not we agree with his entire interpretation, the point I am making here is that he clearly understands Paul's phrase not as a reference to Christ's faith but to our faith in him, which he has bestowed on us as a gift. Later in this work, Augustine gives a similar interpretation:

> Now "*the love of God*" is said to be shed abroad in our hearts, not because He loves us, but because He makes us lovers of Himself; just as "*the righteousness of God*" is used in the sense of our being made righteous by his gift; and "*the salvation of the Lord*," in that we are saved by Him; and "*the faith of Jesus Christ*," because He makes us believers in him.[34]

---

33 Augustine, *On the Spirit and the Letter*, 15, in Philip Schaff, ed., *Nicene and Post-Nicene Fathers*, vol. 5 (Grand Rapids, MI: Eerdmans, 1978).

34 Augustine, *On the Spirit and the Letter*, 56; the italics indicate Scripture quotations. For this reference and the previous one, I am indebted to Harrisville, "Witness of the Fathers," 240.

Here again it is clear that Augustine interprets Paul's phrase "the faith of Jesus Christ" as a reference to our belief in him, which resonates with the few other comments we have noted from the fathers.

Modern Versions

This interpretation of Paul's phrases was probably made explicit in translation for the first time in Luther's monumental German version of the Bible. The followers of Wycliffe had translated the Bible from the Latin Vulgate into English in the fifteenth century and continued the tradition of giving a literal rendering of the eight phrases with the word "of."[35] But in the sixteenth century, Luther gave a more dynamic rendering of seven of the phrases, using the German preposition *an* to show explicitly that Paul was speaking about faith *in Christ*.[36] In Galatians 2:20, Luther preserved the ambiguity of the original with a genitive construction ("glauben des Sons Gottes"), although his lectures on this verse make it clear that he interpreted it as an objective genitive.[37]

William Tyndale, a follower of Luther's theology, made the first translation from Greek into English around the same time that Luther was making his German version. Tyndale tended to translate the ἐκ πίστεως Χριστοῦ phrases literally, expressing the genitive with the preposition "of" in English for five of the eight occurrences. In the three other occurrences, Tyndale, similar to Luther, uses "on" or "in": "him which believeth on Jesus" (Rom. 3:26), "that which springeth of the faith which is in Christ" (Phil. 3:9), "by faith on him" (Eph. 3:12).[38] The influential King James Version, which was highly dependent on

---

35 Conrad Lindberg, *The Earlier Version of the Wycliffite Bible*, vol. 8 (Stockholm: Almqvist and Wiksell, 1997).

36 *The Concordia Bilingual Edition of the Holy Bible, Containing the Old and New Testaments in the English Translation according to the Authorized Version and in the German Translation according to the Original Luther Text* (St. Louis, MO: Concordia, 1925).

37 See the epigraph at the beginning of this chapter, where Luther comments on Gal. 2:20. *Luther's Works*, ed. Jaroslav Pelikan (St. Louis, MO: Concordia, 1963), 26:177.

38 David Daniell, *Tyndale's New Testament* (New Haven, CT: Yale University Press, 1989).

Tyndale's translation, is more literal than Tyndale in these phrases, rendering seven of the eight with "of" and using the preposition "in" only in Romans 3:26: "him which believeth in Jesus." But the Revised Version of 1885 translated all the phrases in Paul with the preposition "in." Perhaps this reflects changes in English usage: in older versions faith directed toward Christ could be referred to as "faith of Christ."[39] But in modern English usage, "faith of Christ" sounds as if it must refer to Christ's own faith. Most English versions today make the genitive relationship explicit with the word "in," including mainline Protestant (NRSV), evangelical Protestant (NIV), and Catholic (NAB) versions. The only variations from the translation "faith in" have come in modern translations published after Hays's influential dissertation. For example, the mainline NRSV now footnotes all eight phrases with the alternative translation "faith of Christ." And the evangelical NET Bible brings the "faithfulness of Christ" translation into the text for each of these phrases.

The suggestion that ἐκ πίστεως Χριστοῦ in Paul's letters should be interpreted as Christ's own faith or faithfulness is really a product of modern exegesis.[40] Many trace this idea back to several German articles written in the late nineteenth and early twentieth centuries.[41] But Benjamin Schliesser has now shown that the idea goes back further to rationalist scholars in the late eighteenth and early nineteenth centuries who exploited the ambiguity of Paul's πίστις Χριστοῦ construction

---

39 For example, The Westminster Confession of Faith 14.2 cites Gal. 2:20 alongside John 1:12 and Acts 16:31 to support the statement "But the principal acts of saving faith are accepting, receiving, and resting upon Christ alone for justification, sanctification, and eternal life, by virtue of the covenant of grace."

40 This does not make the "faithfulness of Christ" view wrong, of course. But it does give us perspective on the view and also supports my approach of interacting primarily with the modern exegetical arguments.

41 Namely, those of Johannes Haussleiter, "Der Glaube Jesu Christi und der christliche Glaube: Ein Beitrag zur Erklärung des Römerbriefes," *NKZ* 2 (1891): 109–45; G. Kittel, "Πίστις Ἰησοῦ Χριστοῦ bei Paulus," *TSK* 79 (1906): 419–36. For example, Hays begins his history with these articles. *Faith of Jesus Christ*, 142–44.

to present Christ not as a vicarious sacrifice for our salvation but as a model for our faith who remained steadfast to death.[42] It is important to observe that Hays explicitly rejects this (liberal) view of the atonement in his understanding of πίστις Χριστοῦ.[43] Several other scholars in the twentieth century argued for the "faithfulness of Christ" translation.[44] Perhaps the most well-known advocate was Karl Barth in his commentary on Romans.[45] But it seems fair to say that, at least in English-speaking scholarship, it was the insightful dissertation of Richard Hays that marked a turning point in this discussion. Hays's dissertation has made the view much more plausible in the eyes of many English-speaking scholars and has opened the floodgates of literature on the topic.

Thus, my goal in the following section is to evaluate Hays's argument, both because it is one of the best arguments for the "faithfulness of Christ" view and because it is the most influential. I have read most of the arguments post-Hays, and I incorporate some of these into the discussion. But my primary goal is to interact with Hays and the text of Paul's letters.

Evaluation of Hays's Christological View of Πίστις

This section is a sustained evaluation of Richard Hays's Christological view of πίστις in Galatians as presented in his published dissertation.[46]

---

42 Namely, H. E. G. Paulus and J. Schulthess. Schliesser, "Exegetical Amnesia," 64–69.

43 Hays says, "I would want to insist that the 'faith of Christ' in Paul must always be understood in the context of the gospel story, in which Christ's faith enables him obediently to carry out his mission of deliverance. We are saved by Christ's faith(fulness), not by having a faith like his." *Faith of Jesus Christ*, 158n135.

44 E.g., A. G. Hebert, "'Faithfulness' and 'Faith,'" *Theology* 58, no. 424 (1955): 373–79; T. F. Torrance, "One Aspect of the Biblical Conception of Faith," *ExpTim* 68, no. 4 (1956–1957): 111–14; Pierre Vallotton, *Le Christ et la foi: Etude de théologie biblique* (Geneva: Labor et Fides, 1961).

45 Specifically, Barth suggested that διὰ πίστεως Ἰησοῦ Χριστοῦ refers to *God's* faithfulness in Jesus Christ. Karl Barth, *The Epistle to the Romans*, trans. from the 6th ed. by Edwyn C. Hoskyns (London: Oxford University Press, 1933), 96–97.

46 Paul's letter to the Galatians is really ground zero for the πίστις Χριστοῦ debate. Four of the eight phrases occur in Galatians, and this letter is both the source of Hays's groundbreaking arguments for the "faithfulness of Christ" translation and Martyn's arguments for the apocalyptic view of Paul's theology.

Here I do not question his primary thesis, that Paul's theological arguments in Galatians presuppose an underlying story about Jesus Christ. Hays supports this primary thesis through complex narrative analyses of Galatians 4:3–6 and 3:13–14, concluding that "we are dealing here with two tellings . . . of the same story,"[47] in which the death of Christ is the central or climactic action.[48] Generally speaking, I agree with Hays's thesis about the narrative substructure of Galatians 3:1–4:11 and the importance of the gospel story of Jesus Christ in Paul's theology. What I question in this section is Hays's secondary thesis, that the word πίστις refers by metonymy to the climax of that story, Jesus's faithful death on the cross.[49]

Hays begins to suggest this thesis about πίστις at the end of his chapter on Galatians 3:13–14 and 4:3–6 by briefly analyzing the narrative structure of Galatians 3:21–22. He concludes,

> This analysis, in agreement with the above analyses of 3:13–14 and
> 4:3–6, places Jesus Christ in the role of Subject, with πίστις as the
> power or quality which enables him to carry out his mandate. If this
> is correct, Gal 3:22 must not be interpreted to mean that believers
> receive the promise by the subjective act of placing their faith in Jesus
> Christ; instead, it must mean that Jesus Christ, by the power of faith,
> has performed an act which allows believers to receive the promise.
> The interpretive problem may be stated the other way around: if
> Gal 3:22 means solely that believers receive the promise by placing
> their faith in Jesus Christ as "object of faith," then the proffered
> analysis of the narrative structure of this verse is erroneous.[50]

Although this conclusion is stated rather strongly, in the next chapter Hays recognizes its tentative nature, that it still awaits exegetical proof:

47 Hays, *Faith of Jesus Christ*, 107.
48 Hays, *Faith of Jesus Christ*, 109.
49 See, e.g., Hays, *Faith of Jesus Christ*, xxx.
50 Hays, *Faith of Jesus Christ*, 115–16.

As we saw in Chapter III, when we become aware of the narrative pattern of Paul's christological formulations, the usual understanding of πίστις becomes at once problematical. Two of these narrative summaries (3:14, 22) seem to speak of πίστις as the power or quality which enables Christ to carry out his mission of deliverance. Is such an interpretation tenable?[51]

Moreover, twenty years later, Hays suggests that his argument rests not on the results of his narrative analyses in chapter 3 of his dissertation but rather on his exegesis in chapter 4:

In my view, however, the argument of the dissertation does not ride upon these methods or upon the results produced by them. Readers who find their eyes glazing over as they seek to decipher the actantial diagrams in Chapter III are hereby absolved of responsibility for making sense of this material and given permission to skip on to Chapter IV.[52]

Thus, in this section, I take Hays up on his generous offer and focus my attention on his careful exegetical argument about πίστις in chapter 4 of his book, a chapter that he titles "The Function of Πίστις in the Narrative Structure of Paul's Gospel." In doing this, I walk alongside Hays as I reexamine the eight uses of the phrase ἐκ πίστεως Χριστοῦ in Paul.

Galatians 2:16a and 2:16c

Hays introduces chapter 4 with the problem in Protestant theology of turning faith into a work or a human achievement that secures our justification. He observes that many exegetes (e.g., Adolf Schlatter)

---

51 Hays, *Faith of Jesus Christ*, 122.
52 Hays, *Faith of Jesus Christ*, xxvii.

have solved this problem by arguing that faith itself is a gift from God. Hays, however, questions whether Galatians speaks of πίστις as a gift of God, which sets up his attempt to redefine the meaning of πίστις as Christ's own action.[53] This way of setting up his argument shows that the theological argument of the "faithfulness of Christ" view, which insists that salvation cannot rest on any human action (including our faith), is not only a conclusion from Hays's new view of πίστις in Galatians but is actually one of the assumptions that led Hays to pursue a new view of πίστις in the first place.

Before his exegesis of Galatians 3, Hays first addresses Galatians 2:16, observing that "many treatments of the problems with which I am dealing here take Gal 2:16 as their point of departure."[54] Two of the eight ἐκ πίστεως Χριστοῦ phrases occur in this verse, and many scholars before Hays had appealed to a standard argument in support of the "faith in Christ" translation: "The expression εἰς Χριστὸν Ἰησοῦν ἐπιστεύσαμεν provides a definitive determination of the sense of πίστις Ἰησοῦ Χριστοῦ, since both expressions occur in this verse."[55] As I observed in chapter 2, Hays concedes that the clause "we . . . have believed in Christ Jesus" (εἰς Χριστὸν Ἰησοῦν ἐπιστεύσαμεν) in Galatians 2:16b "speaks clearly and unambiguously of faith *in* Christ."[56] And many scholars over the years have suggested that this clause disambiguates the two ambiguous phrases that occur before it (διὰ πίστεως Ἰησοῦ Χριστοῦ, Gal. 2:16a) and after it (ἐκ πίστεως Χριστοῦ, Gal. 2:16c), showing that they, too, present Christ as the object of our faith. But Hays rejects this well-worn argument for two reasons.

First, he suggests that "this approach fails to reckon sufficiently with the extreme, almost epigrammatic, concision of this sentence and its

53 Hays, *Faith of Jesus Christ*, 119–22.
54 Hays, *Faith of Jesus Christ*, 122.
55 Hays, *Faith of Jesus Christ*, 122. He notes that scholars who use this standard argument in support of the "faith in Christ" translation include Wilhelm Mundle, Ernest De Witt Burton, Fritz Neugebauer, Hans Dieter Betz, and Dieter Lührmann.
56 Hays, *Faith of Jesus Christ*, 123.

place within the literary structure of the letter."[57] His point is that Galatians 2:16 is a formulaic thesis statement that is explained in Galatians 3–4. Thus "we must seek to unfold their [i.e., the two phrases'] meaning by seeing how Paul uses them in his exposition. Otherwise, we run the risk of merely reading our preconceptions into them."[58] Granted that 2:16 is a summary of Paul's later argument, does it follow that any attempt to explain the meaning of the verse itself is "merely reading our preconceptions into them"? Moreover, does it warrant sidestepping this fundamental (if familiar) argument from 2:16? In his introduction to the second edition of his book, Hays interacts briefly with the argument from 2:16 by appealing to a parallel in Philo's biography of Abraham, one that we have already seen in chapter 1: "God marveling at Abraham's faith in Him [τῆς πρὸς αὐτὸν πίστεως] repaid him with faithfulness [πίστιν] by confirming with an oath the gifts which He had promised."[59] Hays comments,

> If Philo can pivot about in this way in a single sentence, we should hardly be surprised that Paul can similarly speak in the same breath both of our faith in God (καὶ ἡμεῖς εἰς Χριστὸν ’Ιησοῦν ἐπιστεύσαμεν) and of the faithfulness of Jesus Christ (διὰ πίστεως ’Ιησοῦ Χριστοῦ . . . ἐκ πίστεως Χριστοῦ; Gal 2:16).[60]

The problem with this line of argument is that there is no doubt about the meaning of πίστις in Philo's statement.[61] In contrast, Paul's phrases

---

57 Hays, *Faith of Jesus Christ*, 122.

58 Hays, *Faith of Jesus Christ*, 123.

59 Philo, *On Abraham*, §273. English translation from Philo, *On Abraham*, trans. F. H. Colson, LCL 289 (Cambridge, MA: Harvard University Press, 1935).

60 Hays, *Faith of Jesus Christ*, xlvi. It is striking that Hays describes Paul's statement ἡμεῖς εἰς Χριστὸν ’Ιησοῦν ἐπιστεύσαμεν as "our faith in God" rather than "our faith in Christ Jesus."

61 It is clear that Philo's first use of πίστις refers to Abraham's faith in God, which has been his topic of discussion for several paragraphs. And it is clear that his second use of πίστις refers to God's faithfulness, since God is the subject of the verb "repaid" and God's πίστιν is in apposition to (literally) "the confirmation [τὴν . . . βεβαίωσιν] with an oath of the gifts of which he had promised"

διὰ πίστεως Ἰησοῦ Χριστοῦ . . . ἐκ πίστεως Χριστοῦ could genuinely be translated as either "faith in [Jesus] Christ" or "the faithfulness of [Jesus] Christ." How should we decide between these two options? Does it not make sense to read these phrases in light of the clear statement "we . . . have believed in Christ Jesus" (Gal. 2:16b)?

Second, Hays briefly suggests that there may be significance to the fact that Paul uses two different grammatical constructions. Perhaps the apostle intends to distinguish between our faith in Christ and the role of Christ's own faithfulness.[62] But in this case it seems more likely that Paul changes from prepositional phrases to a verbal construction simply because of the flow of his thought:

[a] We know that a person is not justified by works of the law but through faith of Jesus Christ [διὰ πίστεως Ἰησοῦ Χριστοῦ], [b] so we also have believed in Christ Jesus, [c] in order to be justified by faith of Christ [ἐκ πίστεως Χριστοῦ] and not by works of the law, [d] because by works of the law no one will be justified. (Gal. 2:16)[63]

The main clause in this verse is the verbal construction "we also have believed in Christ Jesus" (Gal. 2:16b). The preceding dependent clause probably spells out the reason why Paul and Peter have come to believe (Gal. 2:16a).[64] And the following dependent clause spells out the purpose for which they have come to believe (Gal. 2:16c). Within

---

(cf. Gen. 22:16); that is, it refers to God's faithfulness. Cf. my discussion of Philo's statement in chap. 1, p. 58.

62 Hays, *Faith of Jesus Christ*, 123.

63 Note that throughout this section of the chapter, I change the ESV slightly by rendering Paul's ἐκ πίστεως Χριστοῦ phrases literally.

64 "We know" in Gal. 2:16a translates an adverbial participle (εἰδότες), which most likely modifies "we . . . have believed" in 2:16b, giving the reason why they had come to believe. So Douglas J. Moo, *Galatians*, BECNT (Grand Rapids, MI: Baker Academic, 2013), 157. It is possible, however, that εἰδότες in 2:16a modifies 2:15, especially if δὲ in 2:16a is a later scribal addition (it is omitted in many manuscripts).

these dependent clauses, Paul is forced to use prepositional phrases to indicate the role of faith in justification. Thus, a change in grammatical construction does not necessarily signal an intended change in meaning. We can compare Philippians 3:8 and 10, in which Paul first uses a noun with an objective genitive ("knowing Christ Jesus," τῆς γνώσεως Χριστοῦ ᾽Ιησοῦ) and then changes to a verb (infinitive) with a direct object ("that I may know him," τοῦ γνῶναι αὐτὸν).[65]

In sum, Hays passes too quickly over Galatians 2:16 without considering the importance of this verse in disambiguating Paul's ἐκ πίστεως Χριστοῦ phrases. Ernest De Witt Burton's observation in support of the objective genitive remains potent: "The context in the present case (see esp. the phrase εἰς Χριστὸν ᾽Ιησοῦν ἐπιστεύ-σαμεν) is decisive for its acceptance here; and the meaning here in turn practically decides the meaning of the phrase throughout this epistle."[66] With this said, it must also be recognized that Hays's case rests primarily on his exegesis of Galatians 3, which he correctly identifies as an unfolding of Galatians 2:16. He gives a preview of his argument in two theses: first, "in none of these passages does Paul's emphasis lie upon the salvific efficacy of the individual activity of 'believing'"; and second, "nowhere in Galatians 3 does Paul speak of Jesus Christ as the object toward which human faith is to be directed."[67] Readers will not be surprised that I question both these theses by arguing that Paul does in fact speak about Christ-oriented faith in Galatians 3 and that such faith plays a causal role in salvation.[68]

---

65 Cf. also Gal. 1:12 and 16, where Paul uses a noun with what is probably an objective genitive ("revelation of Jesus Christ," ἀποκαλύψεως ᾽Ιησοῦ Χριστοῦ) and then changes to a verb (infinitive) with a direct object ("to reveal his Son," ἀποκαλύψαι τὸν υἱὸν αὐτοῦ).

66 Ernest De Witt Burton, *A Critical and Exegetical Commentary on the Epistle to the Galatians*, ICC 34 (Edinburgh: T&T Clark, 1921), 121. Note that Burton is responding to Haussleiter in this sentence.

67 Hays, *Faith of Jesus Christ*, 124.

68 As I have observed in previous chapters, I am using the word *causal* broadly and not in a sense that would deny the imputation of Christ's righteousness.

Galatians 3:22 (and Ephesians 3:12)

Galatians 3 begins a series of arguments about justification by faith, appealing to the evidence of the Galatians' own experience: they had not received the Spirit of God by works of the law but "by hearing with faith [ἐξ ἀκοῆς πίστεως]" (Gal. 3:2, 5). Hays views this piece of evidence as "of central importance in the argumentative logic of Galatians."[69] The problem is that the meaning of ἐξ ἀκοῆς πίστεως is actually opaque. The word πίστις could mean the act of "faith" or "the body of faith" in this context. Similarly, the word ἀκοή could mean the act of "hearing" or "the message heard." Hays helpfully lays out the four resulting possibilities:[70]

1. "by hearing with faith" (so ESV)
2. "by hearing 'the faith'" (i.e., the gospel)
3. "from the message that enables faith"
4. "from the message of 'the faith'" (i.e., the gospel message)

He then argues for one of the last two translations, preferring the final one (option 4), and showing that the emphasis of ἐξ ἀκοῆς πίστεως in Galatians 3:2 and 5 is on the gospel message rather than on the individual's faith.

First, Hays argues that ἀκοή means "the message," based on its usage in 1 Thessalonians 2:13 and Romans 10:16–17.[71] This translation is possible, and it is not essential to my thesis, so I do not contest it here.[72] This translation is, however, essential to Hays's thesis, for he concludes

---

69 Hays, *Faith of Jesus Christ*, 125.

70 Hays, *Faith of Jesus Christ*, 125–28.

71 Hays, *Faith of Jesus Christ*, 129.

72 That said, I am convinced that ἀκοή in Gal. 3:2 and 5 probably means "hearing" the gospel in light of its linguistic relationship with Rom. 10:14–17 (see chap. 1, p. 68). Cf. Harmon's conclusion: "Based then on our analysis of an allusion to Isa 53:1 in Gal 3:2, 5 and the citation of Isa 53:1 in Rom 10:16–17, we conclude that the best way to render ἐξ ἀκοῆς πίστεως in Gal 3:2, 5 is 'on the basis of hearing accompanied by faith.' Paul has transformed Isaiah's question into an affirmation of the proper way to respond to God's self-revelation in Christ." Matthew S.

from it that "Paul's emphasis lies not upon the individual act of *believing* as the means of receiving the Spirit, but upon the proclaimed *message* (ἀκοή), which calls forth faith, as the means by which the Spirit is given."[73] We see here the theological argument that, for Paul, we receive the Spirit not by our faith but by the gospel message of Christ. What is interesting is that this theological argument functions not only as a *conclusion from* Hays's translation of ἀκοή but as a *reason for* his translation. He first observes the common argument that Paul is contrasting two lines of human action in Galatians 3:2 and 5: works of the law and hearing with faith (option 1).[74] Then, in response, he argues that the passage makes better sense if Paul is contrasting a human activity with a divine activity:

Paul's formulation here has a facetious tone; it would be ridiculous to say that God supplies the Spirit and works miracles ἐξ ἔργων νόμου ["by works of the law"]. That is precisely the point, but it would be equally ridiculous to say (as the *RSV* does) that God works miracles "through the hearing with faith." Thus, ἀκοὴ πίστεως in Gal 3:5 is best understood as a designation for the proclamation of the gospel.[75]

Here we see that his translation rests on ("Thus") the argument that it would be "equally ridiculous" to say that God works miracles through our faith. Why? Because faith is a human activity just like works of the law, and God cannot give the Spirit or work miracles by human action. My point here is not necessarily to prove that ἀκοή refers to a human activity in Galatians 3:2 and 5. It is rather to observe that

---

Harmon, *She Must and Shall Go Free: Paul's Isaianic Gospel in Galatians*, BZNW 168 (Berlin: de Gruyter, 2010), 132.

73 Hays, *Faith of Jesus Christ*, 132.

74 Hays, *Faith of Jesus Christ*, 126. He notes that scholars who make this argument include J. B. Lightfoot, Ernest De Witt Burton, Adolf Schlatter, and Herman Ridderbos.

75 Hays, *Faith of Jesus Christ*, 130.

Hays precludes such an understanding *because of* his arguably hyper-Protestant theological claims.

Second, Hays argues that it is possible that πίστις does not refer explicitly to a human activity but rather to "the body of faith," based on its usage in Galatians 1:23; 3:23–26; and 6:10.[76] His argument proceeds with characteristic caution. It is not that such a translation would rule out a human response: "Even if πίστις is a quasi-technical term for 'the gospel,' the implication of some human response is scarcely thereby excluded."[77] As I observed in the introduction, Hays never excludes our faith from Paul's thought entirely but rather argues that our faith cannot be a means by which we are saved.[78] His conclusions regarding πίστις in Galatians 3:2 and 5 are twofold: first, "even if πίστις here means 'believing' (*das Glauben*), no object of faith is specified"; and second, "it is at least possible that πίστις here, as in other texts in Galatians, functions as a collective designation for 'that which is believed' and does not refer explicitly to the Galatians' act or attitude of faith."[79] While his first conclusion is technically correct, is not the object of the Galatians' faith clearly implied in this context to be the message about Jesus Christ crucified (Gal. 3:1)?[80] It is the second conclusion, however, that seems most significant to me for the argument of this chapter. Let us grant the conclusion that πίστις in Galatians 3:2 and 5 refers not to the Galatians' act of faith but rather to the body of faith that they had believed.[81] Even if Hays is correct about this translation, the word

76 Hays, *Faith of Jesus Christ*, 131.

77 Hays, *Faith of Jesus Christ*, 132.

78 See the introduction, p. 31.

79 Hays, *Faith of Jesus Christ*, 132.

80 Hays states his conclusion about πίστις in Gal. 3:2 and 5 in contrast with Marie-Joseph Lagrange's point that "it goes without saying that this faith has for its object Christ [*il va sans dire que cette foi a pour objet le Christ*]." Quoted in Hays, *Faith of Jesus Christ*, 132n49. Lagrange's point seems correct in light of Gal. 3:1.

81 I am granting this point for the sake of argument, but I think it is unlikely. Paul goes on immediately to compare this πίστις in Gal. 3:2 and 5 with Abraham's faith in God: "Just as Abraham 'believed God, and it was counted to him as righteousness' (Gal. 3:6).

πίστις in Galatians 3:2 and 5 does not mean "faithfulness," and it does not refer to Jesus's faithfulness. Rather, it means "what is believed" (the body of faith) and refers to the object of the Galatians' faith.

Hays's exegesis turns next to Paul's citation of Habakkuk 2:4 in Galatians 3:11, since he views this Old Testament verse as the likely source of an important phrase occurring often in Galatians 3: ἐκ πίστεως (Gal. 3:7, 8, 9, 11, 12, 22, 24).[82] I have already evaluated the messianic view of Habakkuk 2:4 adopted by Hays and others.[83] Here I interact specifically with Hays's argument about the meaning and referent of πίστις in Galatians 3:11. He considers three possible referents of πίστις in Paul's citation of Habakkuk 2:4: God's faithfulness, the Messiah's faith(fulness), or people's faith in God. He then argues that Galatians 3:11 does not refer to God's faithfulness because, unlike Romans, God's faithfulness is not mentioned in Galatians. But interestingly, rather than choosing between the two remaining options, he suggests that the phrase ἐκ πίστεως is ambiguous and refers to both the Messiah's faith(fulness) *and* our faith.[84] He sees three possible interpretations of Galatians 3:11:[85]

1. The Messiah will live by (his own) faith(fulness).
2. The righteous person will live as a result of the Messiah's faith(fulness).
3. The righteous person will live by (his own) faith (in the Messiah).

And he suggests that all three are correct: "Paul's thought is rendered wholly intelligible only if all three of these interpretations are held together and affirmed as correct. The ambiguity of Paul's formulation allows him to draw multiple implications out of the Habakkuk

---

82 Hays, *Faith of Jesus Christ*, 132.
83 See chap. 1, p. 90.
84 Hays, *Faith of Jesus Christ*, 140.
85 Hays, *Faith of Jesus Christ*, 140.

text."[86] Strangely, though, in his final conclusion, Hays suggests that Galatians 3:11 "does not explicitly point to Christ as the object of faith" and that the verse "places the primary emphasis upon Christ's faith rather than upon the faith of the individual Christian as a means of attaining life."[87] Thus, even though he argues that ἐκ πίστεως in Galatians 3:11 refers to both Christ's faith and our faith in him, his conclusion significantly de-emphasizes the role of our faith in Galatians 3.

Why not simply argue that Paul's citation of Habakkuk 2:4 in Galatians 3:11 refers to Christ's faith(fulness) *and not* to our faith in Christ? Hays says that Paul's thought in Galatians 3 is only "wholly intelligible" if it refers to both. It seems that he is sensing the difficulty of the fact that the phrase ἐκ πίστεως so clearly refers to our faith in Galatians 3:6–9. If Hays is to uphold his messianic interpretation of Habakkuk 2:4 in the context of Galatians 3:11, Paul's citation must be ambiguous and must refer to both our faith and Christ's faith(fulness). But consider the plausibility of this supposed ambiguity. It would mean that Paul intended one use of πίστις in Galatians 3:11 to simultaneously mean both "faith," in the sense of our believing in God or Christ, and "faithfulness," in the sense of Christ faithfully going to the cross. Further, it would mean that this one use of πίστις refers to both *our* faith and *Christ's* faith(fulness). Would it not be a much simpler solution in the context of Galatians 3:6–9 to say that Paul takes Habakkuk 2:4 to mean that the righteous person will live by his or her faith?

Finally, we come to Hays's exegesis of Galatians 3:22: "But the Scripture imprisoned everything under sin, so that the promise by faith of Jesus Christ [ἐκ πίστεως Ἰησοῦ Χριστοῦ] might be given to those who believe [τοῖς πιστεύουσιν]." Hays's translation of ἐκ πίστεως Ἰησοῦ Χριστοῦ in this verse rests on three pillars: (1) an argument

86 Hays, *Faith of Jesus Christ*, 140.
87 Hays, *Faith of Jesus Christ*, 141.

from redundancy, (2) an argument from grammar, and (3) an argument from theology. He mentions the problem of redundancy only briefly in the beginning of his discussion: "First of all, the sentence, when so translated [as 'faith in Jesus Christ'] is redundant. Paul could have omitted either ἐκ πίστεως ’Ιησοῦ Χριστοῦ or τοῖς πιστεύουσιν without changing the meaning."[88] This argument from redundancy has been applied by others to Romans 3:22; Galatians 2:16; and Philippians 3:9 as well.[89] Hays himself recognizes that an argument from redundancy is not decisive and that "one could easily enough point out other places where Paul's writing would benefit from the judicious application of a red pencil."[90] But to take his imagery further, we may envision Paul protesting such editorial changes, since repetition is a common way for authors to emphasize their most important ideas. Hays's main two arguments, however, are from grammar and theology. Recounting a brief history of the question, he suggests that many still advocate the "faith of Jesus Christ" translation even after James Barr's criticism of Gabriel Hebert and T. F. Torrance because "'faith *in* Jesus Christ' is not the most natural translation of πίστις ’Ιησοῦ Χριστοῦ" and because we are in a time when "the fundamental contours of Pauline thought are being reassessed."[91] These two observations set up his grammatical and theological argument for "the faith of Jesus Christ" in Galatians 3:22.

First, Hays argues that the grammatical evidence favors a subjective genitive in Galatians 3:22 because of the exact parallel in Romans 4:16. He approaches the issue with caution in that he allows that πίστις with the genitive could at least hypothetically indicate the object of faith,

---

88 Hays, *Faith of Jesus Christ*, 142. He briefly mentions this argument from redundancy again at the end of his argument for Gal. 3:22, suggesting that his interpretation "gives a clear meaning to an expression which would otherwise be a redundancy." Hays, 153.

89 Ulrichs observes that the redundancy argument goes all the way back to Haussleiter. *Christusglaube*, 8. For a summary of this argument and a sophisticated response, see R. Barry Matlock, "The Rhetoric of Πίστις in Paul: Galatians 2.16, 3.22, Romans 3.22, and Philippians 3.9," *JSNT* 30, no. 2 (2007): 173–203.

90 Hays, *Faith of Jesus Christ*, 142n80.

91 Hays, *Faith of Jesus Christ*, 147.

as it does in Mark 11:22. But in his view, "the really significant point
. . . is that this construction cannot be demonstrated in the Pauline
corpus."[92] One might object that he seems to be assuming what he
is to prove about the eight debated phrases, and there are some clear
examples of the objective genitive in Paul's disputed letters (Col. 2:12;
2 Thess. 2:13). Nevertheless, it is also true that there are examples of
the subjective genitive with πίστις in Paul's letters. In Hays's view, the
most telling example is Romans 4:16, to which both Romans 3:26 and
Galatians 3:22 can be compared:

ἐκ πίστεως Ἀβραάμ (Rom. 4:16)
ἐκ πίστεως Ἰησοῦ (Rom. 3:26)
ἐκ πίστεως Ἰησοῦ Χριστοῦ (Gal. 3:22)

Hays concludes that this grammatical evidence favors the translation
"faith of Jesus Christ" in Galatians 3:22 and that the case for "faith in
Jesus Christ" is "really very weak."[93]

I have already observed above that this construction in Paul can be
translated either way. While it is true that Paul has many examples
of πίστις with a subjective genitive, arguments from statistics can
be misleading because Paul so often speaks to his readers about
"your faith" (e.g., Rom. 1:8).[94] Hays's comparison with ἐκ πίστεως
Ἀβραάμ in Romans 4:16, however, is a very compelling argument
in my view. Paul speaks in this text of the promise being given to
the one who shares in the faith of Abraham (ἐκ πίστεως Ἀβραάμ).
Perhaps, then, Paul is making a similar argument in Galatians 3:22:
the promise is given to the one who shares in the faith of Jesus Christ

---

92 Hays, *Faith of Jesus Christ*, 149.

93 Hays, *Faith of Jesus Christ*, 150.

94 Almost all the examples in Paul's letters that Wallace lists as examples of the "predominant usage"
of the subjective genitive with πίστις in the New Testament are places where Paul is speaking to
his readers of "your faith." Wallace, *Greek Grammar*, 116n121. On this phrase in Paul, see chap. 5,
p. 250.

(ἐκ πίστεως ᾿Ιησοῦ Χριστοῦ). The problem with this comparison is that in Romans 4, Paul explicitly describes Abraham as one who believes in God (Rom. 4:3–5, 18–21), and he explicitly describes believers as those who "walk in the footsteps of the faith that our father Abraham had before he was circumcised" (Rom. 4:12). But in Galatians 3, Paul does not explicitly describe Christ as one who has believed in God (or been faithful to God), nor does he explicitly speak of believers sharing in his faith(fulness). Thus, I conclude that Hays's grammatical argument is making a superficial comparison between Romans 4:16 and Galatians 3:22. Further, since Paul speaks clearly about believing in Christ Jesus in Galatians 2:16b, it seems better to translate the ambiguous construction in Galatians 3:22 according to the clear statement.

Second, Hays suggests that the translation "faithfulness of Jesus Christ" in Galatians 3:22 might better fit Paul's theology—namely, his representative Christology. He questions "whether it is more intelligible to suppose that 'believing in Jesus Christ' is the basis upon which 'the promise' is given to those who believe."[95] His main reason is that Abraham, whom Paul invokes as our prototype, was justified by trusting in God, so why would we need to trust in Christ to receive Abraham's inheritance? Instead, Hays suggests, "Paul's entire discussion makes much better sense if he is interpreted as presupposing that Jesus Christ, like Abraham, is justified ἐκ πί-στεως and that we, as a consequence, are justified *in* him . . . as a result of his faith(fulness)."[96] Hays sees this kind of representative Christology in Ephesians 3:12: "in whom we have boldness and access with confidence through our faith in him [διὰ τῆς πίστεως αὐτοῦ]."[97] He suggests that "through our faith in him" is a "very

---

95 Hays, *Faith of Jesus Christ*, 150.
96 Hays, *Faith of Jesus Christ*, 151.
97 Hays also mentions Heb. 12:2, which speaks of Jesus as "the founder and perfecter of our faith." Hays, *Faith of Jesus Christ*, 151.

strained translation" of Ephesians 3:12 and that a more natural reading would be "through his faith(fulness)."[98] He also appeals to the
two texts in Paul that speak of Jesus's representative obedience for
our salvation (Rom. 5:19; Phil. 2:8), arguing that "if Paul can speak
so compellingly in Rom. 5:19 of the soteriological consequences of
Christ's ὑπακοή ['obedience'], there is no a priori reason to deny
that Paul could intend the expression πίστις Ἰησοῦ Χριστοῦ to refer
to Christ's soteriologically efficacious faith(fulness)."[99]

In response to Hays's argument from theology, I do not deny
that it is *possible* that the apostle could have spoken of Jesus Christ's
faithfulness in Galatians 3:22 as a representative action for our salvation. Does he though? Hays himself, in his debate with Dunn, later
retracted his main argument that "Abraham's theocentric faith is
not properly analogous to Christocentric Christian faith" and now
acknowledges that Galatians 3 does present Abraham as a paradigm
for our faith.[100] And his argument based on representative Christology in Ephesians 3:12 seems to assume what he is trying to prove
(that the πίστις Χριστοῦ phrases mean "faithfulness of Christ").
Hays does not explain why he considers "through our faith in him"
to be a "very strained translation" of διὰ τῆς πίστεως αὐτοῦ in
Ephesians 3:12, but perhaps he is thinking about the article τῆς
before πίστεως and the pronoun αὐτοῦ, which seems to indicate
possession. I admit that this syntax would incline me to translate
the phrase as "through his faithfulness" were it not for Paul's consistent use of the phrase "by faith" elsewhere (see the argument of
my next section). Nevertheless, the phrase διὰ τῆς πίστεως αὐτοῦ
in Ephesians 3:12 can really be translated either way, which is why

---

98 Hays, *Faith of Jesus Christ*, 151.

99 Hays, *Faith of Jesus Christ*, 152. Many others have also suggested that Jesus's obedience in Rom.
5:12–21 and Phil. 2:5–11 is a conceptual parallel to the faithfulness of Christ.

100 Hays, *Faith of Jesus Christ*, 290. He wrongly concludes from this, however, that our faith is fundamentally theocentric (rather than Christocentric). Hays, 290. For an argument that our faith
is fundamentally oriented toward Christ in Pauline theology, see chap. 5, p. 241.

the commentaries are divided.[101] What about the suggested parallel between Jesus's faithfulness and Jesus's representative obedience in Romans 5:19 and Philippians 2:8? The problem with this argument is that Paul does not use the word πίστις to describe Jesus's obedience in either of these passages. Hays points to the close relationship between faith and obedience in Romans 1:5 ("the obedience of faith").[102] But Paul's description of the obedience of our faith in submitting to the truth of the gospel message is conceptually very different from Jesus's obedience to the point of death, which the apostle describes in Romans 5:12–21 and Philippians 2:5–11.[103] And once again, Paul does not describe Jesus's obedience as πίστις in either of these passages. At the end of the day, Hays's argument from representative Christology in support of his translation of ἐκ πίστεως Ἰησοῦ Χριστοῦ in Galatians 3:22 rests on very slim evidence. It is more likely that Paul is simply emphasizing in this verse that the inheritance of the Abrahamic promise comes by means of our faith in Jesus Christ (cf. Rom. 4:13–16).

Galatians 2:20

Hays next considers two other texts from Galatians that have bearing on this debate: Galatians 2:20b and 3:26. The latter text does not contain one of Paul's ἐκ πίστεως Χριστοῦ phrases, and I have already addressed it in chapter 2.[104] Here I focus on Galatians 2:20: "[a] It is no longer I who live, but Christ who lives in me. [b] And the life I now live in the flesh I live by faith of the Son of God [ἐν πίστει . . . τῇ τοῦ υἱοῦ τοῦ θεοῦ], [c] who loved me and gave himself for me."[105]

---

101 Compare the same grammatical construction in 2 Cor. 2:14, which is clearly an objective genitive: τῆς γνώσεως αὐτοῦ, "the knowledge of him."

102 Hays, *Faith of Jesus Christ*, 152.

103 For a discussion of obedience to the gospel, see chap. 3, p. 160.

104 See chap. 2, p. 125.

105 Note that the versification in the Greek text is slightly different from the ESV, which includes "I have been crucified with Christ" as part of Gal. 2:20.

Before explaining Hays's argument, I need to address a significant textual problem in this verse, since Galatians 2:20 is the source of my book's title. Several important ancient copies of Paul's letters read, "by faith of God and Christ [ἐν πίστει . . . τῇ τοῦ θεοῦ καὶ Χριστοῦ]."[106] Arguably, the external evidence in support of the translation "by faith of the Son of God" is slightly better.[107] Evaluating internal evidence is also difficult because Paul never uses the exact phrase "faith of God and Christ" or "faith of the Son of God" outside Galatians 2:20b. It is significant, however, that all Paul's other ἐκ πίστεως Χριστοῦ phrases speak about "faith of Christ" and not "faith of God and Christ." It is unlikely that a scribe has attempted a correction in this verse because neither reading is a typical Pauline expression.[108] Thus it seems most likely that we have evidence of a scribal mistake. Therefore, because of slightly better external evidence and internal evidence suggesting that Paul would have written about Christ in one of these phrases, I follow the typical reading, "faith of the Son of God."[109] This is a difficult textual decision, so I am not resting any weight on it. The title of my book is meant to reflect an emphasis in Paul's theology (cf. Rom. 1:1–17; 1 Thess. 1:10), not the wording of this particular verse.

106 These include P46, our earliest copy of Paul's letters; B, a fourth-century copy of the Greek Bible; and several manuscripts in the Western tradition (D, F, G).

107 Witnesses include the fourth-century Codex Sinaiticus (ℵ), the fifth-century Codex Alexandrinus (A), the important ninth-century manuscript 33, and the important tenth-century manuscript 1739. The majority of manuscripts, which are in the Byzantine text tradition, also have this reading. All the ancient versions have this reading as well.

108 Though Carlson suggests that "an anti-Patripassionist [sic] scribe could well have misread the τοῦ θεοῦ καὶ Χριστοῦ as a single person, which would suggest the possibility of God in this context, and fixed the reading to avoid that implication." Stephen C. Carlson, *The Text of Galatians and Its History*, WUNT, 2nd ser., vol. 385 (Tübingen: Mohr Siebeck, 2015), 101.

109 So Richard N. Longenecker, *Galatians*, WBC 41 (Dallas, TX: Word Books, 1990), 82. The most recent study of the text of Galatians by Carlson concludes that "faith of God and Christ" is the correct reading. This conclusion, however, is based solely on the internal evidence, because he sees the external evidence as evenly divided. And part of the internal evidence is his argument for the subjective genitive. Carlson, *Text of Galatians*, 96–101. Thus, it seems like a stretch to say that "this reading has a significant bearing on the *pistis Christou* debate" (Carlson, 251) when the reading itself actually rests on a conclusion about the debate.

Hays follows the normal reading of the text ("by faith of the Son of God") but argues that this phrase makes much better sense if it is taken as either a subjective genitive or a genitive of author. He sees a parallel in Romans 5:15: "by the grace of that one man Jesus Christ [ἐν χάριτι τῇ τοῦ ἑνὸς ἀνθρώπου Ἰησοῦ Χριστοῦ]." Hays observes that "it would never occur to anyone to translate τοῦ ἑνὸς ἀνθρώπου Ἰησοῦ Χριστοῦ as an objective genitive" in Romans 5:15.[110] This is correct, of course, because such a translation is not grammatically or logically possible with the noun "grace" (χάρις) as it is with the noun "faith" (πίστις). Arguably, a closer parallel is found in the historical record of Paul's defense before Agrippa. Paul relates his encounter at Damascus when the Lord Jesus said he was sending him to the Gentiles "that they may receive forgiveness of sins and a place among those who are sanctified by faith in me [πίστει τῇ εἰς ἐμέ]" (Acts 26:18). Here we have πίστις followed by an attributive phrase, which indicates the object of faith.

Hays's second argument is that the conjunction δὲ in Galatians 2:20b is continuative rather than adversative. His point seems to be that Paul is not correcting his statement about himself no longer living (Gal. 2:20a) by now saying that he actually does live by his faith (Gal. 2:20b). Rather, Galatians 2:20b is continuing the line of thought in 2:20a, where he says that he no longer lives but that *Christ* now lives in him as the "acting subject" of faith.[111] This argument does not have much substance, however, because no matter how one interprets the genitive "of the Son of God," Paul still says "*I* live" (ζῶ) two times in Galatians 2:20b. This means that there must be some sense in which Paul is paradoxically saying both that he does not live (Gal. 2:20a) and yet that he does live (Gal. 2:20b). The question is whether he now lives by his own faith in the Son or by the Son's faithfulness.

---

110 Hays, *Faith of Jesus Christ*, 154. In his later debate with Dunn, he makes the same argument. Hays, 291.

111 Hays, *Faith of Jesus Christ*, 155.

Hays reserves his most substantive argument, in my view, for last. In the preceding and following context of Galatians 2:20b, Christ is depicted as the active agent or subject: "Christ who lives in me" (Gal. 2:20a); "who loved me and gave himself for me" (Gal. 2:20c). In fact, Hays sees these phrases resonating with a broader theological theme in Galatians: "Indeed, this unrelenting emphasis on the priority of Christ's (or God's) willing and doing *over any human will or action* is the theological keynote of the whole letter."[112] Here we see again that the theological argument of the "faithfulness of Christ" view goes all the way back to Hays's dissertation. But is this theological view of Galatians correct? I have already argued in chapter 2 that Galatians 2:16b presents Paul and Peter's faith as a cause of their justification.[113] In the following verse, Paul describes their faith as a human "endeavor to be justified in Christ" (Gal. 2:17).[114] And even in Galatians 2:20, we have just seen that not only is Christ an active subject ("Christ . . . lives in me"), but Paul himself is an active subject ("I now live"; "I live"). Clearly, Paul is not opposing Christ's action with *any* human action in Galatians. Perhaps, then, Galatians 2:20b is in fact a statement about Paul's own confident faith in God's Son, who has loved him and given himself for him. As Martin Luther comments, "Here you have the true meaning of justification described, together with an example of the certainty of faith. 'I live by faith in the Son of God, who loved me and gave himself for me'—anyone who could say these words with Paul in a certain and constant faith would be truly blessed."[115]

---

112 Hays, *Faith of Jesus Christ*, 155; emphasis mine.

113 See chap. 2, p. 110. Once again, it must be noted that I am using the word *cause* generally in this book and not in a way that denies the imputation of Christ's righteousness.

114 Literally, Paul says they are "seeking to be justified" (ζητοῦντες δικαιωθῆναι). Here I am indebted to Pifer for her observation that this clause "has already given place to human agency." Jeanette Hagen Pifer, *Faith as Participation*, WUNT, 2nd ser., vol. 486 (Tübingen: Mohr Siebeck, 2019), 155.

115 *Luther's Works*, ed. Jaroslav Pelikan (St. Louis, MO: Concordia, 1963), 26:172.

Romans 3:22 and 26

Hays concludes his influential argument about πίστις with a look at Romans 3:21–26, which he believes is even more conducive to his interpretation. It is difficult to overestimate the importance of this paragraph for Pauline theology, since it clearly explains Paul's thesis statement about the revelation of God's righteousness ἐκ πίστεως (Rom. 1:17). It also contains two examples of the phrase under consideration in this chapter: "the righteousness of God through faith of Jesus Christ [διὰ πίστεως 'Ιησοῦ Χριστοῦ]" (Rom. 3:22), and "the one who has faith of Jesus [τὸν ἐκ πίστεως 'Ιησοῦ]" (Rom. 3:26).

Hays's argument about this passage rests on five pieces of evidence. First, he suggests that Romans is "thoroughly theocentric" and that there is no statement in the letter that "unambiguously presents Christ as an object of faith."[116] But as I have already observed in chapter 2, Paul's theocentrism should not be played off against his Christocentrism, and the apostle clearly presents Christ as the object of faith in Roman 9:33 and 10:11.

Second, Hays follows Gerhard Kittel in noting that Romans 3:22 and 26 are sandwiched between subjective-genitive references in Romans 3:3 (πίστις θεοῦ) and 4:12 and 16 (πίστις 'Αβραάμ). "Furthermore," he argues, "there is no indication anywhere in the surrounding context that Jesus Christ is to be considered the object of faith."[117] I have already argued in chapter 2 that Romans 1:1–17 speaks of the gospel about the Son of God as the object of the Romans' faith and that Romans 4:23–25 speaks of our faith in God as also oriented toward the resurrection of Christ. Here I observe that the supposed subjective-genitive parallels in 3:3; 4:12; and 4:16 are really only superficially related to each other. Romans 3:3 refers to "the faithfulness of God" to do what he has said in the oracles he

---

116 Hays, *Faith of Jesus Christ*, 156.
117 Hays, *Faith of Jesus Christ*, 157.

revealed to Israel, despite their unfaithfulness. But Romans 4:12 and 16 refer to Abraham's faith in God and his promise as recorded in Genesis 15:6. Thus, although the Greek wording and grammar are similar, these two passages refer to very different concepts. Hays acknowledges in a footnote that "the meaning of πίστις is not the same in both cases."[118] But then he invalidly draws the conclusion that "our strict distinction between 'faith' and 'faithfulness' is not applicable to the Greek word πίστις, which contains both ideas."[119] Certainly, this word "contains both ideas" in the sense that it has various meanings in its different contexts, such as Romans 3:3 and 4:12. But Hays is arguing that it "contains both ideas" in each use of the word, a lexical fallacy that Barr calls "illegitimate totality transfer."[120] We will soon see that this fallacy lies at the heart of Hays's argument. Here my point is simply that the parallels with the subjective genitives πίστις θεοῦ in Romans 3:3 and πίστις Ἀβραάμ in Romans 4:12 and 16 are only superficial.[121]

Third, Hays makes the related observation that "ἐκ πίστεως Ἀβραάμ (Rom. 4:16) forms a precise formal parallel to the phrase ἐκ πίστεως Ἰησοῦ in 3:26."[122] This is the same observation he has made about ἐκ πίστεως Ἰησοῦ Χριστοῦ in his argument about Galatians 3:22. Again, the question is whether this parallel is substantive or superficial. The phase ἐκ πίστεως Ἰησοῦ in Romans 3:26 could refer to either our faith in Jesus or Jesus's own faithfulness. It is compelling to suggest that there is a true parallel with Romans 4:16 and that just as our inheritance is secured by sharing in the faith of Abraham,

---

118 Hays, *Faith of Jesus Christ*, 157n133.

119 Hays, *Faith of Jesus Christ*, 157n133.

120 See James Barr, *The Semantics of Biblical Language* (New York: Oxford University Press, 1961), 218.

121 Further, Ulrichs is probably correct to observe that the genitive in Rom. 4:16 is not technically a subjective genitive but refers to the *Abrahamic* faith of the patriarch's offspring, with the genitive naming a quality of faith, which is then explained in Rom. 4:17–21. Ulrichs, *Christusglaube*, 208.

122 Hays, *Faith of Jesus Christ*, 157.

so our justification is secured by sharing in the faith of Jesus. The difficulty with this view, as I have already observed about Galatians 3:22, is that Paul never explicitly says that we share in Jesus's faith as he says that we share in Abraham's faith (cf. Rom. 4:12, 23–25; Gal. 3:6). This view of Paul's theology is entirely a product of the novel translation of πίστις Χριστοῦ. And I argue below that it is more consistent to view these eight phrases as a reference to Christ-oriented faith within Pauline theology.

Fourth, Hays briefly mentions the "ponderous redundancy" of Romans 3:22 if διὰ πίστεως ᾿Ιησοῦ Χριστοῦ refers to our faith in Christ: "Why then would Paul need to add εἰς πάντας τοὺς πιστεύοντας?"[123] In this case the charge of redundancy is again easily explained as emphasis, and many have observed that Paul also advances his argument by using the word "all" (πάντας) in his second reference to our faith in Romans 3:22.

Fifth, Hays observes that in Romans 3:21–22, the righteousness of God is said to have been revealed διὰ πίστεως ᾿Ιησοῦ Χριστοῦ. He suggests that "it is difficult to see what possible sense this could make if the phrase is translated as 'through believing in Jesus Christ.'"[124] This difficulty is resolved, Hays argues, if we say that God's righteousness "has been manifested" through the faithful death of Jesus rather than through our faith. Hays's interpretation also makes better sense of the perfect tense of the verb "manifested" (πεφανέρωται), which indicates something that has been accomplished in the past.[125] These issues are complex, and so my response is necessarily complex. I agree with Hays that in Romans 3:21, Paul refers to the death of Christ in which God's righteousness has now been manifested or revealed (see Rom. 3:24–26).

123 Hays, *Faith of Jesus Christ*, 158.
124 Hays, *Faith of Jesus Christ*, 158. Campbell has made a similar argument in many places; for example, "The key point is simply this: human 'faith' *cannot function instrumentally within a process of divine disclosure. This is semantically impossible.*" Douglas A. Campbell, *The Quest for Paul's Gospel: A Suggested Strategy* (New York: T&T Clark, 2005), 197; emphasis original.
125 Hays, *Faith of Jesus Christ*, 158.

But then in Romans 3:22, Paul explains the significance of that event for the believer. Paul's phrase διὰ πίστεως ᾽Ιησοῦ Χριστοῦ in 3:22 does not actually modify the verb "has been revealed" in 3:21 but rather the noun "righteousness" in 3:22, explaining the means of righteousness or justification. When we compare Romans 3:21–22 with the very similar 1:17, we can see that Paul's point is not only that God's righteousness has been revealed in the cross but that it is continually revealed as the good news of the cross that is proclaimed and believed: "In it [the good news] the righteousness of God is revealed by faith to faith, as it is written, 'The righteous shall live by faith.'"[126] Here Paul uses the present tense of the verb "revealed" (ἀποκαλύπτεται), referring to an ongoing revelation of God's righteousness as the gospel of Christ is proclaimed and believed.[127] It is in this sense that God's righteousness is said to be "revealed by faith" in Romans 1:17. Thus, in light of Romans 1:17, Paul's point in Romans 3:21–22 is *both* that God's righteousness has been revealed in the cross (Rom. 3:21) *and* that this righteousness is a righteousness or justification that comes about by means of people believing in the message about this cross that has been proclaimed to them (Rom. 3:22).[128]

In conclusion, Hays explains how his view of πίστις in Romans 3:21–26 fits into the argument of Romans 3. He argues that in this chapter "Paul's fundamental concern is to assert the integrity of God," or his faithfulness

---

126 The ESV renders the first occurrence of ἐκ πίστεως in Rom. 1:17 as "from faith," but I have changed this to "by faith" to show that it is the same phrase used later in the verse in the citation of Hab. 2:4. I have also changed "for faith" to "to faith" to show that it is an idiom of progression (see below, p. 230n151).

127 Longenecker comments that the form of the verb ἀποκαλύπτεται in Rom. 1:17 "suggests the ongoing proclamation of the 'good news' of the Christian message as it was preached throughout the Greco-Roman world." Richard N. Longenecker, *The Epistle to the Romans*, NIGTC (Grand Rapids, MI: Eerdmans, 2016), 167. Cf. 2 Cor. 2:14: "But thanks be to God, who in Christ always leads us in triumphal procession, and through us spreads [literally, 'manifests,' φανεροῦντι] the fragrance of the knowledge of him everywhere."

128 Cf. also Taylor's observation: "In Rom. 3:5 human wickedness is said to display the righteousness of God. Why should human faith not also be a means for the display of his righteousness?" John W. Taylor, "From Faith to Faith: Romans 1.17 in the Light of Greek Idiom," *NTS* 50, no. 3 (2004): 341.

(Rom. 3:3) and righteousness (Rom. 3:5, 25).[129] He asks rhetorically, "Does it make sense to say that our faith in Jesus Christ somehow manifests the righteousness of God or proves his integrity?"[130] Instead, Hays posits that the phrase "through faith of Jesus Christ" here, as in Galatians 3, is a metonym for the story of the cross, which Paul uses in Romans 3 "to prove that God's integrity is still intact, that he has not abandoned his promises, because he has overcome humanity's unfaithfulness through the [representative] faithfulness of Jesus Christ."[131] Here we see the relationship of the πίστις Χριστοῦ debate with an equally thorny debate in Pauline theology, the meaning of the phrase "the righteousness of God" (δικαιοσύνη θεοῦ). Until the nineteenth century, most Christians understood this phrase as a reference to the righteousness God gives to the believer (whether imputed or imparted, the main distinction between Protestants and Catholics). But after the work of Hermann Cremer, many now argue that the phrase refers to God's own righteousness and that it is a relational and covenantal concept rather than a reference to a norm of righteousness.[132] Hays, in his debate with Dunn, suggests that

> the pivotal point in this discussion is the meaning of δικαιοσύνη θεοῦ. As long as interpreters maintained the notion that this phrase signified a status of righteousness imputed by God to believers, it was possible to make sense of ᾽Ιησοῦ Χριστοῦ in [Romans] 3:22 as an objective genitive: the status of righteousness is conferred through the believer's faith in Jesus Christ. . . . However, it should be beyond dispute that the "righteousness" in question in 3:21–22 is God's own righteousness.[133]

129 Hays, *Faith of Jesus Christ*, 159.
130 Hays, *Faith of Jesus Christ*, 159.
131 Hays, *Faith of Jesus Christ*, 161; see 159–61 for the entire argument.
132 See the history of interpretation in Charles Lee Irons, *The Righteousness of God: A Lexical Examination of the Covenant-Faithfulness Interpretation*, WUNT, 2nd ser., vol. 386 (Tübingen: Mohr Siebeck, 2015), 9–60.
133 Hays, *Faith of Jesus Christ*, 283. Similarly, in N. T. Wright's interpretation of Rom. 3:21–22, God's faithfulness to his covenant (δικαιοσύνη θεοῦ) has now been revealed through the faithfulness of

While I cannot enter into this other debate here, Cremer's view of δικαιοσύνη θεοῦ is not beyond dispute, because it has been thoroughly
and convincingly critiqued in the recent work of Charles Lee Irons.[134]
Perhaps, then, it is still possible to make sense of Ἰησοῦ Χριστοῦ in
Romans 3:22 (and Ἰησοῦ in Rom. 3:26) as an objective genitive.

Philippians 3:9

Philippians 3:9 is the only use of ἐκ πίστεως Χριστοῦ that Hays does
not discuss in his dissertation, and perhaps this is the reason the verse
has played such a small part in the debate.[135] As in Galatians 2:16 and
20, the context of Philippians 3:9 is an autobiographical statement
about Paul's own experience:[136]

> Indeed, I count everything as loss because of the surpassing worth
> of knowing Christ Jesus my Lord. For his sake I have suffered the
> loss of all things and count them as rubbish, in order that I may
> gain Christ and be found in him, not having a righteousness of my
> own that comes from the law, but that which comes through faith
> of Christ [διὰ πίστεως Χριστοῦ], the righteousness from God that
> depends on faith [ἐπὶ τῇ πίστει]. (Phil. 3:8–9)

And like Romans 3:22, the phrase διὰ πίστεως Χριστοῦ modifies the
noun "righteousness."[137] Most scholars agree that the final phrase of

---

Christ (πίστις Χριστοῦ), the one who was faithful where Israel was unfaithful (cf. Rom. 3:2–4).
Paul and the Faithfulness of God, COQG 4 (Minneapolis: Fortress, 2013), 841; see also 839.

134 Irons, *Righteousness of God*.

135 Ulrichs also observes the little discussion on this verse in the πίστις Χριστοῦ debate. *Christusglaube*,
223. For a helpful summary of the debate over Phil. 3:9, mostly in the commentaries, see Foster,
who concludes in favor of the subjective genitive. Paul Foster, "Πίστις Χριστοῦ Terminology in
Philippians and Ephesians," in *The Faith of Jesus Christ: Exegetical, Biblical, and Theological Studies*, ed. Michael F. Bird and Preston M. Sprinkle (Peabody, MA: Hendrickson, 2009), 93–100.
For a thorough study of Phil. 3:9 and a conclusion in favor of the objective genitive, see Veronica
Koperski, "The Meaning of *Pistis Christou* in Philippians 3:9," *LS* 18, no. 3 (1993): 198–216.

136 For this observation I am indebted to Ulrichs, *Christusglaube*, 222.

137 The feminine article τὴν that governs διὰ πίστεως Χριστοῦ is clearly intended to stand for the
feminine noun "righteousness" (δικαιοσύνην), which Paul has just mentioned.

Philippians 3:9 (ἐπὶ τῇ πίστει) refers to Paul's own faith as the basis of the "righteousness from God" that he longs to have.[138] And because this phrase further explains "that which comes through faith of Christ," it makes best sense to see διὰ πίστεως Χριστοῦ as a reference to Paul's own faith in Christ as well.[139]

Ambiguity in the Meaning and Referent of Πίστις*?*
Hays concludes his influential argument about πίστις with these words:

> It should be clear that πίστις is not a univocal concept for Paul. His use of it is extensive and flexible, and its meaning in any particular sentence must be determined in view of a whole range of considerations. To take a clear example, πίστις in Gal 1:23 (εὐαγγελίζεται τὴν πίστιν) demands a different interpretation from πίστις in 3:11 (ὁ δίκαιος ἐκ πίστεως ζήσεται). Some studies . . . suffer from a tendency to seek a single comprehensive definition that will account for every instance in which the word πίστις occurs. This has the result of leveling out Paul's uneven usage and suppressing the connotative diversity inherent in Paul's language. We should be willing to recognize that Paul's language may sometimes be ambiguous by design, allowing him to speak in one breath of Christ's faith and our faith.[140]

Here we see the appeal to ambiguity that we saw above in Hays's exposition of Habakkuk 2:4 in Galatians 3:11 and his comparison of πίστις θεοῦ in

---

138 Wallis, however, argues that ἐπὶ indicates purpose, interpreting the verse to mean that God's righteousness, which comes through Christ's faith, leads to faith in believers. *Faith of Jesus Christ*, 124.

139 So Koperski, "Philippians 3:9," 214. Some also point to the constellation of ideas in Phil. 3 that may be considered parallels to Christ-oriented faith: boasting in Christ Jesus (Phil. 3:3), knowing Christ Jesus our Lord (Phil. 3:8, 10), gaining Christ (Phil. 3:8), and being found in Christ (Phil. 3:9). See, e.g., Ulrichs, *Christusglaube*, 229–40. Because Paul, however, seems to present these ideas as the *goal* of his new valuation of Christ (i.e., his Christ-oriented faith), I think they are better classified as ways in which the apostle speaks about the more general category of participation with Christ.

140 Hays, *Faith of Jesus Christ*, 161.

Romans 3:3 to πίστις Ἀβραάμ in Romans 4:12 and 16. In the next chapter of Hays's dissertation, we see more clearly that his appeal to ambiguity is not tangential but fundamental to his understanding of Paul's argument in Galatians 3. Hays reinterprets the phrase οἱ ἐκ πίστεως in the beginning of Paul's argument (Gal. 3:7, 9) as a reference to both the faith of believers and Christ's own faith, although his emphasis falls on the latter meaning:

> We may suggest that οἱ ἐκ πίστεως carries not primarily the connotation of "those who have faith" but rather the connotation of "those who are given life on the basis of [Christ's] faith."
>
> Caution is demanded: Paul's language here is by no means as unambiguous as my interpretive paraphrase might suggest. Paul, as we have repeatedly emphasized, does regard Christ's people as "believers"; those who receive life "out of" Christ's faith in turn trust in him (cf. 3:22) and live their lives also in a manner characterized by faith (cf. 2 Cor 5:7—διὰ πίστεως γὰρ περιπατοῦμεν). Thus, οἱ ἐκ πίστεως is a phrase capable of sustaining several interpretations. It would be a mistake to attempt to exclude "those who believe" as one part of Paul's meaning. However, this is not the exclusive or even primary meaning demanded by context; Paul is not concerned here with developing the parallelism between Abraham's faith and the faith of Christians.[141]

Here he appeals to ambiguity, arguing that οἱ ἐκ πίστεως refers primarily to Christ's faith(fulness) but also to our faith. He makes a similar appeal to ambiguity in his discussion of Galatians 3:23 and 25 at the end of Paul's argument:

> Because the Christian's life is a reenactment of the pattern of faithfulness revealed in Jesus, it is futile to ask, in a formulation such as ἵνα ἐκ πίστεως δικαιωθῶμεν (3:24), *whose* faith is meant. It is of course

141 Hays, *Faith of Jesus Christ*, 172.

"the faith of Jesus Christ," but it is also the faith of the Christian. . . . Thus, the coming of πίστις [in Gal. 3:23 and 25] is indeed the coming of a new possible mode of disposing one's self toward God, but this mode is possible precisely because it was first of all actualized in and by Jesus Christ.[142]

Thus we see that the appeal to ambiguity lies at the very heart of Hays's understanding of πίστις in Galatians 3. Is Hays correct that Paul is being purposely ambiguous in his language of πίστις?

First, we should observe that the "clear example" of the ambiguity of πίστις in Galatians 1:23 and 3:11 is not actually an example of ambiguity, because it refers to *two different uses of the word* πίστις. When a word has different meanings in different contexts, it is an example not of ambiguity but rather of a word's multiple meanings (polysemy).[143] True ambiguity is found *when a word is used one time with multiple levels of meaning*. John's Gospel, for example, famously uses ambiguity when Jesus tells Nicodemus, "Unless one is born again he cannot see the kingdom of God" (John 3:3). The word "again" (ἄνωθεν) can also mean "from above," and in this context, the one use of the word is probably purposely ambiguous, intended to communicate both meanings. Nicodemus clearly takes Jesus to mean born "again" (John 3:4), but the narrator probably intends his readers to see the need for a heavenly birth "from above" and by the Spirit (John 3:5–13).[144] As with most things in interpretation, context is the key to determining ambiguity. John 3 clearly shows two levels of meaning in one use of a word. But ambiguity is a stretching of the normal use of language. Normally words do not have two levels of meaning. This is what makes wordplay so interesting.[145]

---

142 Hays, *Faith of Jesus Christ*, 203–4.
143 See my argument in chap. 1, p. 54.
144 So BDAG, s.v. "ἄνωθεν."
145 In his discussion of ambiguity, Silva observes that context typically "serves to *eliminate* multiple meanings" and that ambiguity is *not* a "pervasive phenomenon" in Scripture. Moisés Silva, *Biblical Words and Their Meaning: An Introduction to Lexical Semantics*, rev. ed. (Grand Rapids, MI:

Why does Hays so often appeal to ambiguity in the meaning and referent of πίστις within Paul's argument in Galatians 3? Why not simply argue that πίστις in this context refers to Christ's faithfulness and not to our faith? Why say that it refers to both? Is it because the context indicates that Paul is being intentionally ambiguous in his language of πίστις? Or could it be that Hays's new interpretation of πίστις settles so poorly within the context of Paul's argument, which so clearly speaks about our faith, that Hays must say the word refers to both? Readers must decide for themselves. In what follows I suggest that there is no need to appeal to ambiguity in Paul's use of πίστις. In fact, Paul consistently uses the phrase "by faith" throughout his letters as an idiom referring to our faith, specifically our faith in Christ.

"By Faith" as a Consistent Pauline Idiom

There is something distinctly Pauline about the phrase "by faith." This phrase appears a few times in Greek literature before Paul.[146] But in the Pauline corpus, variations of this phrase occur over forty times, typically with the prepositional phrases ἐκ πίστεως and διὰ [τῆς] πίστεως and occasionally with the phrase ἐν πίστει or just the instrumental dative [τῇ] πίστει. The phrase occurs a few more times in the New Testament (e.g., 1 Pet. 1:5). Most significant is Hebrews 11, which uses "by faith" twenty times—eighteen with the instrumental dative πίστει, which is

---

Zondervan, 1994), 150–51. Ironically, to say that in normal usage a word contains all its multiple meanings in one use of the word, as Hays often does, is to fall into the very trap he is trying to avoid: the trap of seeking "a single comprehensive definition that will account for every instance in which the word πίστις occurs." Hays, *Faith of Jesus Christ*, 161. That is, in Hays's view, the word always has a single comprehensive definition in Gal. 3: "faith(fulness)."

146 Most important for Paul is the use of "by faith," ἐκ πίστεώς, in Hab. 2:4 LXX, since he quotes this verse in Rom. 1:17 and Gal. 3:11. Another example is Xenophon of Athens, who uses the phrase διὰ πίστεως as an adjective, referring to generals "who trustingly [διὰ πίστεως] put themselves" in the hands of the barbarians (*Anabasis III*, 2.8). The Skeptic philosopher Sextus Empiricus lived after Paul but has two interesting examples of οἱ ἐκ πίστεως (cf. Gal. 3:7, 9), referring specifically to those who depend on faith and memory (*Against the Logicians II*, 308; *Outlines of Pyrrhonism*, 141).

rare for Paul, and two with διὰ [τῆς] πίστεως.[147] "By faith" is also found occasionally in the Apostolic Fathers, perhaps under the influence of Paul.[148] Thus we see that the phrase "by faith" characterizes Paul's letters in a way that is not really characteristic of other Greek literature, with the exception of Hebrews 11. The phrase is not formulaic because Paul uses different variations in his letters. But it is a distinct manner of speaking—that is, an idiom of the apostle. Specifically, it is an idiom that typically presents our faith as a means or cause of salvation.[149] Table 4.1 lists each occurrence of the idiom in canonical order of the Pauline corpus, including the debated ἐκ πίστεως Χριστοῦ phrases.

Table 4.1   "By Faith" in the Pauline Corpus*

Rom. 1:12	". . . that is, that we may be mutually encouraged by each other's faith [διὰ τῆς ἐν ἀλλήλοις πίστεως], both yours and mine."
Rom. 1:17a	"For in it the righteousness of God is revealed from faith [ἐκ πίστεως] for faith . . ."
Rom. 1:17b	". . . as it is written, 'The righteous shall live by faith [ἐκ πίστεως].'"
Rom. 3:22	". . . the righteousness of God through faith in Jesus Christ [διὰ πίστεως 'Ιησοῦ Χριστοῦ] for all who believe."
Rom. 3:25	". . . whom God put forward as a propitiation by his blood, to be received by faith [διὰ (τῆς) πίστεως]."†
Rom. 3:26	". . . so that he might be just and the justifier of the one who has faith in Jesus [τὸν ἐκ πίστεως 'Ιησοῦ]."
Rom. 3:28	"For we hold that one is justified by faith [πίστει] apart from works of the law."

147 Note also δι' ἧς (2x), δι' αὐτῆς, and κατὰ πίστιν (2x) in Heb. 11.

148 E.g., 1 Clement 31.2; Epistle to Diognetus 8.6.

149 Grammatically, the categories of means/instrument and cause can be distinguished in some cases. But in the case of Paul's "by faith" idiom, they are overlapping categories because "by faith" indicates a means that is also a cause. Wallace, for example, compares the dative of means (instrumental dative) with the dative of cause and observes that sometimes "it is impossible to distinguish the two." *Greek Grammar*, 167. Cf. BDAG, s.v. "ἐκ," use 3; s.v. "διὰ," use A.3.

Table 4.1 (cont.)

Rom. 3:30a	"... who will justify the circumcised by faith [ἐκ πίστεως] ..."
Rom. 3:30b	"... and the uncircumcised through faith [διὰ τῆς πίστεως]."
Rom. 3:31	"Do we then overthrow the law by this faith [διὰ τῆς πίστεως]?"
Rom. 4:16a	"That is why it [the promise] depends on faith [ἐκ πίστεως] ..."
Rom. 4:16c	"... not only to the adherent of the law but also to the one who shares the faith of Abraham [τῷ ἐκ πίστεως Ἀβραάμ]."
Rom. 5:1	"Therefore, since we have been justified by faith [ἐκ πίστεως] ..."
Rom. 5:2	"Through him we have also obtained access by faith [τῇ πίστει] into this grace in which we stand, and we rejoice in hope of the glory of God."‡
Rom. 9:30	"What shall we say, then? That Gentiles who did not pursue righteousness have attained it, that is, a righteousness that is by faith [ἐκ πίστεως]."
Rom. 9:32	"Why? Because they [Israel] did not pursue it by faith [ἐκ πίστεως], but as if it were based on works."
Rom. 10:6	"But the righteousness based on faith [ἐκ πίστεως] says ..."
Rom. 11:20	"They were broken off because of their unbelief, but you stand fast through faith [τῇ πίστει]."
Rom. 14:23a	"But whoever has doubts is condemned if he eats, because the eating is not from faith [ἐκ πίστεως] ..."
Rom. 14:23b	"... For whatever does not proceed from faith [ἐκ πίστεως] is sin."
2 Cor. 1:24	"You stand firm in your faith [τῇ ... πίστει]."
2 Cor. 5:7	"For we walk by faith [διὰ πίστεως], not by sight."
Gal. 2:16a	"Yet we know that a person is not justified by works of the law but through faith in Jesus Christ [διὰ πίστεως Ἰησοῦ Χριστοῦ]."
Gal. 2:16c	"... in order to be justified by faith in Christ [ἐκ πίστεως Χριστοῦ] and not by works of the law."

Table 4.1 (cont.)

Gal. 2:20	"And the life I now live in the flesh I live by faith in the Son of God [ἐν πίστει . . . τῇ τοῦ υἱοῦ τοῦ θεοῦ], who loved me and gave himself for me."
Gal. 3:7	"Know then that it is those of faith [οἱ ἐκ πίστεως] who are the sons of Abraham."
Gal. 3:8	"And the Scripture, foreseeing that God would justify the Gentiles by faith [ἐκ πίστεως] . . ."
Gal. 3:9	"So then, those who are of faith [οἱ ἐκ πίστεως] are blessed along with Abraham, the man of faith."
Gal. 3:11	"Now it is evident that no one is justified before God by the law, for 'The righteous shall live by faith [ἐκ πίστεως].'"
Gal. 3:12	"But the law is not of faith [ἐκ πίστεως], rather 'The one who does them shall live by them.'"
Gal. 3:14	". . . so that we might receive the promised Spirit through faith [διὰ τῆς πίστεως]."
Gal. 3:22	"But the Scripture imprisoned everything under sin, so that the promise by faith in Jesus Christ [ἐκ πίστεως Ἰησοῦ Χριστοῦ] might be given to those who believe."
Gal. 3:24	"So then, the law was our guardian until Christ came, in order that we might be justified by faith [ἐκ πίστεως]."
Gal. 3:26	"For in Christ Jesus you are all sons of God, through faith [διὰ τῆς πίστεως]."
Gal. 5:5	"For through the Spirit, by faith [ἐκ πίστεως], we ourselves eagerly wait for the hope of righteousness."
Eph. 2:8	"For by grace you have been saved through faith [διὰ πίστεως]. And this is not your own doing; it is the gift of God."
Eph. 3:12	". . . in whom we have boldness and access with confidence through our faith in him [διὰ τῆς πίστεως αὐτοῦ]."

Table 4.1 (cont.)

Eph. 3:17	". . . so that Christ may dwell in your hearts through faith [διὰ τῆς πίστεως]."
Phil. 3:9	". . . not having a righteousness of my own that comes from the law, but that which comes through faith in Christ [διὰ πίστεως Χριστοῦ], the righteousness from God that depends on faith."
Col. 2:12	"You were also raised with him through faith [διὰ τῆς πίστεως] in the powerful working of God."
2 Thess. 2:13	"But we ought always to give thanks to God for you, brothers beloved by the Lord, because God chose you as the firstfruits to be saved, through sanctification by the Spirit and belief in the truth [ἐν . . . πίστει ἀληθείας]."
1 Tim. 1:4	". . . the stewardship from God that is by faith [ἐν πίστει]."
2 Tim. 3:15	"From childhood you have been acquainted with the sacred writings, which are able to make you wise for salvation through faith in Christ Jesus [διὰ πίστεως τῆς ἐν Χριστῷ Ἰησοῦ]."

* Note also some phrases that are similar to "by faith" in Paul's letters: "by the law of faith [διὰ νόμου πίστεως]" (Rom. 3:27); "through the righteousness of faith [διὰ δικαιοσύνης πίστεως]" (Rom. 4:13); "by hearing with faith [ἐξ ἀκοῆς πίστεως]" (Gal. 3:2, 5); and "on the basis of faith [ἐπὶ τῇ πίστει]" (Phil. 3:9, my trans.).

† Some manuscripts omit the article τῆς.

‡ "By faith" in Rom. 5:2 is omitted in several manuscripts (e.g., B, D, F, G), but the external evidence slightly favors its originality (e.g., ℵ, A, C, 1739, Majority Text)—so Thomas R. Schreiner, *Romans*, 2nd ed. BECNT (Grand Rapids, MI: Baker Academic, 2018), 266. It is difficult to know why it would have been omitted or added by a scribe, so this decision should probably rest on the weight of the external evidence.

My goal in this section is to show that, unlike Hays's view, this idiom can be consistently interpreted in Paul's letters as a reference to our faith without any need to appeal to ambiguity. I am not aiming to give a thorough exegesis of any of these texts that will convince readers of my interpretation. Rather, I am aiming to show the plausibility of a simple and consistent interpretation of the phrase "by faith" in Paul's letters, including the eight ἐκ πίστεως Χριστοῦ phrases. In other words,

I am aiming to show that there is no need to appeal to ambiguity if we simply view this idiom as a reference to our faith. I close by arguing that the genitive in the ἐκ πίστεως Χριστοῦ phrases most likely means that Christ is the object of our faith and thus refers to Christ-oriented faith as a cause of salvation.

By Faith

We start with Paul's many uses of the phrase "by faith" in his letter to the Romans. His first use explains why he wants to visit the saints in Rome: "that we may be mutually encouraged by each other's faith [διὰ τῆς ἐν ἀλλήλοις πίστεως], both yours and mine" (Rom. 1:12). The next two uses occur within the thesis statement of the letter and are highly debated: "For in it [the gospel] the righteousness of God is revealed from faith [ἐκ πίστεως] for faith, as it is written, 'The righteous shall live by faith [ἐκ πίστεως]'" (Rom. 1:17). Most interpreters agree that "for faith" (or better, "to faith") in this verse refers to our faith. But many have argued in the last few decades that "from faith" (or better, "by faith") refers to either the faithfulness of God or the faith(fulness) of Christ.[150] These readings, however, falter on the context. Paul has just spoken about faith as our obedient response to the proclamation of the gospel about God's Son (Rom. 1:1–7); he has just thanked God for the Romans' faith in that gospel (Rom. 1:8); and most importantly, he has just said that the gospel is God's power "for salvation to everyone who believes, to the Jew first and also to the Greek" (Rom. 1:16). In this context, the progression

150 Dunn is perhaps best known for arguing that the phrase is a play on words meaning "from God's faithfulness to man's faith," based in part on the theme of God's faithfulness in Rom. 3:3 and on the phrase "righteousness of God," which he takes as the covenant faithfulness of God. James D. G. Dunn, *Romans 1–8*, WBC 38A (Nashville: Thomas Nelson, 1988), 44. Against Dunn, Campbell argues that the phrase means "by Christ's faithfulness," based mainly on his messianic interpretation of Hab. 2:4 in Rom. 1:17b. Douglas A. Campbell, "Romans 1:17—A *Crux Interpretum* for the Πιστις Χριστου Debate," *JBL* 113, no. 2 (1994): 277–85. For a refutation of the messianic interpretation of Hab. 2:4 in Paul's citation, see chap. 1, p. 90.

"by faith to faith" is likely a reference to our faith, perhaps referring specifically to the progress of the gospel around the world as more and more people believe it.[151] Paul's citation of Habakkuk 2:4, then, supports what is happening in Paul's proclamation of the gospel: "The righteous shall live by [their] faith."

Paul picks up this idea of our faith again in Romans 3:21–31. Here he says that the righteousness of God comes "through faith [διὰ πίστεως] . . . for all who believe" (Rom. 3:22),[152] that the propitiatory sacrifice of the cross is applied "by faith [διὰ (τῆς) πίστεως]" (Rom. 3:25), that God justifies "the one who has faith [τὸν ἐκ πίστεως]" (Rom. 3:26), that a person is "justified by faith [πίστει]" (Rom. 3:28), and that the one God justifies "the circumcised by faith [ἐκ πίστεως] and the uncircumcised through faith [διὰ τῆς πίστεως]" (Rom. 3:30). Paul then argues that the promised Abrahamic inheritance "depends on faith [ἐκ πίστεως]" and comes "to the one who shares the faith of Abraham [τῷ ἐκ πίστεως Ἀβραάμ]" (Rom. 4:16), concluding that "we have been justified by faith [ἐκ πίστεως]" (Rom. 5:1) and that "we have also obtained access by faith [τῇ πίστει] into this grace in which we stand" (Rom. 5:2).[153] In Romans 9–11, he addresses faith as a response to the gospel in explaining why the Gentiles have attained "a righteousness that is by faith [ἐκ πίστεως]" (Rom. 9:30), but most of Israel has not: "Why? Because they [Israel] did not pursue it [the

---

151 The studies of both Quarles and Taylor have confirmed that "by faith to faith" in Rom. 1:17 is an idiom of progression of some sort (and not emphatic, as many commentators have suggested). Charles L. Quarles, "From Faith to Faith: A Fresh Examination of the Prepositional Series in Romans 1:17," *NovT* 45, no. 1 (2003): 1–21; Taylor, "From Faith to Faith," 337–48. I follow Taylor's view that it specifically refers to the progress of the gospel. Taylor, "From Faith to Faith," 346.

152 Many interpreters have suggested a parallel between ἐκ πίστεως εἰς πίστιν in Rom. 1:17 and διὰ πίστεως . . . εἰς πάντας τοὺς πιστεύοντας in Rom. 3:22; e.g., Ulrichs, *Christusglaube*, 171. Although the similar wording is striking, in my view the two verses are not truly parallel in substance.

153 Murray has observed how similar Rom. 5:2 is to Eph. 3:12: "in whom we have boldness and access with confidence through our faith in him [διὰ τῆς πίστεως αὐτοῦ]." John Murray, *The Epistle to the Romans*, NICNT (Grand Rapids, MI: Eerdmans, 1959), 1:370.

law] by faith [ἐκ πίστεως]" (Rom. 9:32)—that is, they did not believe in the Christ (Rom. 9:33). They pursued the righteousness based on the law (Rom. 10:5) rather than "the righteousness based on faith [ἐκ πίστεως]" (Rom. 10:6). "They were broken off because of their unbelief [τῇ ἀπιστίᾳ], but you [Gentiles] stand fast through faith [τῇ πίστει]" (Rom. 11:20). Finally in Romans, Paul addresses believers who are weak in their faith and unable to affirm with Paul that the Lord Jesus has declared all foods to be clean (Rom. 14:1–2, 14). He warns that "whoever has doubts is condemned if he eats, because the eating is not from faith [ἐκ πίστεως]. For whatever does not proceed from faith [ἐκ πίστεως] is sin" (Rom. 14:23).

In 2 Corinthians 1:24, Paul says that he does not "lord it over your faith . . . for you stand firm in [or 'by'] your faith [τῇ . . . πίστει]" and not by his ministry among them. He then summarizes a larger argument with iconic words about his own faith: "For we walk by faith [διὰ πίστεως], not by sight" (2 Cor. 5:7). And in Galatians he uses the idiom many times to support his argument about justification by faith. Along with other Jewish Christians, he knows that "a person is not justified by works of the law but through faith [διὰ πίστεως]" (Gal. 2:16a), and so he has come to believe in Christ Jesus "in order to be justified by faith [ἐκ πίστεως]" (Gal. 2:16c). The life he now lives in the flesh he lives "by faith [ἐν πίστει]" (Gal. 2:20). Abraham also was righteous by faith (Gal. 3:6), so these Gentile believers can know that "it is those of faith [οἱ ἐκ πίστεως] who are the sons of Abraham" (Gal. 3:7), or again that "those who are of faith [οἱ ἐκ πίστεως] are blessed along with Abraham, the man of faith" (Gal. 3:9). Scripture, too, supports the idea that justification is by faith rather than the law for everyone: "The righteous shall live by faith [ἐκ πίστεως]" (Gal. 3:11). And Christ redeemed us from the curse of the law "so that we might receive the promised Spirit through faith [διὰ τῆς πίστεως]" (Gal. 3:14). In fact, God's ultimate purpose in the law was to give the promise to believers: "Scripture imprisoned everything under sin, so that the promise by faith [ἐκ πίστεως] . . . might be given to those who believe" (Gal. 3:22). Paul concludes that "the law was our guardian until Christ came, in order that we might be justified by faith [ἐκ πίστεως]" (Gal. 3:24). But now that the faith has come, we are not under this law-guardian, because we "are all sons of God, through faith [διὰ τῆς πίστεως]" (Gal. 3:26). Then making one final warning about circumcision and the law, he reminds the Galatians that we await final justification by faith: "For through the Spirit, by faith [ἐκ πίστεως], we ourselves eagerly wait for the hope of righteousness" (Gal. 5:5). What counts in Christ Jesus is only our "faith working through love" (Gal. 5:6).[154]

Several uses of this idiom occur in the disputed letter to the Ephesians. One is the classic soteriological statement "by grace you have been saved through faith [διὰ πίστεως]" (Eph. 2:8; cf. Rom. 3:24–25). The second speaks of our access to God "through our faith [διὰ τῆς πίστεως]" (Eph. 3:12; cf. Rom. 5:2). And a third comes within Paul's prayer for the Gentiles that "Christ may dwell in your hearts through faith [διὰ τῆς πίστεως]" (Eph. 3:17). Perhaps the articles in these latter two verses are anaphoric, pointing back to the "faith" mentioned in the fundamental statement of Ephesians 2:8. A scattering of occurrences are found in four other letters of Paul. One is biographical, recalling Paul's loss of all things to gain Christ and be found in him by "not having a righteousness of my own that comes from the law, but that which comes through faith [διὰ πίστεως] . . . , the righteousness from God that depends on faith" (Phil. 3:9). Another occurrence reminds the Colossians of their own biography of union with Christ: "You were also raised with him through faith [διὰ

---

154 Hays follows Klaus Berger and J. Christiaan Beker, who claim that it is logically incoherent for Paul to argue that *believers* are the heirs of Abraham in Gal. 3:6–9 and then that *Christ* is the sole heir in Gal. 3:16–19. Hays, *Faith of Jesus Christ*, 164, also 165–66. He resolves this supposed incoherence with his argument that πίστις actually refers primarily to *Christ's* faith (and only secondarily to our faith). But a better interpretive approach takes πίστις in Paul's argument as a consistent reference to our faith and still avoids incoherence—namely, that our faith unites us to Christ so that we are now heirs along with Christ, the one heir of Abraham (Gal. 3:26–29).

τῆς πίστεως] in the powerful working of God" (Col. 2:12). Paul recalls the Thessalonians' acceptance of the gospel, thanking God for them because he "chose [them] as the firstfruits to be saved, through sanctification by the Spirit and belief in the truth [ἐν . . . πίστει ἀληθείας]" (2 Thess. 2:13). And finally, Paul reminds Timothy that God's plan of salvation is "by faith [ἐν πίστει]" (1 Tim. 1:4),[155] and that Timothy himself has known the sacred writings from childhood, "which are able to make you wise for salvation through faith [διὰ πίστεως]" (2 Tim. 3:15).

My point in these last four paragraphs has been that the "by faith" idiom in Paul's letters can be consistently interpreted as a reference to our faith without any need to appeal to ambiguity in the meaning or referent of πίστις, as Hays does. In my reading of Paul's letters, at least, the apostle consistently uses these phrases to refer to our faith as a means or cause of salvation.[156]

By Faith in Christ

Included within Paul's "by faith" idiom are his eight ἐκ πίστεως Χριστοῦ phrases. I have mentioned each of these in the last section but have purposely left out the debated genitives. Now comes the time to address them. If I am correct in my evaluation of Hays, and if Paul uses "by faith" consistently as a reference to our faith, then the genitives cannot indicate that Christ is the subject of faith or faithfulness. But

---

155 The ESV translates οἰκονομίαν θεοῦ as "the stewardship from God," but I take it to refer to "God's plan" (BDAG, use 2), specifically, "God's work of redemption in the world, particularly in the church itself (called God's *oikos* [household] in 1 Tim 3:15)." Robert W. Yarbrough, *The Letters to Timothy and Titus*, PNTC (Grand Rapids, MI: Eerdmans, 2018), 105.

156 Cf. Dunn's conclusion in his congenial "letter" to Hays: "In many ways the most persuasive argument for πίστις Χριστοῦ as referring to 'faith in Christ' is that it ensures that Paul's πίστις phrases can and should be taken consistently as referring to the act of believing, of hearing and responding to the gospel with the commitment to Christ as Lord for which the gospel calls." James D. G. Dunn, "Ἐκ Πίστεως: A Key to the Meaning of Πίστις Χριστου," in *The Word Leaps the Gap: Essays on Scripture and Theology in Honor of Richard B. Hays*, ed. J. Ross Wagner, C. Kavin Rowe, and A. Katherine Grieb (Grand Rapids, MI: Eerdmans, 2008), 365.

does this necessarily mean that Paul is presenting Christ as the object of our faith? Some have argued for other alternatives, a commendable approach in such a polarized debate.

The most promising alternative is the genitive of source (or *genitive auctoris*), which would yield the translation "by faith from Christ."[157] This view was advocated by several scholars in Leiden, was initially adopted by Johannes Haussleiter, and has recently been defended by Mark Seifrid.[158] In this view, the genitive Χριστοῦ shows that our faith is given to us by Christ. Seifrid defends the position, drawing our attention to the similar idea seen in Acts 3:16, which speaks of "the faith that is through Jesus [δι' αὐτοῦ]."[159] He observes the "theocentric thrust" of Romans 3:21–26 and the fact that Paul describes *God* as the object of our faith in the context (Rom. 4:24–25).[160] And he appeals to the passivity of Paul and the participatory thrust of Philippians 3:9 to conclude that "'the faith of Christ' signifies faith which comes as a gift from Christ."[161] This grammatical interpretation is certainly possible and resonates with the close relationship between faith and grace in Paul's theology. But the arguments may also be questioned. Is Paul's "pressing on" and "straining forward" in Philippians 3 rightly characterized as "passive"? Is there a reason to oppose believing in God with believing in Christ in Paul's theology?

---

157 Most other alternatives are uncompelling. Gustav Adolf Deissmann famously invented a genitive category, the *genitivus mysticus*, to explain the relationship, but Seifrid rightly observes that with such an approach, there could be "as many categories of the genitive as there are genitive constructs." Mark A. Seifrid, "The Faith of Christ," in Bird and Sprinkle, *Faith of Jesus Christ*, 133. Others use generic categories like genitive of quality or characterizing genitive. See Garwood P. Anderson, *Paul's New Perspective: Charting a Soteriological Journey* (Downers Grove, IL: IVP Academic, 2016), 148–51. The problem with this approach is that it fails to actually explain the meaning of the genitive. Finally, some appeal to ambiguity and say that the genitive is both subjective *and* objective; e.g., Morna D. Hooker, "Another Look at πίστις Χριστοῦ," *SJT* 69, no. 1 (2016): 48. But there is nothing in the context signaling that Paul is being purposely ambiguous.

158 Schliesser, "Exegetical Amnesia," 80–83.

159 Seifrid, "Faith of Christ," 137.

160 Seifrid, "Faith of Christ," 141–42.

161 Seifrid, "Faith of Christ," 145.

Much of this study has been dedicated to showing that these are two ways of referring to the same thing.

Another alternative has been suggested by Benjamin Schliesser, who has made many contributions to the recent study of faith in the New Testament. In his published dissertation on Romans 4, he calls scholars to move beyond the polarity of objective genitive and subjective genitive.[162] And one can see hints of an alternative view in his dissertation. For example, he argues that "δια [της] πιστεως [in Rom. 3:25] describes the means through which God publicly and universally established Christ as the means of atonement. Here, our personal faith is not the primary issue. . . . Faith is here a phenomenon that transcends human subjectivity."[163] Similarly, πίστις in Romans 1:17 and 3:22, 25, and 26 refers not to "Jesus' own faithfulness, nor God's faithfulness in Christ, nor [n.b.] a human attitude, but the new reality that has been instigated upon his coming and has received a universal dimension through his death."[164] Now Schliesser has clearly articulated this view in an article carving out a bona fide third position in the πίστις Χριστοῦ debate based on Galatians 3:23 and 25, where Paul personifies faith by saying that it "came" and "was revealed." Many advocates of the "faithfulness of Christ" view have appealed to these verses to prove that πίστις refers to Christ.[165] But Schliesser argues that πίστις (and thus πίστις Χριστοῦ) refers not to a subjective disposition of faith or faithfulness but to the transsubjective, eschatological event of the coming of Christ.[166] Schliesser has done Pauline theology a great service in

---

162 Schliesser, *Abraham's Faith*, 261–63.

163 Schliesser, *Abraham's Faith*, 290.

164 Schliesser, *Abraham's Faith*, 291–92; cf. 300–301, 309, 399.

165 For example, Hays observes that "for Paul the coming of πίστις (vv. 23, 25) is virtually identified with the coming of Christ himself." *Faith of Jesus Christ*, 203. And de Boer sees this text as "decisive in this matter." Martinus C. de Boer, *Galatians: A Commentary*, NTL (Louisville: Westminster John Knox, 2011), 193.

166 Benjamin Schliesser, "'Christ-Faith' as an Eschatological Event (Galatians 3.23–26): A 'Third-View' on Πίστις Χριστοῦ," *JSNT* 38, no. 3 (2016): 277–300. Similar is Preston M. Sprinkle, "Πίστις Χριστοῦ as an Eschatological Event," in Bird and Sprinkle, *Faith of Jesus Christ*, 165–84. Gupta

moving the debate out of the trenches, both in his deep exploration of the history of the debate and the attempt to carve out a third view.[167] He has also brought together German- and English-speaking scholarship as a German scholar who writes in English. But I believe that his insights about the eschatological nature of πίστις in Galatians 3:23 and 25 are better integrated into Pauline theology as one aspect of our Christ-oriented faith rather than as an alternative to the objective genitive view. In Galatians 3:23 and 25, Paul personifies πίστις as the "body of faith," or the gospel, that has now come and been eschatologically revealed with Christ and that we now believe. But in Paul's "by faith" idiom, πίστις refers to our subjective act of faith in the gospel. These two meanings of πίστις are closely related in that "body of faith" is an objectified extension of the meaning "faith."[168] They are also closely related in the context of Galatians 3 (see "by faith" in Gal. 3:24). But they are not identical. Πίστις in Paul's ἐκ πίστεως Χριστοῦ phrases does not refer to the eschatological coming of the gospel but to our belief in that gospel.

How, then, does the genitive "of Christ" relate to our faith? In chapter 2, I observed that in 1 Corinthians 15:11–12, Paul speaks interchangeably about proclaiming the gospel (1 Cor. 15:11) and proclaiming Christ (1 Cor. 15:12).[169] I also observed that one of Paul's most common ways of specifying the object of our faith is to speak about our faith in the gospel. Would it then be surprising for him to use "faith of Christ" as a shorthand way to refer to our faith in Christ and the good news about him? The two clear examples of πίστις with an objective genitive in Paul's disputed letters seem to speak this way. One speaks about salvation "by . . . belief in the truth [ἐν . . . πίστει

---

is now sympathetic to Schliesser's new view as well. Nijay K. Gupta, *Paul and the Language of Faith* (Grand Rapids, MI: Eerdmans, 2020), 174–75.

167 On the former, see Schliesser, "Exegetical Amnesia"; on the latter, see Schliesser, "Eschatological Event."

168 See chap. 1, p. 54.

169 See chap. 2, p. 148.

ἀληθείας]" (2 Thess. 2:13)—that is, salvation by faith in the gospel. The other says we have been raised with Christ "through faith in the powerful working of God [διὰ τῆς πίστεως τῆς ἐνεργείας τοῦ θεοῦ]" (Col. 2:12). This latter example is not unlike what Paul says about our faith in the God who raised Christ from the dead. Thus, I conclude that it is most likely that ἐκ πίστεως Χριστοῦ means "by faith in Christ" in Paul's letters. Not only is this view grammatically possible, it also fits with the many passages we discussed in chapters 2 and 3, in which Christ-oriented faith is a cause of our salvation, which leads to my final point.

In each occurrence of the "by faith" idiom, πίστις plays an instrumental role. Paul seems to use the different constructions that make up this idiom as semantically equivalent. For example, in Romans 3:21–31, he uses διὰ [τῆς] πίστεως (Rom. 3:22, 25), ἐκ πίστεως (Rom. 3:26), and the dative πίστει (Rom. 3:28) with no clear difference in meaning. Similarly, in Galatians 2:15–21, he uses διὰ πίστεως (Gal. 2:16a), ἐκ πίστεως (Gal. 2:16b), and ἐν πίστει (Gal. 2:20) with no clear difference in meaning. In some of these uses, πίστις is simply the means by which a Christian conducts his or her life: walking by faith, not by sight (2 Cor. 5:7); eating meat that the Lord has declared clean by faith (Rom. 14:23a; cf. 14:14); or really doing anything by faith (Rom. 14:23b). In one instance, Paul considers a possible objection that faith might be the means by which we "overthrow the law" (Rom. 3:31). But in most of these occurrences, Paul is speaking about the causal role of πίστις in his soteriology as a means of justification, inheritance, access, resurrection life, blessing, adoption to sonship, Christ dwelling in our hearts, and salvation itself. In these cases, the category of instrument or means is basically identical to the category of cause. In other words, the majority of these uses refer to the causal role of πίστις in salvation. It is not surprising, then, that over half the uses of Paul's "by faith" idiom occur in Romans 1:1–5:11 and Galatians 2:11–5:12, Paul's most lengthy discussions about justification "by faith," that is, justification "by faith in Christ."

Conclusion

This chapter has argued that the eight ἐκ πίστεως Χριστοῦ phrases in Paul's letters refer to our faith in Christ, reinforcing my larger thesis that Paul significantly emphasizes Christ-oriented faith in his theology. The suggestion that these phrases refer to Christ's own faithfulness is a product of modern exegesis and especially the influential dissertation of Richard Hays. I have evaluated Hays's Christological view of πίστις and observed that it can work only by an unwarranted appeal to ambiguity in Paul's language of πίστις. In contrast, I have shown that one can simply and consistently translate the "by faith" idiom in Paul as a reference to our faith—namely, our faith in the gospel about Jesus Christ or in Christ himself. My work in this chapter suggests that Hays's view of πίστις in Paul is incorrect. And yet I am not questioning his primary thesis that Paul's arguments are rooted in the gospel story and especially the climactic moment of the cross. I am simply questioning whether πίστις refers to that climactic moment. Similarly, I am not questioning the importance of Christology or participation with Christ in Paul's theology. In the next chapter, I address some of these broader theological issues in an attempt to synthesize the role of our faith, God's grace, and Christ's work in Paul's soteriology.

5

Theological Synthesis

Christ-Oriented Faith within Pauline Theology

It is not faith that saves, but faith in Jesus Christ.
. . . It is not, strictly speaking, even faith in Christ
that saves, but Christ that saves through faith.

B. B. WARFIELD, "FAITH"

DOES PAUL TEACH THAT we are justified by our faith in Christ or by Christ's faithfulness? Much of this book has been arguing that Paul, in many different ways, teaches that we are justified by our faith in Christ. But it does not follow from this that he denies that we are justified by Christ himself. In the same paragraph, Paul can say both that "we have been justified by faith" (Rom. 5:1) and that "we have now been justified by [Christ's] blood" (Rom. 5:9). There is a very close relationship between faith and Christ in many places in Paul's letters, as Hays has rightly observed.[1] Paul speaks in the same context about his proclaiming the good news of God's Son (εὐαγγελίζωμαι αὐτὸν, Gal. 1:16) and his proclaiming the good news of the faith (εὐαγγελίζεται τὴν

---

1 For example, "For Paul [in Gal. 3:23–25] the coming of πίστις (vv. 23, 25) is virtually identified with the coming of Christ himself." Richard B. Hays, *The Faith of Jesus Christ: The Narrative Substructure of Galatians 3:1–4:11*, 2nd ed. (Grand Rapids, MI: Eerdmans, 2002), 203.

πίστιν, Gal. 1:23).[2] He says that Christ, the offspring of Abraham, has come (Gal. 3:19) and that the faith itself has come (Gal. 3:23, 25). He calls the gospel message both the "word of faith" (Rom. 10:8) and the "word of Christ" (Rom. 10:17). He tells the Corinthians that they should examine themselves to see if they are "in the faith," that is, if "Jesus Christ is in you" (2 Cor. 13:5).[3] He tells the Galatians that those who have been baptized have "put on Christ" (Gal. 3:27), and he tells the Thessalonians that they have "put on the breastplate of faith and love, and for a helmet the hope of salvation" (1 Thess. 5:8). And as he speaks to the Romans of faith as our common possession ("yours and mine," Rom. 1:12), so he speaks to the Corinthians of Christ as our common possession ("their Lord and ours," 1 Cor. 1:2). But how exactly are faith and Christ related for Paul? In the last chapter, I argued that πίστις refers not to the story of Christ's faithfulness in Paul's letters but rather to our faith. The goal of this chapter is to synthesize how exactly the apostle relates our faith and Christ.

This chapter is organized by four theological categories that Pauline scholars often use in the πίστις Χριστοῦ debate: Christology, anthropology, soteriology, and eschatology. Some might object that these categories squeeze Paul's thinking into modern theological thought. Not only are these categories, however, often used by Pauline scholars, but Paul's faith discourse has a lot to say about Christ, people, salvation, and the end of time. In synthesizing his teaching under these four umbrella categories, I have attempted to explain the theology contained in Paul's letters.[4] I use the apostle's own categories as much as possible and employ modern categories only to illuminate what Paul says. For

---

2   For this observation I am indebted to Karl Friedrich Ulrichs, *Christusglaube: Studien zum Syntagma πίστις Χριστοῦ und zum paulinischen Verständnis von Glaube und Rechtfertigung*, WUNT, 2nd ser., vol. 227 (Tübingen: Mohr Siebeck, 2007), 97.

3   Here I am indebted to Seifrid's observation from 2 Cor. 13:5 that "to be 'in the faith' is to be indwelt by Christ." Mark A. Seifrid, *Christ, Our Righteousness: Paul's Theology of Justification*, NSBT 9 (Downers Grove, IL: InterVarsity Press, 2000), 131.

4   Thus this chapter is an exercise in biblical theology rather than systematic theology.

example, I use the grammatical terms *subject* and *object* because they illuminate what Paul teaches about faith and Christ. My synthesis relies on the exegesis of the previous three chapters, but it also appeals to texts in Paul's letters that have not yet been discussed. Overall, my goal is to reinforce and sharpen the major thesis of the book, that Paul significantly emphasizes Christ-oriented faith in his theology.

Faith and Christology in Paul

Paul's teaching about faith is Christological in the highest sense because our faith is fundamentally oriented toward Jesus Christ, the faithful Son of God. Paul's letters consistently speak about faith as oriented toward Christ.[5] In chapter 2, I observed that Paul speaks explicitly about faith in Christ more often than many scholars recognize.[6] In chapter 3, I discussed several parallels to Christ-oriented faith, such as hoping in Christ (1 Cor. 15:17) and seeing the glory of the Lord (2 Cor. 3:18; 4:4–6). And in chapter 4, I argued that the simplest and most consistent translation of the phrase ἐκ πίστεως Χριστοῦ in Paul's letters is "by faith in Christ." Even though this phrase occurs only eight times in his letters, it is highly significant for understanding Paul's theology of faith because it adds a level of specificity to his more common phrase "by faith," and it typically occurs within important statements about justification (Rom. 3:21–26 [2x]; Gal. 2:15–21 [3x]; Phil. 3:2–11 [1x]). It is striking that Paul does not say "by faith in God" (ἐκ πίστεως θεοῦ) in these passages, even though he surely could have.[7] Instead, he specifies the object of justifying faith as Christ. Thus, in light of Paul's

---

5   One exception to this pattern is Paul's use of πιστεύω to refer to the idea that God has trusted, or "entrusted," Paul and the apostles with the gospel (e.g., Gal. 2:7; cf. 1 Cor. 4:1–5). But this is a very different line of thinking from Paul's normal use of πίστις and πιστεύω.

6   See Rom. 9:33 and 10:11 (quoting Isa. 28:16); Rom. 10:14; Gal. 2:16b; Eph. 1:15–16; Phil. 1:29; Col. 1:3–4; 2:5; 1 Tim. 1:16; 3:16; Philem. 4–5. It is possible that Paul also speaks explicitly about faith in Christ in Rom. 3:25; Gal. 3:26; 1 Tim. 3:13; 2 Tim. 1:12; 3:15.

7   In chap. 4, I argued that the difficult textual variant in Gal. 2:20 (ἐν πίστει . . . τῇ τοῦ θεοῦ καὶ Χριστοῦ) is most likely a scribal mistake (see p. 212). Nevertheless, it demonstrates that a Greek speaker like Paul could have written "by faith in God."

explicit statements, conceptual parallels, and use of ἐκ πίστεως Χριστοῦ, it seems best to say that Paul viewed Christ as the fundamental
object of our faith.

Some scholars think that to speak of Christ as the object of our faith
is to depersonalize or objectify him. G. M. Taylor argues that "a system
of justification simply by faith in Christ . . . (so far as the mechanism of
justification is concerned) leaves Christ in the passive rôle of being
the object of our justifying faith."[8] Benjamin Schliesser warns that
"the language of 'object' or 'content' is deeply inadequate and confus-
ing, since Christ the Lord is pressed into the category of a disposable
neuter."[9] And Teresa Morgan sees the binary approach of subject and
object as a problematic model for studying faith in early Christianity,
specifically the influential Augustinian distinction between the faith
that believes (*fides qua*) and the faith that is believed (*fides quae*). She is
concerned that such an approach seems to present our faith in contractual rather than relational terms and fails to do credit to the idea that
as persons, God the Father and Christ are also acting subjects.[10] But to
speak of Christ as the object of our faith is not meant to depersonalize
him. Paul certainly speaks of Christ as a real person who was an acting subject in our salvation. Actually, it is more complex because Paul
speaks of Christ as both a subject who gave himself up (παραδόντος
ἑαυτὸν, Gal. 2:20) and as an object who was given up by God for us
all (παρεδόθη, Rom. 4:25; cf. 8:32). Arguably, however, one cannot
understand Paul's teaching about faith without positing some kind of
subject-object distinction. Paul never speaks about Christ as the subject
of faith in his letters; rather, he is everywhere spoken of as the object of

8   G. M. Taylor, "The Function of Πιστις Χριστου in Galatians," *JBL* 85, no. 1 (1966): 75. Note
    that Hays quotes this sentence in the beginning of his own argument for the "faithfulness of
    Christ" translation. *Faith of Jesus Christ*, 121.
9   Benjamin Schliesser, *Abraham's Faith in Romans 4: Paul's Concept of Faith in Light of the History of
    Reception of Genesis 15:6*, WUNT, 2nd ser., vol. 224 (Tübingen: Mohr Siebeck, 2007), 263n318.
10 Teresa Morgan, *Roman Faith and Christian Faith: Pistis and Fides in the Early Roman Empire and
    Early Churches* (New York: Oxford University Press, 2015), 28–29.

our faith. Once again, this is not to depersonalize Christ, because Paul presents the object of our faith as a living person. In fact, the apostle speaks about Christ as the object of his own faith in strikingly personal and experiential terms (Gal. 2:18–21; Phil. 3:8–11; 2 Tim. 1:11–12).

Faith in Christ is also faith in certain truths about him that have been and are being proclaimed in the gospel. In fact, one of Paul's most common ways of specifying the object of our faith is to speak about faith in the gospel or the message that he and the other apostles had proclaimed—that is, the kerygma (Rom. 1:1–17; 10:6–13; 1 Cor. 1:18–2:5; 15:1–19; cf. 1 Thess. 1:2–10; 1 Tim. 3:16). This gospel is the message about God's Son (Rom. 1:3), incarnate and descended from David (Rom. 1:3; 10:6), crucified for our sins and buried (1 Cor. 1:23; 15:3), raised from the dead and appearing to Cephas (Peter) and others (Rom. 1:4; 10:7; 1 Cor. 15:4–8), taken up in glory and enthroned in power (Rom. 1:4; 1 Tim. 3:16), and coming from heaven to deliver us from the final judgment (1 Thess. 1:10). If one asks what for Paul is the heart of this gospel, the answer is surely the death and resurrection of Christ. These two elements are highlighted in his most important summary of the apostolic kerygma (1 Cor. 15:3–4). In 1 Corinthians 1:18, he identifies the kerygma with the label "word of the cross." And in other texts, he speaks about our faith as oriented specifically toward the death and resurrection of Christ (Rom. 4:25; 1 Thess. 4:14).[11] Thus, the object of our faith in Paul's theology is rightly described as the gospel proclaimed. To believe *in* Christ for Paul is by definition also to believe *that* Christ—namely, "that Christ died for our sins in

---

11 Timmins, in an insightful review, observes that Bates wrongly shifts the center of the gospel from what God has done in Christ's death and resurrection to what Jesus is doing now in his current reign as King. Will N. Timmins, "A Faith unlike Abraham's: Matthew Bates on Salvation by Allegiance Alone," *JETS* 61, no. 3 (2018): 598–600. Bates argues that "the gospel climaxes with the enthronement of Jesus as the cosmic king." Matthew W. Bates, *Salvation by Allegiance Alone: Rethinking Faith, Works, and the Gospel of Jesus the King* (Grand Rapids, MI: Baker Academic, 2017), 77. But while Paul certainly speaks about Jesus's enthronement as an important part of the gospel (Rom. 1:4), his emphasis is on Christ's death and resurrection.

accordance with the Scriptures, that he was buried, that he was raised on the third day in accordance with the Scriptures" (1 Cor. 15:3–4).

Further, in Paul's letters, to believe in Christ is also to believe in God. Paul describes the pagan Thessalonians' reception of the gospel word as their "faith in God," a turning from idols "to serve the living and true God" and "to wait for his Son from heaven" (1 Thess. 1:6–10). Paul compares the Galatians' faith in what they had heard about Jesus Christ crucified to Abraham's faith in God (Gal. 3:1–6). And he passes imperceptibly in Romans from speaking about our faith in Jesus (Rom. 3:22, 26) to speaking about Abraham's faith in the God who raises the dead (Rom. 4:17) and our faith in this same God (Rom. 4:24). Why is Christ-oriented faith at the same time oriented toward God in Paul's letters? There seem to be two interrelated reasons, which are bound up with the gospel. First, in the gospel Abraham's God has now been identified as the one who raised Jesus our Lord from the dead (Rom. 4:24; cf. 2 Cor. 4:13–14; 1 Thess. 1:10). To believe that Jesus was raised from the dead is to believe that Abraham's God raised him from the dead and thus to believe in the living and true God (1 Thess. 1:9). Second, in the gospel the resurrected Christ is himself proclaimed as Israel's "Lord" (2 Cor. 4:5), partaking in the very identity of Israel's God (cf. 1 Cor. 8:4–6). To believe that God has raised Christ from the dead is to confess that Jesus is the risen Lord (Rom. 10:9) and to call on the name of the Lord in worship and prayer (Rom. 10:13).[12] Here we see

---

12 See "Calling on the Name of the Lord" in chap. 3, p. 167. Cf. Hurtado: "In Paul's inherited religious vocabulary the term *Kyrios* ['Lord'] could serve to designate God, and functioned as a Greek substitute for God's name." Larry W. Hurtado, *Lord Jesus Christ: Devotion to Jesus in Earliest Christianity* (Grand Rapids, MI: Eerdmans, 2003), 112. Perhaps "Son of God" implies Jesus's divinity for Paul as well since the apostle uses this title to refer to God sending the preexistent Son into the world for our justification and redemption (Rom. 8:3; Gal. 4:4). But Hurtado observes that "Jesus' status as God's 'Son' does not particularly function in Paul's epistles to indicate Jesus' own divinity (for which *Kyrios* much more clearly serves . . .). Ironically it is even possible that Paul's desire to avoid among his converts the sort of misunderstanding of Jesus' sonship that Bultmann fell into, likening him to divine heroes and demigods, may help account for the infrequency of Paul's references to Jesus as God's 'Son'" [17x]. Hurtado, 107.

the complexity and mystery in Paul's teaching about Christ, the Son of God, as the object of our faith.[13] For Paul, Israel's Christ is also "God over all, blessed forever" (Rom. 9:5).[14] Thus, faith in Christ is not at odds with faith in God in Paul's theology. Those with Christ-oriented faith confess both that Abraham's God has raised Christ from the dead and that Christ himself is Israel's Lord.[15]

The faithfulness of Jesus Christ in Pauline theology is a function of his identity with God rather than his participation with us. There has been much confusion on this point because of the πίστις Χριστοῦ debate and because the only explicit references to Jesus's faithfulness are in Paul's disputed letters (2 Thess. 3:3; 2 Tim. 2:13). Pauline scholars who hold to the "faithfulness of Christ" translation often say that we participate in Christ's faith or faithfulness. But while Paul clearly says, for example, that we participate in Christ's death and resurrection (Rom. 6:4), he never explicitly says that we participate in his faith or faithfulness. Instead, this idea is read out of the subjective-genitive translation of Paul's eight ἐκ πίστεως Χριστοῦ phrases and the related (but unlikely) messianic interpretations of Paul's Old Testament citations in Romans 1:17 (Hab. 2:4) and 2 Corinthians 4:13 (Ps. 116:10). So much is read out of (or into?) these eight phrases and the word πίστις in Paul, and there is a corresponding lack of clarity and disagreement

---

13 We also see how Christ-oriented faith in Paul goes beyond other biblical statements about faith in God's messengers like Moses (Ex. 14:31) or Philip (Acts 8:12).

14 Paul very rarely calls Jesus "God" (θεός) (only Rom. 9:5 and Titus 2:13). Some scholars question whether Paul does so in Rom. 9:5, but see Carraway's argument that Paul does so here "because of the need for Israel to join the Gentiles in confessing the [divine] identity of Christ." George Carraway, *Christ Is God over All: Romans 9:5 in the Context of Romans 9–11*, LNTS 489 (New York: Bloomsbury, 2013), 185.

15 Thus, in Paul's view, our faith is not of a fundamentally different type or even content than that of Abraham, who also believed in the God who justifies the ungodly and raises the dead (Rom. 4:5, 17). Yeung observes in the conclusion of her important study that "it is the failure to appreciate the theocentric nature of faith in Jesus and Paul that results in the dichotomy between Jesus' 'miracle-faith' and Paul's 'salvation-faith.'" Maureen W. Yeung, *Faith in Jesus and Paul: A Comparison with Special Reference to "Faith That Can Remove Mountains" and "Your Faith Has Healed/Saved You,"* WUNT, 2nd ser., vol. 147 (Tübingen: Mohr Siebeck, 2002), 294.

about what the "faithfulness of Christ" even means in Paul's theology. The standard view, following Hays, is that the "faithfulness of Christ" refers to Christ's self-sacrificial death, which was "*simultaneously* an act of human fidelity to God and an act of divine fidelity to humanity."[16] Thus, Christ's faithfulness means both his human faithfulness to (and faith in) God and his divine faithfulness to us in going to the cross. Moreover, as I observed in chapter 4, Hays often appeals to ambiguity and suggests that πίστις refers to our faith (and faithfulness) as well, as we participate in Christ's faith(fulness).[17] A recent book by David Downs and Benjamin Lappenga now challenges the standard view and argues that πίστις Χριστοῦ refers not only to Christ's faithfulness in death but primarily to his ongoing faithfulness *to us* as the *risen* Christ.[18] Downs and Lappenga are to be commended for focusing on Jesus's resurrection in Paul's theology and for considering the apostle's explicit references to Christ's faithfulness, even though they are in his disputed letters. But it seems to me that their overall project further muddies the waters of Pauline theology by reading *even more* out of Paul's ἐκ πίστεως Χριστοῦ phrases.[19] One walks away from this view with the idea that the faithfulness of Christ is a very important theme in Paul's theology but without a clear understanding of what exactly that means.

When we understand the eight phrases, however, as references to Christ as the object of our faith, Paul's explicit statements about Christ's faithfulness become clearer. Paul often speaks about God's faithfulness in his letters to assure his readers that the object of their faith is secure because God will be true to his word. An interesting example is Paul's two uses of Psalm 116: both declare the apostle's confidence in God and

---

16 Hays, *Faith of Jesus Christ*, xxxi; emphasis original.

17 See chap. 4, p. 221.

18 David J. Downs and Benjamin J. Lappenga, *The Faithfulness of the Risen Christ: Pistis and the Exalted Lord in the Pauline Letters* (Waco, TX: Baylor University Press, 2019).

19 As someone who holds to the "faith in Christ" translation, it is difficult to evaluate their argument since they purposely assume the "faithfulness of Christ" translation without arguing for it. In other words, their book is more of an "in-house" discussion among "faithfulness of Christ" advocates.

his word, but one does so from the perspective of Paul as the subject who believes ("We also believe, and so we also speak," 2 Cor. 4:13, quoting Ps. 116:10), and the other does so from the perspective of God as the object who is true and trustworthy ("Let God be true though every one were a liar," Rom. 3:4, alluding to Ps. 116:11). Here Paul says that God will be faithful to the oracles he has revealed in Scripture even though some of the Jewish people have been unfaithful to him (Rom. 3:2–4). That is, he and his word are worthy objects of our faith.

Paul particularly assures his converts that God will be faithful to continue his saving work in them until the day of Christ:

> God is faithful [πιστός], and he will not let you be tempted beyond your ability. (1 Cor. 10:13)

> Now may the God of peace himself sanctify you completely, and may your whole spirit and soul and body be kept blameless at the coming of our Lord Jesus Christ. He who calls you is faithful [πιστός]; he will surely do it. (1 Thess. 5:23–24)

> . . . who will sustain you to the end, guiltless in the day of our Lord Jesus Christ. God is faithful [πιστός], by whom you were called into the fellowship of his Son, Jesus Christ our Lord. (1 Cor. 1:8–9)

This last text is interesting because it is unclear in context whether the "who" (ὅς) doing the sustaining refers to God or to Christ.[20] Does the faithfulness of God underwrite the guarantee that *God* will sustain the Corinthian believers to the end or that *Christ* will sustain the Corinthian believers to the end? Whichever antecedent is correct, it is clear that Paul closely associates the faithfulness of God with the

---

20 Note a similar problem in 2 Tim. 1:12, where it is unclear whether the one in "whom" (ᾧ) Paul has believed is God or Christ.

trustworthiness of the gospel of his Son: "As surely as God is faithful, our word to you has not been Yes and No. For the Son of God, Jesus Christ, whom we proclaimed among you, Silvanus and Timothy and I, was not Yes and No, but in him it is always Yes. For all the promises of God find their Yes in him" (2 Cor. 1:18–20a). Here the Son of God confirms the faithfulness of God because in the gospel he has made good on the promises that God had previously made in Scripture (cf. Rom. 1:2; 15:8). Thus in the gospel the Son joins God as the sure object of our faith. In fact, the gospel of Christ is a more sure object of our faith than the ancient promises of God because the gospel proclaims that God's promises have been fulfilled: "That is why it is through him [Christ] that we utter our Amen to God for his glory" (2 Cor. 1:20b).

It should not be surprising, then, to see Paul speak very similarly about the faithfulness of Christ in keeping believers to the end, as he does twice in his disputed letters. He assures the Thessalonian believers, who are living in the midst of unbelievers (2 Thess. 3:2), that "the Lord is faithful" and thus will "establish you and guard you against the evil one" (2 Thess. 3:3).[21] And he reminds Timothy of the faithfulness both of the word or saying about Christ and of Christ himself:

The saying is trustworthy [πιστὸς]:[22]

> If we have died with him, we will also live with him;
> if we endure, we will also reign with him;
> if we deny him, he also will deny us;
> if we are faithless, he remains faithful [πιστὸς]—

for he cannot deny himself. (2 Tim. 2:11–13)

---

21 Downs and Lappenga rightly observe that here "the faithfulness of God is attributed to the Lord Jesus Christ." *Faithfulness of the Risen Christ*, 37.

22 The ESV adds the word "for" to the Greek text of 2 Tim. 2:11, which I have removed here.

Although this saying warns that Jesus Christ will deny those who deny him (cf. Mark 8:38), it also encourages Timothy that Christ cannot deny himself. It is in his very nature to remain immutably faithful in salvation, even if we are faithless (cf. Rom. 3:3–4).[23] Thus, Christ is the worthy object of our faith. Just as Paul reminds readers of God's faithfulness in order to assure them that the object of their faith is trustworthy, so he does with Christ. In other words, in Paul's theology, it is not that we participate in Jesus's faithfulness (cf. 2 Tim. 2:13) but that he participates in the very faithfulness of God.[24]

Finally, to understand Paul's teaching about faith, we need to observe that Christ, the object of our faith, is God's gift of grace to us. The grace of God is so central in Paul's letters. And it finds its greatest expression in the gift of his own Son, so much so that now that he has been given to us, we can expect God to give us all things: "He who did not spare his own Son but gave him up for us all, how will he not also with him graciously give us all things?" (Rom. 8:32). Moreover, Christ also gave *himself* for us and for our sins (Gal. 1:4; 2:20).[25] To be severed from Christ, then, is to fall from grace (Gal. 5:4; cf. 2:21). For Paul, the reason our faith is "according to grace" (Rom. 4:4–5, 16, my trans.) is because the object of our faith is the God of grace who "justifies the ungodly" (Rom. 4:5) through the death and resurrection of Jesus our Lord (Rom. 4:25).[26] Surely, then, it is wrong to label the

---

23   It seems more likely that "he remains faithful" is a promise to save the unfaithful (like Peter) rather than a warning that "he remains faithful" to judge the unfaithful (like Judas), because the previous line has already warned about apostasy. So most commentators, according to William D. Mounce, *Pastoral Epistles*, WBC 47A (Nashville: Thomas Nelson, 2000), 518.

24   This is not to question the importance of our participation with Christ in Paul's theology but rather to question the specific idea that we participate *in his faith or faithfulness*. Theologically, of course, we could suggest that participation with Christ in the new life of the resurrection is a kind of participation in his faithfulness. But Paul never says anything like this.

25   I am indebted to Barclay for the observation that in Gal. 2:20, Paul adapts the opening phrase of Gal. 1:4, which was perhaps taken from early Christian tradition. John M. G. Barclay, *Paul and the Gift* (Grand Rapids, MI: Eerdmans, 2015), 331.

26   Ridderbos penetratingly observes that faith is so closely associated with grace in Paul because of the *redemptive-historical* reality of Christ (i.e., the object) rather than a *psychological* experience

"faith in Christ" view of πίστις Χριστοῦ as *anthropocentric*, because the whole point of Paul's construction is that our faith orients us toward the grace of God given to us in Christ. Christ-oriented faith is Christological in the highest sense.[27]

Faith and Anthropology in Paul

In Paul's letters, faith is human belief or trust in the gospel proclaimed by the apostles. Paul often describes his readers as those who possess faith with the words "your faith" (ἡ πίστις ὑμῶν).[28] An interesting variation of this description refers to the faith dwelling "in" (ἐν) believers.[29] And in at least two places, Paul speaks of "my faith" (Rom. 1:12; 2 Tim. 3:10).[30] This faith dwelling in Paul and his readers begins with and corresponds to the preaching of the gospel. Michael Wolter rightly observes that "in Paul everything begins with the proclamation of the gospel" and that "faith is that which the proclaimer of the gospel hopes to achieve on the part of his hearers: that they concur with his message and adhere to it."[31] The goal of Paul's own apostolic calling was "to bring about the obedience of faith for the sake of [Christ's] name among all the nations" (Rom. 1:5; cf. 10:14–15). We see a concrete example of this goal accomplished in one of his earliest letters, written soon after

---

(i.e., the subject). Herman Ridderbos, *Paul: An Outline of His Theology*, trans. John Richard de Witt (Grand Rapids, MI: Eerdmans, 1975), 173–74.

27 Cf. Seifrid: "The necessity of faith does not in the least diminish the centrality of Christ in salvation. It signals just the opposite." *Christ, Our Righteousness*, 135.

28 The following texts have these exact words, although the word order varies: Rom. 1:8, 12; 1 Cor. 2:5; 15:14, 17; 2 Cor. 1:24; 10:15; Phil. 2:17; Col. 1:4; 2:5; 1 Thess. 1:8; 3:2, 5, 6, 7, 10; 2 Thess. 1:3. In Philem. 6, we see the singular "your faith [τῆς πίστεώς σου]" (cf. σου . . . τὴν πίστιν in Philem. 5). In Eph. 1:15, we see the variation "your faith [τὴν καθ᾽ ὑμᾶς πίστιν]."

29 In Rom. 1:12, Paul speaks of being "mutually encouraged by the faith, which is [dwelling] in one another [τῆς ἐν ἀλλήλοις πίστεως, my trans.]." And in 2 Tim. 1:5, he says, "I am reminded of your sincere faith [τῆς ἐν σοὶ ἀνυποκρίτου πίστεως], a faith that dwelt first in [ἐν] your grandmother Lois and your mother Eunice and now, I am sure, dwells in you [ἐν σοί] as well."

30 Note also the textual variant in 1 Cor. 15:14, which says "our faith [ἡ πίστις ἡμῶν]" (in manuscripts B, D, and 1739).

31 Michael Wolter, *Paul: An Outline of His Theology*, trans. Robert L. Brawley (Waco, TX: Baylor University Press, 2015), 4.

the Thessalonians had heard Paul preach the gospel and had believed: "And we also thank God constantly for this, that when you received the word of God, which you heard from us, you accepted it not as the word of men but as what it really is, the word of God, which is at work in you believers" (1 Thess. 2:13; cf. 1:4–10). The Corinthians, too, had come to believe through the preaching of Paul and Apollos (1 Cor. 3:5). Paul sums it up to them in this way: "So we preach and so you believed" (1 Cor. 15:11). Thus, in Paul's letters, people are the subjects or agents of faith who believe in the proclaimed gospel.[32]

This means that *faith* for Paul is best defined and understood in light of its orientation toward the gospel. Therefore, the English words *belief* and *trust* best describe this concept in Paul, although the apostle makes no clear distinction between the concepts of belief and trust.[33] On the one hand, faith is rightly described as *belief* because it is a reception of the gospel or an assent to the gospel "as it truly [ἀληθῶς] is, the word of God" (1 Thess. 2:13, my trans.). Faith believes the gospel to be true— that Christ has truly died for our sins, and that God has truly raised him from the dead (and that we have died and will be raised with him, Rom. 6:1–11).[34] Paul speaks of "faith" as "knowing" (εἰδότες) certain things to be true (2 Cor. 4:13–14; 5:6–7).[35] Even when he speaks of faith as "obedience" or submission to the gospel, he describes it in terms of the "*knowledge* of God" and the submission of "every *thought*" to

---

32 Paul observes that even Abraham's faith in Gen. 15:6 began with the prior word of God in Gen. 15:5 (cf. Rom. 4:18). For this observation I am indebted to Roy A. Harrisville III, *The Faith of St. Paul: Transformative Gift of Divine Power* (Eugene, OR: Pickwick, 2019), 62.

33 Cf. the definitions of πιστεύω offered by the standard lexicon: "to consider someth[ing] to be true and therefore worthy of one's trust, *believe*" (BDAG, use 1); "to entrust oneself to an entity in complete confidence, *believe (in), trust*" (BDAG, use 2).

34 Note how Paul talks about the gospel as "the truth of the gospel" (Gal. 2:5) or "the word of truth" (Eph. 1:13). Cf. 2 Thess. 2:13: "God chose you as the firstfruits to be saved, through sanctification by the Spirit and belief in the truth [πίστει ἀληθείας]."

35 Cf. "those who believe and know the truth" (1 Tim. 4:3). Pifer's study of faith in Paul's letters concludes that "at a foundational level, *faith is knowledge.*" Jeanette Hagen Pifer, *Faith as Participation*, WUNT, 2nd ser., vol. 486 (Tübingen: Mohr Siebeck, 2019), 217.

Christ (2 Cor. 10:5). On the other hand, faith is also rightly described as *trust* in Paul, because it is confidence in the gospel, even in the midst of contradicting circumstances.[36] We see such confidence in the faith of Abraham, whom Paul presents as the fatherly example in whose footsteps believers now walk (Rom. 4:12). Even though it was physically impossible for the promise to be fulfilled, he became "fully convinced that God was able to do what he had promised" (Rom. 4:21). We also see this confidence in Paul's own reliance on the God who raises the dead to deliver him from his deepest afflictions (2 Cor. 1:9–10). Similarly, the Thessalonians' faith is described as "waiting" for God's Son to come and deliver them from the final judgment (1 Thess. 1:10). To summarize, in Paul faith is best described as belief that the gospel is the true word of God and trust that God will do what he has promised in the gospel. As such, faith is an internal function of the human mind and heart that we then express externally in worship and prayer as we confess the gospel with our lips (Rom. 10:9).[37]

Conversely, in Paul faith is wrongly defined with an orientation toward the self. This is where Rudolf Bultmann's profound reading of Paul falters. He severs the link between the true, saving events of the gospel and the present proclamation of the gospel, arguing that "*the*

---

36 Thus, I think the Reformers were fundamentally right in passionately rejecting the scholastic distinction between an unformed faith (intellectual assent) and a faith formed by love. I say this because in Paul faith is never merely intellectual assent but always includes trust, or "confidence and assurance of heart." John Calvin, *Institutes of the Christian Religion*, ed. John T. McNeill, trans. Ford Lewis Battles (Louisville: Westminster, 1960), 3.2.33. On the scholastic distinction, see Aquinas, *Summa Theologica*, 2a2ae.4.3–4. On the Protestant response, see *Luther's Works*, ed. Jaroslav Pelikan (St. Louis, MO: Concordia, 1963), 26:160–61, 167, 208, 269–70, 273; 27:28–29; Calvin, *Institutes*, 3.2.8–10, 33.

37 Thus, I find Augustine's distinction between "the faith that believes" (*fides qua*) and "the faith that is believed" (*fides quae*) to be a helpful distinction for understanding how Paul relates our faith to the gospel. Morgan argues that Augustine's focus on the interiority of faith misses the more prominent emphasis on the relational aspects of faith, which are of more interest in the ancient sources. *Roman Faith and Christian Faith*, 503. She also acknowledges, however, that in these sources (including Paul), faith "has a substantial and at times complex interiority to match its relational and active aspects." Morgan, 472.

salvation-occurrence is nowhere present except in the proclaiming, accosting, demanding, and promising word of preaching."[38] He then argues that the present proclamation of the gospel demands not only the "acknowledgment of the crucified Jesus as Lord" but also "the surrender of [the individual's] previous understanding of himself."[39] Finally, he radicalizes Paul's language about faith as obedience and defines faith fundamentally as a human decision, "the free deed [or act] of obedience in which the new self constitutes itself in place of the old."[40] Bultmann sought to avoid the errors of turning faith into a work and of orienting faith toward self rather than the kerygma, which is the object of our faith.[41] But his separation of the kerygma from the history of Christ and his definition of faith as a decision and as "a new understanding of one's self"[42] focuses our faith acutely on our own action. In contrast, Paul's teaching about faith is acutely focused on the truth about Christ. It is true that Paul closely associates faith with the knowledge that no one will be justified by works (Gal. 2:16a) and the abandonment of "confidence in the flesh" (Phil. 3:3) and reliance on the self (2 Cor. 1:9). But this kind of self-negation is probably better described as a *reason* for Christ-oriented faith rather than as part of the definition of faith.[43] The discovery of the sinful self for Paul is a function not of faith but of the law (Rom. 3:20; 7:7). In one text Paul does include self as part of the object of our faith: "We believe that we will also live with him"

---

38 Rudolf Bultmann, *Theology of the New Testament*, trans. Kendrick Grobel (New York: Scribner, 1951), 1:302; emphasis original.

39 Bultmann, *Theology*, 1:315.

40 Bultmann, *Theology*, 1:316.

41 Bultmann, *Theology*, 1:315, 319. See the introduction, p. 30n25.

42 Bultmann, *Theology*, 1:318.

43 I am in substantial agreement with Pifer's careful exegetical and theological work, although I am not sure that she is correct to *define* faith in Paul as "self-negating." *Faith as Participation*, 219. Note the logic of Gal. 2:16: "We know that a person is not justified by works of the law but through faith in Jesus Christ, *so* we also have believed in Christ Jesus" (the word *so* is an interpretive translation showing how "we know" [εἰδότες] is an adverbial participle of cause). Here self-negation seems to be the *reason* Paul has come to believe in Christ.

(Rom. 6:8). But even this statement is really an expression of our faith in God and his promise in the gospel to raise us from the dead with Jesus (cf. 2 Cor. 4:14; 1 Thess. 4:14).

In a very different way, some recent scholars have, in my view, wrongly defined faith with an orientation toward the self. I am thinking of those who now argue that we should translate πίστις in Paul's letters as "faithfulness" much more often and therefore conceive of faith in Paul's theology not only as our faith in Christ but also as our faithfulness or loyalty to him.[44] This view consciously downplays the Pauline contrast of faith and works and suggests that our works are a part of our faith.[45] In so doing, it subtly shifts the orientation of our faith toward our works of loyalty rather than toward Christ and his death and resurrection.[46] But Paul so clearly opposes the worker who earns a wage with the believer "who does not work but believes in him who justifies the ungodly" (Rom. 4:4–5). Here we see as well that the object of our faith according to Paul includes the idea that the God of grace justifies the ungodly.[47] Paul goes on to describe this as the blessing of God counting righteousness "apart from works" (Rom. 4:6). Thus, to include works as a part of the definition of our faith seems to run the risk that Paul warns the Galatians of—namely, the risk of nullifying the object of our faith: "I do not nullify the grace of God, for if righteousness were through the law, then Christ died for no purpose" (Gal. 2:21).[48] Moreover, as I have argued throughout the book, πίστις does not actually mean "faithfulness" in the contexts

---

44 Bates, *Allegiance Alone*, 77–100; Nijay K. Gupta, *Paul and the Language of Faith* (Grand Rapids, MI: Eerdmans, 2020), 178.

45 Bates, *Allegiance Alone*, 109; Gupta, *Paul and the Language of Faith*, 183–85. Gupta is more nuanced than Bates in that he views our faithfulness/loyalty as "preobedience" rather than explicitly defining faith as including works.

46 As I note above, Bates has wrongly shifted the emphasis of the gospel away from Christ's accomplished death and resurrection to his current reign as King (see above, p. 243n11).

47 Recall that for Paul believing *in* God is the same as believing *that* God.

48 I am not arguing that the grace of which Paul speaks is a pure gift that demands no response (see Bates, *Allegiance Alone*, 104). This is the teaching of the free-grace movement, which seems to

suggested by these scholars. Rather, it means belief and trust in the gospel.[49]

Wolter observes that "as consent to the gospel, faith therefore first marks conversion and then functions as an abiding characteristic of the Christian life. Accordingly, speaking of faith also forms the most stable theological constant that is found in the Pauline letters."[50] Paul uses a textbook definition of conversion to describe the faith of the Thessalonians: "You turned to God from idols" (1 Thess. 1:9). And he sometimes uses the aorist of πιστεύω in an ingressive sense to speak of the time when he or Peter or the Corinthians had first come to believe in Christ and the gospel (1 Cor. 3:5; 15:2; Gal. 2:16b; cf. Rom. 13:11). But Paul was also very concerned that the initial faith of his converts would endure and grow, especially in the face of opposition and affliction (Phil. 1:27–30; 1 Thess. 3:1–10).[51] He labored for the Philippians' "progress and joy in the faith" (Phil. 1:25; cf. 2 Cor. 1:24), and he urged them to "stand firm . . . in the Lord" (Phil. 4:1; cf. 1 Thess. 3:8).[52] He speaks of the final goal of all ministry as an attainment of the "unity of the faith and of the knowledge of the Son of God" (Eph. 4:13). Nevertheless, he also recognizes that God has assigned different measures of faith (Rom. 12:3; cf. 12:6) so that some are "weak in faith" (Rom. 14:1) and others are strong in faith (Rom. 15:1). This is probably

---

be the real foil and concern of Bates's thesis and which he unfortunately fails to distinguish from classic Protestant or evangelical teaching. See Timmins, "Faith unlike Abraham's," 607–8.

49 This is not to say that πίστις *never* means "faithfulness" in Paul. It occasionally means "faithfulness"; for example, in describing the "faithfulness of God" (Rom. 3:3) or in describing "faithfulness," or intercommunity trust, as a fruit of the Spirit (Gal. 5:22). But this is a rare meaning of the word in Paul's letters.

50 Wolter, *Paul*, 4.

51 Cf. Stuhlmacher: "When believers confess Christ as their Lord and lead their new life in freedom, they must be prepared for hostility and persecution. *Faith for Paul is always a threatened faith.*" Peter Stuhlmacher, *Biblical Theology of the New Testament*, trans. and ed. Daniel P. Bailey (Grand Rapids, MI: Eerdmans, 2018), 380; emphasis original.

52 Paul speaks of the same reality as standing in "the faith" (1 Cor. 16:13; 2 Cor. 1:24), standing in the gospel (1 Cor. 15:1), standing in grace (Rom. 5:2), or even just standing: "For freedom Christ has set us free; stand firm therefore, and do not submit again to a yoke of slavery" (Gal. 5:1).

how he thought of the Spirit's discriminate gift of faith (1 Cor. 12:9). Some Christians might have such strong and complete faith that it can move mountains, although Paul warns that this is nothing without love (1 Cor. 13:2).[53] Faith, after all, works through love (Gal. 5:6), and love for neighbor fulfills the law (Rom. 13:10; cf. Gal. 5:14).[54] Thus, faith in Christ and love for the saints are tightly bound together for Paul as things for which he is thankful as he prays for his converts from prison (Eph. 1:15–16; Col. 1:3–4; Philem. 4–7).

Nevertheless, it is striking that Paul designates his converts not as "lovers" but as "believers."[55] Christ-oriented faith marks out the fundamental identity of his converts. Paul occasionally uses the designation "those who belong to Christ [οἱ τοῦ Χριστοῦ]" (1 Cor. 15:23; Gal. 5:24).[56] But more frequent is his use of "those who believe [οἱ πιστεύοντες]" (1 Cor. 1:21; 14:22; 1 Thess. 1:7; 2:10, 13; cf. Rom. 3:22; 4:11; Gal. 3:22).[57] His typical use of the present-tense participle in these designations shows that he is thinking not merely about coming to faith but about the ongoing faith that is at work in his converts' lives (cf. 1 Thess. 2:13).[58] And his typical use of the plural in these

---

53 So Gordon D. Fee, *The First Epistle to the Corinthians*, rev. ed., NICNT (Grand Rapids, MI: Eerdmans, 2014), 658. Fee observes that some see an example of such faith in Elijah when he stood off with the prophets of Baal (1 Kings 18). Fee, 658n128.

54 Note that it seems unhelpful to speak of faith with the theological terms *passive* or *active* since faith both passively receives and waits for Christ and also actively works through love. Cf. Pifer, who speaks about the "active passivity" of faith, although in a slightly different sense; e.g., *Faith as Participation*, 76, 205.

55 Nor does he identify them as "those who are baptized," as Wolter observes. *Paul*, 144, 254. Note that Paul does speak once of "all who love our Lord Jesus Christ" (Eph. 6:24). But this designation is referring to our love for the Lord, not our love for the saints, which is the typical way Paul speaks about our love.

56 Cf. "those who are in Christ Jesus [τοῖς ἐν Χριστῷ Ἰησοῦ]" (Rom. 8:1).

57 Cf. also "those of faith [οἱ ἐκ πίστεως]" in Gal. 3:7 and 9. Paul also uses πιστός as both a substantive and an adjective to describe believers (2 Cor. 6:15; Gal. 3:9; 1 Tim. 4:12; 5:16; 6:2). Perhaps, then, contra most English translations, we should translate the word πιστοῖς in Eph. 1:1 and Col. 1:2 as "believers" rather than "faithful," since these are statements of Christian identity.

58 But note also his use of the aorist participle to describe "all who have believed [πᾶσιν τοῖς πιστεύσασιν]" (2 Thess. 1:10) and those "who did not believe [οἱ μὴ πιστεύσαντες]" (2 Thess. 2:12).

designations shows that he is thinking not only of faith as a possession of individuals but of faith as the common possession of a community and even a family.[59] Believers are "members of the household of faith" (Gal. 6:10, my trans.). Paul views this family as spanning geographic distance, writing to the Romans from Corinth about faith as their common possession: "both yours and mine" (Rom. 1:12).[60] He also views it as spanning the generations, since the Abrahamic promise is given "to the one who shares the faith of Abraham, who is the father of us all" (Rom. 4:16). And in a letter that was probably sent to a number of different churches in the province of Asia, he famously says that there is only "one faith" (Eph. 4:5).[61] Faith also marks the dividing line between those who are inside the family and those who are outside it. In his letters to the Corinthians, Paul uses the opposite designation "unbeliever(s)" to describe those outside.[62] Wolter perceptively observes that "it is not that they believe something else; they do not believe at all."[63] This shows that the designation "believer" for Paul means specifically "believer in the truth of the gospel."[64] Unbelievers believe what is false, but they do not believe in the truth (2 Thess. 2:11–12). Thus, for Paul, they are not really believers at all, because genuine faith is always oriented toward Christ.

Finally, building on my previous section, it is important to observe that just as Paul speaks of Christ as the gift of God, so he occasionally speaks of even our faith as a part of the divine gift of salvation (Eph.

---

59 Paul, though, is also concerned with the individual. This can be seen in his use of the singular participle (ὁ πιστεύων, Rom. 1:16; 9:33; 10:4, 11).

60 Cf. "my true child in a common faith" (Titus 1:4).

61 It is best to take πίστις in Rom. 1:12; 4:16; Eph. 4:5; and Titus 1:4 to mean "body of faith." Faith is "one" in terms of its common object and "many" in terms of its human subjects. See Aquinas, *Summa Theologica*, 2a2ae.4.6; cf. Augustine, *The Trinity*, 13.2.5.

62 Paul uses the plural ἄπιστοι (1 Cor. 6:6; 10:27; 14:22–23; 2 Cor. 4:4; 6:14) and the singular ἄπιστος as both a noun (1 Cor. 7:15; 14:22; 2 Cor. 6:15; 1 Tim. 5:8) and an adjective (1 Cor. 7:12–14).

63 Wolter, *Paul*, 82n47. This entire paragraph is deeply indebted to Wolter, 253–54.

64 Here my understanding seems slightly different from Wolter. *Paul*, 254.

2:8; Phil. 1:29). God has caused his new-creation light to shine into our hearts, and it is by this light that we now see the glory of the Lord (2 Cor. 4:6). Paul often thanks God for the faith of his readers, which assumes divine agency behind their faith (Rom. 1:8; Eph. 1:15–16; Col. 1:3–5; 1 Thess. 1:2–3; 2 Thess. 1:3; Philem. 4–5; cf. also Rom. 6:17; 2 Cor. 9:13).[65] And he associates our faith closely with the divine gift of the Spirit, although interpreters struggle to discern the relationship between the Spirit and faith in Paul's letters. He reminds the Galatians that they received the Spirit by faith (Gal. 3:2, 5, 14); that is, faith results in the reception of the Spirit (cf. Eph. 1:13). But he tells the Corinthians that "no one can say 'Jesus is Lord' except in the Holy Spirit" (1 Cor. 12:3)—that is, the Spirit results in the confession of our faith.[66] Perhaps, then, Paul understands the Spirit to be the enabler of our faith, but he also has seen his converts' faith result in the Spirit's miraculous works of confirmation, such as their speaking in tongues (Gal. 3:5).[67] Paul certainly does not emphasize the efficacy of the Spirit in our faith as much as later theologians like John Calvin.[68] But my point is simply to observe that *the apostle does not oppose divine and human agency when it comes to our faith, as his modern interpreters often do.*[69] Hays's concern about turning faith into a meritorious work

---

65 Paul even sees divine agency behind unbelief (e.g., Rom. 9:32–33).

66 Pifer makes the interesting observation that Gal. 4:6—"God has sent the Spirit of his Son into our hearts, crying, 'Abba! Father!'"—also speaks about the Spirit enabling the articulation of our faith. *Faith as Participation*, 182.

67 Another approach is Seifrid's suggestion that Paul purposely does not say that the Spirit works faith because "for Paul, the Spirit does not transform the old, fallen person that we are" but rather "constitutes the entrance of the new creation, the presence of Christ." *Christ, Our Righteousness*, 132–33. Or Pifer suggests that "rather than a sequential process, Paul presents a sort of reciprocal relationship between faith and the Spirit." *Faith as Participation*, 182.

68 Calvin begins book 3 of his *Institutes* with a discussion of the Spirit and then a discussion of faith, observing that "faith is the principal work of the Holy Spirit" (3.1.4). One of the conclusions of Barclay's important study of grace in Paul is that "*efficacy* is given less attention [in Paul] than the Augustinian tradition might suggest." *Paul and the Gift*, 569.

69 Allen rightly observes that "scholars working within Pauline studies have a difficult time making coherent sense of the relationship between divine and human action." R. Michael Allen, *Justification and the Gospel: Understanding the Contexts and Controversies* (Grand Rapids, MI: Baker Academic, 2013), 102.

is more of a critique of Bultmann than of Paul (or of Martin Luther for that matter).[70] Bultmann rejected the idea that faith could be a gift in order to preserve his understanding of faith as an act of genuine obedience and human decision.[71] With this view of faith, perhaps we could say that faith is a kind of work. But not with Paul's view of faith. For Paul, our belief and trust in Christ is a part of the gift of salvation given to us by God. Christ-oriented faith is anthropological in that it involves human agency, but it is at the same time theological in that it involves divine agency.

Faith and Soteriology in Paul

Christ-oriented faith is a proximate cause of salvation in Pauline theology. In the introduction I attempted to articulate the theological argument of the "faithfulness of Christ" view: Paul teaches not that we are justified by our own faith in Christ but that we are justified by Christ's faith or faithfulness. In chapter 1, however, I observed that Paul's teaching about faith alludes to several texts that speak about our faith as a cause of righteousness (e.g., Gen. 15:6) or condition of salvation (e.g., Isa. 28:16). And in chapter 2, I argued that Paul himself also talks about our faith, specifically our faith in Christ, as a cause of justification (e.g., Gal. 2:16b) and as a condition of salvation (e.g., Rom. 10:9). It is important to observe that all these references are *outside the eight debated ἐκ πίστεως Χριστοῦ phrases* and thus are not a part of the πίστις Χριστοῦ debate in the proper sense. In other words, the theological argument of the "faithfulness of Christ" view can be shown to be a wrong view of Paul's theology no matter how we translate these phrases. Paul clearly teaches that we are justified by our faith in Christ.

---

70 Hays himself notes that his criticism is not really of Luther's own theology but of "the post-Kantian interpretation of it which has been popularized by Bultmann and his followers." *Faith of Jesus Christ*, 120n3.

71 Bultmann, *Theology*, 1:329–30. Faith is only "God-wrought to the extent that prevenient grace first made the human decision possible." Bultmann, 1:330.

In chapter 4, I entered the πίστις Χριστοῦ debate proper and argued that Paul typically uses the phrase "by faith" (including the eight ἐκ πίστεως Χριστοῦ phrases) to present our faith as a means or cause of salvation. Throughout these discussions, however, I attempted to show that Paul *also* presents Christ himself as a cause of our salvation. The goal of this section is to explain how Paul conceives of faith and Christ as causes in his soteriology.

A classic attempt to explain the causes of salvation in Paul is found in Calvin's *Commentary on Romans* (where he treats Rom. 3:21–26) and in his *Institutes*. Calvin appeals to the four kinds of causes postulated by the philosophers.[72] Aristotle was the first to articulate these four kinds of causes in his book on the natural world:

> Plainly, then, these are the causes, and this is how many there are. They are four, and the student of nature should know about them all, and it will be his method, when stating on account of what, to get back to them all: the matter, the form, the thing which effects the change, and what the thing is for.[73]

Later, Aristotle used these four causes as a method for understanding the things that come after nature as well (i.e., *meta-physics*).[74] Calvin appropriates these causes to make the key point that "as far as the establishment of our salvation is concerned, *none of them has anything to do with works*."[75] Calvin then explains the causes in his *Institutes*, appealing to Romans 3:21–26 but also saying that "Scripture everywhere proclaims" this.[76] First, the efficient cause of salvation, or what Aristotle

---

72 My discussion in this paragraph is drawn from Calvin, *Institutes*, 3.14.17, 21, and from John Calvin, *The Epistles of Paul to the Romans and to the Thessalonians*, trans. Ross Mackenzie, ed. David W. Torrance and Thomas F. Torrance (Grand Rapids, MI: Eerdmans, 1960), 73–75.

73 Aristotle, *Physics*, trans. W. Charlton (Oxford: Clarendon, 1970), 2.7.

74 See Aristotle, *Metaphysics*, 1.3.

75 Calvin, *Institutes*, 3.14.17; emphasis mine.

76 Calvin, *Institutes*, 3.14.17.

calls the "thing which effects the change," is the mercy of God and his "freely given love toward us."[77] Second, the material cause of salvation ("the matter") is Christ and his obedience, or, as Calvin says in his commentary, "Christ with his blood."[78] Third, "what shall we say is the formal or instrumental cause but faith?"[79] This statement is interesting because in the subsequent discussion, he identifies the formal or instrumental cause as "the Spirit's illumination, that is, faith," and in his commentary, he identifies it as "the Word, with faith," or as "faith conceived by the Word."[80] Clearly, for Calvin there is a close relationship between the Word, the Spirit, and faith as the formal or instrumental cause of salvation. Fourth, Calvin identifies the final cause of salvation ("what the thing is for") with "the proof of divine justice and in the praise of God's goodness" or "the glory of God's great generosity" or "the glory of both the divine justice and goodness."[81]

Calvin's appropriation of Aristotle's four causes is a helpful tool for analyzing Paul's theology. First, it teaches us something the philosophers have always recognized but biblical scholars sometimes forget—that causality is complex. Second, I think that Calvin rightly observes that when it comes to explaining the causes of salvation in Paul, one thing the apostle teaches is clear: salvation is "not by works [οὐκ ἐξ ἔργων]" (Rom. 9:11 [Gk. 9:12]; Gal. 2:16; Eph. 2:9; Titus 3:5, my trans.).[82] Thus, we should not speak of our works as a cause of salvation in Paul. Third, I think Calvin's explanation of Christ as the material cause of salvation and faith as the formal or instrumental cause is helpful.[83] Calvin explains, "Faith is therefore said to justify,

---

77 Calvin, *Institutes*, 3.14.17.

78 Calvin, *Romans*, 75.

79 Calvin, *Institutes*, 3.14.17.

80 Respectively, Calvin, *Institutes*, 3.14.21; Calvin, *Romans*, 73; Calvin, *Romans*, 75.

81 Respectively, Calvin, *Institutes*, 3.14.17; Calvin, *Institutes*, 3.14.21; Calvin, *Romans*, 75.

82 I should qualify that the exact meaning of "works" in Gal. 2:16 is part of another thorny debate in Pauline theology: the New Perspective on Paul.

83 I am not sure, however, that it is correct to put *the word* alongside *faith* as the formal or instrumental cause of salvation. Rather, as I observed in chap. 2, *the word about Christ* and *the body*

because it is the instrument by which we receive Christ, in whom righteousness is communicated to us."[84] We have seen that Paul often uses prepositions of instrument or cause (ἐκ, διά, ἐν) with πίστις and πίστις Χριστοῦ to show the role that our faith in Christ plays in salvation. And he occasionally uses the instrumental dative πίστει in the same way (e.g., Rom. 3:28). Further, although Paul does not emphasize the Spirit's role in producing faith like Calvin does, he does associate our faith with the Spirit, who also plays an instrumental role (dative πνεύματι) in the beginning and end of our justification (Gal. 3:3; 5:5; cf. 1 Cor. 6:11). Finally, with my focus on faith and Christ in this book, it is helpful to keep in mind the importance of God himself as the efficient and final cause of salvation in Paul's theology. For while Paul says that everything, including our salvation, comes about "through" (δι') the Lord Jesus Christ, it is ultimately "from" (ἐξ, efficient cause) God the Father (1 Cor. 8:6; cf. Rom. 11:36) and "for" (εἰς, final cause) both the Father and the Son (1 Cor. 8:6; Col. 1:16; cf. Rom. 11:36).[85]

In Paul's letters, faith is also rightly described as a proximate cause of salvation that rests on the more ultimate cause of Christ. At least two texts in Paul's letters explain the logical relationship between Christ, faith, and salvation. First, in 1 Corinthians 15:17, Paul gives the chain of reasoning shown in table 5.1.

Table 5.1   Paul's Logic in 1 Corinthians 15:17

Christ	17a And if Christ has not been raised,
Faith	17b your faith is futile
Salvation	17c and you are still in your sins.

of faith and *Christ himself* are all ways of denoting the saving object of our faith in Paul's letters. Thus, it seems better to view *the word about Christ* alongside *Christ himself* as the material cause of our salvation in Paul's theology.

84 Calvin, *Romans*, 73.

85 Note that the antecedent of "him" in Col. 1:16 is "his beloved Son" in Col. 1:13.

The logical connection between 1 Corinthians 15:17a and 15:17b is clearly conditional (if-then). But in Greek there is no conjunction "and" between 15:17b and 15:17c. How are these two phrases related? It seems most likely that the ESV's addition of "and" is correct and that Paul adds a further "then" statement or conclusion that follows from both 15:17a and 15:17b. Thus, Paul's meaning is this: if Christ has not been raised, then your faith is futile, and if your faith is futile, then you are still in your sins. Here we see a chain of reasoning in which our salvation from sin rests proximately on our faith in Christ but ultimately on the resurrection of Christ.

Second, in Romans 4:24b–25, Paul gives a similar chain of reasoning but in the opposite direction (see table 5.2).

Table 5.2   Paul's Logic in Romans 4:24b–25

Justification	24b It [righteousness/justification] will be counted
Faith	24c to us who believe in him who raised from the dead Jesus our Lord,
Christ	25 who was delivered up for our trespasses and raised for our justification.

The logical connection between these three propositions is a series of grounds: like Abraham, we will be counted righteous (Rom. 4:24b), because of our faith in him who raised Jesus (Rom. 4:24c), because Jesus's death and resurrection secures our justification. Thus, in both these texts, faith occupies the middle position in a chain of causality between Christ and salvation. It is important to observe that the logic cannot be turned around: Paul does not say that Christ saves because faith saves but rather that faith saves because Christ saves. Thus, in Pauline theology, faith is rightly viewed as a proximate cause of salvation because it rests on the more ultimate cause of Jesus's death and resurrection in Pauline theology. Notably, the more ultimate cause of salvation on which our faith rests according to 1 Corinthians 15:17

and Romans 4:25 is *Jesus's death and resurrection.* That is, Paul does not locate the cause of our salvation in Jesus's faith or faithfulness, his *motivation* for going to the cross, but rather in the *accomplishment* of the cross and resurrection itself, in which God gave up his own Son for our trespasses and raised him from the dead for our justification.[86]

This logical relationship between Christ, faith, and salvation is the reason Paul can summarize his position by saying, "We hold that one is justified by faith" (Rom. 3:28). He does not mean that one's justification rests entirely and only on one's faith but rather that it rests on faith because faith rests on Christ (note the context of Rom. 3:21–26). This point should alleviate some of the theological and pastoral concerns of the "faithfulness of Christ" view.[87] It is also a point that seems to have been grasped well by theologians in the Protestant tradition, which makes it strange that Hays, following Gerhard Ebeling, critiques "the traditional post-Reformation understanding of 'faith' and 'justification' in Paul" as offering "no coherent account of the relation between the doctrine of justification and *christology.*"[88] Luther famously says that "faith takes hold of Christ and has Him present, enclosing Him as the ring encloses the gem. And whoever is found having this faith in the Christ who is grasped in the heart, him God accounts as righteous."[89] And he spells out Paul's logic explicitly: "We are justified by faith alone, because faith alone grasps this victory of Christ."[90] Douglas Moo, writing a commentary in the Lutheran tradition, observes that "what gives rise to Paul's confidence in the ability of faith 'alone' to justify is his insistence that faith brings

---

86   Here I am indebted to Ulrichs for his perceptive observation: "Is the relevant event for salvation now the motivation of Jesus for suffering death on the cross, or is it the dying of Jesus Christ for us?" *Christusglaube,* 193 (my trans.). It is also striking to me that in both 1 Cor. 15:17 and Rom. 4:25, Paul speaks about *God's* agency in Jesus's death and resurrection as the cause of our salvation.
87   See the introduction, p. 45.
88   Hays, *Faith of Jesus Christ,* xxix; see also 119, 150, 203, 293.
89   *Luther's Works,* 26:132.
90   *Luther's Works,* 26:284.

people into union with Christ. . . . It therefore is Paul's conviction about the utter adequacy of *Christ* that engenders his insistence on the adequacy of *faith*."[91] Calvin offers this concession to his teaching about justification by faith: "I willingly concede Osiander's objection that faith of itself does not possess the power of justifying, but only in so far as it receives Christ."[92] And B. B. Warfield, writing in the Reformed tradition, clarifies that "it is not faith that saves, but faith in Jesus Christ. . . . It is not, strictly speaking, even faith in Christ that saves, but Christ that saves through faith. The saving power resides exclusively, not in the act of faith or the attitude of faith, or the nature of faith, but in the object of faith."[93] Perhaps, then, Hays's concern is more of a response to the liberal Protestant view of faith as a religious disposition of absolute dependence rather than the orthodox Protestant reading of Paul.[94] Karl Barth, whose writing responds so much to liberal Protestantism, has perhaps given one of the most memorable formulations of the relationship between faith and Christ: "What is the *sola fide* but a faint yet necessary echo of the *solus Christus*?"[95]

Finally, this middle position of faith between Christ and salvation is also the reason that the apostle can speak about faith as a condition

---

91 Douglas J. Moo, *Galatians*, BECNT (Grand Rapids, MI: Baker Academic, 2013), 193; emphasis original. I am indebted to this statement for guiding my initial thinking about how to conceive of the relationship between faith and Christ in Paul's theology.

92 Calvin, *Institutes*, 3.11.7.

93 Benjamin Breckinridge Warfield, "Faith," in *Biblical and Theological Studies* (Philadelphia: Presbyterian and Reformed, 1952), 425.

94 Allen observes that "the modern era saw a number of liberal Protestant theologians sever the doctrine of faith from an operative doctrine of Christ, thereby giving faith an autonomous value that it never warranted in traditional Protestant dogmatics. Friedrich Schleiermacher and Albrecht Ritschl are indicative of this trend, inasmuch as faith ceases functioning as an instrument uniting one to Christ and serves more as a cipher for human self-divestment or a sense of absolute dependence." *Justification and the Gospel*, 112.

95 Karl Barth, *Church Dogmatics*, ed. G. W. Bromiley and T. F. Torrance, trans. G. W. Bromiley, G. T. Thomson, and Harold Knight (London: T&T Clark, 2009), 4.1:632. For pointing me to this reference, I am indebted to Jonathan A. Linebaugh, "The Christo-Centrism of Faith in Christ: Martin Luther's Reading of Galatians 2.16, 19–20," *NTS* 59, no. 4 (2013): 235.

for salvation.[96] Romans 10:9 and 1 Corinthians 15:2 are the clearest examples of Paul's conditional logic regarding faith, but we have also seen conditional logic in the statements in which Paul limits the saving power of the gospel to those who believe (Rom. 1:16; 10:4; 1 Cor. 1:21; cf. 1 Tim. 4:10).[97] For Paul, our faith is what receives and then stands in the death and resurrection of Christ and binds us to Christ himself. In this sense it is a condition for salvation.[98] Perhaps this proximate position of faith is also why Paul chooses to associate faith and Christ so closely with a genitive in his "by faith in Christ" (ἐκ πίστεως Χριστοῦ) phrases. These phrases allow him to speak of both the causal role of our faith *and* the causal role of Christ in salvation at the same time. Thus, there is no hint of an opposition between our faith and Christ's work in Paul's soteriology (or between justification by faith and participation with Christ).[99] It is as we participate in Christ's death and life *by faith* that we are justified or saved. For Paul, the gospel saves *as it is believed,* because faith is a proximate cause of salvation in his theology.

Faith and Eschatology in Paul

The last thing to briefly observe about faith in Paul's letters is that its orientation toward Christ gives it an eschatological character. Our faith has an eschatological character because the object of our faith has "already" come. Paul personifies πίστις as the body of faith that has come and been

---

96 It must be remembered, though, that faith is a condition granted by God, as observed above (p. 257). Cf. John Owen: "Salvation, indeed, is bestowed conditionally; but faith, which is the condition, is absolutely procured [i.e., purchased by the death of Christ]." *The Death of Death in the Death of Christ,* in *The Works of John Owen,* ed. William H. Goold (Edinburgh: Banner of Truth, 1967), 10:235.

97 Wolter observes that "no one can deny that Paul makes faith the prerequisite and condition for participating in God's salvation." *Paul,* 80.

98 Paul also speaks of our works as a condition for salvation: for example, he says, "If you live according to the flesh you will die, but if by the Spirit you put to death the deeds of the body, you will live" (Rom. 8:13). But he denies that works are a cause of our salvation (see above, p. 261).

99 See, e.g., Gal. 2:15–21. See also Pifer's careful work in *Faith as Participation,* which shows, among other things, that in Paul's theology our faith is as much a part of participation as it is a part of justification.

revealed in the coming of Christ and has ended the era of the law (Gal. 3:23, 25).[100] He does this because the object of our faith is Christ, in whom is the new creation (2 Cor. 5:17). In fact, our faith in Christ is a part of the new creation.[101] There were believers in God and his promises long before the coming of Christ, with our father Abraham being the prime example for Paul. Abraham's faith foreshadows our faith, and we now walk in his footsteps (Rom. 4:12, 23–25). But the faith has now "come" with Christ because our faith is fundamentally oriented toward the Christ who has already come.

Faith, however, also has an eschatological (and paradoxical) character because the object of our faith has "not yet" come. Believers "wait for [God's] Son from heaven, whom he raised from the dead, Jesus who delivers us from the wrath to come" (1 Thess. 1:10). Our faith in Christ overlaps with hope because it is oriented toward the eschatological future. This is why Paul can describe Abraham's faith and our faith in paradoxical terms. Abraham believed "against hope" and at the same time "in hope" because his present reality was characterized by death and yet God had given him the promise of life (Rom. 4:18–21). Believers now see the glory of the Lord by faith and at the same time walk by faith and *not by sight* because in our present reality we are away from the Lord and live in dying bodies but our hope is to be with him and partake in his resurrection (2 Cor. 3–5). This is the paradoxical element of our faith—and perhaps the closest Paul comes to what is sometimes called fideism. Luther vividly describes this aspect of faith as the darkness of faith.[102] Faith sees what cannot be seen with the

---

100 Perhaps similar is Paul's personification of the "righteousness based on faith" in Rom. 10:6–8, who "voices Moses' prohibition of pride" (Seifrid, *Christ, Our Righteousness*, 134) and proclaims to us the good tidings that Christ has already been incarnate and raised from the dead.

101 Compare these two statements in Galatians: "For in Christ Jesus neither circumcision nor uncircumcision counts for anything, but only faith working through love" (Gal. 5:6); "For neither circumcision counts for anything, nor uncircumcision, but a new creation" (Gal. 6:15).

102 For example, "All devout people enter with Abraham into the darkness of faith, kill reason, and say: 'Reason, you are foolish. You do not understand the things that belong to God (Matt. 16:23). Therefore do not speak against me, but keep quiet. Do not judge; but listen to the Word of God,

human eye apart from the Spirit.[103] It is the assurance of reality not as it appears to be but as it really is as defined by the word of God.[104] Faith is not fully paradoxical for Paul, however, because Christ has already been raised.[105] Thus, the eschatological character of our faith is shaped by the object of our faith.

Conclusion

Faith and Christ are so closely related in Pauline theology because our faith rests on the death and resurrection of Christ for salvation in the present and future. In Paul faith is belief and trust in the truth of the gospel and the God of the gospel, with Christ as the fundamental object of our faith. We believe *in* Christ, and we believe *that* Christ—especially that he died for our sins and was raised for our justification by the God of Abraham. God's gift of salvation to us includes both the object of our faith and our faith itself. And this Christ-oriented faith is a proximate cause of our salvation in that it rests on the more ultimate cause of Jesus's death and resurrection. It is also a part of the eschatological new creation because the object of our faith has already come, and yet it paradoxically sees what cannot yet be seen because we await God's Son to come and deliver us from the final judgment.

So in conclusion, on the one hand, if we are to be true to the apostle's theology, we should be wary of separating faith and Christ by speaking about faith without at the same time speaking about the object of our faith: Christ. If Søren Kierkegaard rightly said that we never move beyond faith, perhaps Paul would clarify that

---

and believe it.' Thus devout people, by their faith, kill a beast that is greater than the world; and so they offer a highly pleasing sacrifice and worship to God." *Luther's Works*, 26:228.

103 See Gupta, who highlights faith as a new epistemology that embraces the folly of the cross in his discussion of Paul's letters to the Corinthians. *Paul and the Language of Faith*, 95–133, 178–79.

104 See Wolter, who highlights faith as assurance of reality. *Paul*, 84–94.

105 Ridderbos observes that "the kerygma of Christ's resurrection is foundational and indispensable for preaching (1 Cor. 15:3–8, 14ff.), and one cannot for this reason seek the essence of the gospel in paradox." *Paul*, 249.

this means we never move beyond Christ. On the other hand, we should be wary of separating Christ from our faith as I think the "faithfulness of Christ" view has. Twenty years after the publication of his groundbreaking thesis, Richard Hays reflected on the pastoral importance of his work:

> I have grown increasingly convinced that the struggles of the church in our time are a result of losing touch with its own gospel story. We have gotten "off message" and therefore lost our way in a culture that tells us many other stories about who we are and where our hope lies. In both the evangelical and the liberal wings of Protestantism, there is too much emphasis on individual faith-experience and not enough grounding of our theological discourse in the story of Jesus Christ.[106]

I could not agree with Hays's concern more. But the burden of my work has been to emphasize the significance of Hays's words "where our hope lies." It is paramount to proclaim Christ afresh for every generation. The Christian religion is not about "individual faith-experience" but about what God has done for us in Christ. But it also really matters whether we believe in this Christ.

106 Hays, *Faith of Jesus Christ*, lii.

Bibliography

Adams, Edward. "Abraham's Faith and Gentile Disobedience: Textual Links between Romans 1 and 4." *JSNT* 19, no. 65 (1997): 47–66.

Allen, R. Michael. *Justification and the Gospel: Understanding the Contexts and Controversies*. Grand Rapids, MI: Baker Academic, 2013.

Anderson, Garwood P. *Paul's New Perspective: Charting a Soteriological Journey*. Downers Grove, IL: IVP Academic, 2016.

Aristotle. *Physics*. Translated by W. Charlton. Oxford: Clarendon, 1970.

Augustine. *Augustine's Commentary on Galatians: Introduction, Text, Translation, and Notes*. Translated by Eric Plumer. OECS. New York: Oxford University Press, 2003.

Augustine. *Confessions*. Translated by Henry Chadwick. Oxford: Oxford University Press, 1991.

Balla, Peter. "2 Corinthians." In Beale and Carson, *Commentary on the New Testament Use of the Old Testament*, 753–83.

Barclay, John M. G. *Paul and the Gift*. Grand Rapids, MI: Eerdmans, 2015.

Barnett, Paul. *The Second Epistle to the Corinthians*. NICNT. Grand Rapids, MI: Eerdmans, 1997.

Barr, James. *The Semantics of Biblical Language*. London: Oxford University Press, 1961.

Barth, Karl. *Church Dogmatics*. Edited by G. W. Bromiley and T. F. Torrance. Translated by G. W. Bromiley, G. T. Thomson, and Harold Knight. London: T&T Clark, 2009.

Barth, Karl. *The Epistle to the Romans*. Translated from the 6th ed. by Edwyn C. Hoskyns. London: Oxford University Press, 1933.

Barth, Markus. "The Faith of the Messiah." *Heythrop Journal* 10, no. 4 (1969): 363–70.

Bates, Matthew W. "A Christology of Incarnation and Enthronement: Romans 1:3–4 as Unified, Nonadoptionist, and Nonconciliatory." *CBQ* 77, no. 1 (2015): 107–27.

Bates, Matthew W. *Salvation by Allegiance Alone: Rethinking Faith, Works, and the Gospel of Jesus the King.* Grand Rapids, MI: Baker Academic, 2017.

Beale, G. K. *A New Testament Biblical Theology: The Unfolding of the Old Testament in the New.* Grand Rapids, MI: Baker Academic, 2011.

Beale, G. K., and D. A. Carson, eds. *Commentary on the New Testament Use of the Old Testament.* Grand Rapids, MI: Baker Academic, 2007.

Beentjes, Pancratius C. *The Book of Ben Sira in Hebrew: A Text Edition of All Extant Hebrew Manuscripts and a Synopsis of All Parallel Hebrew Ben Sira Texts.* VTSup 68. Leiden: Brill, 1997.

Bird, Michael F., and Michael R. Whitenton. "The Faithfulness of Jesus Christ in Hippolytus's *De Christo et Antichristo*: Overlooked Patristic Evidence in the Πίστις Χριστοῦ Debate." *NTS* 55, no. 4 (2009): 552–62.

Bird, Michael F., and Preston M. Sprinkle, eds. *The Faith of Jesus Christ: Exegetical, Biblical, and Theological Studies.* Peabody, MA: Hendrickson, 2009.

Blackwell, Ben C., John K. Goodrich, and Jason Maston, eds. *Paul and the Apocalyptic Imagination.* Minneapolis: Fortress, 2016.

Bockmuehl, Markus. *The Epistle to the Philippians.* BNTC. Peabody, MA: Hendrickson, 1998.

Bolt, Peter G. "The Faith of Jesus Christ in the Synoptic Gospels and Acts." In Bird and Sprinkle, *Faith of Jesus Christ*, 210–22.

Bortone, Pietro. *Greek Prepositions: From Antiquity to the Present.* New York: Oxford University Press, 2010.

Bultmann, Rudolf. "Πιστεύω κτλ." In *Theological Dictionary of the New Testament*, edited by Gerhard Kittel and Gerhard Friedrich, translated by Geoffrey W. Bromiley, 6:174–228. Grand Rapids, MI: Eerdmans, 1968.

Bultmann, Rudolf. *Theology of the New Testament.* Translated by Kendrick Grobel. Vol. 1. New York: Charles Scribner's Sons, 1951.

Burton, Ernest De Witt. *A Critical and Exegetical Commentary on the Epistle to the Galatians.* ICC 34. Edinburgh: T&T Clark, 1921.

Calvin, John. *The Epistles of Paul to the Romans and Thessalonians.* Translated by Ross Mackenzie. Vol. 8 of *Calvin's New Testament Commentary.* Edited by David W. Torrance and Thomas F. Torrance. Grand Rapids, MI: Eerdmans, 1960.

Calvin, John. *Institutes of the Christian Religion.* Edited by John T. McNeill. Translated by Ford Lewis Battles. Louisville: Westminster, 1960.

Campbell, Constantine R. *Paul and Union with Christ: An Exegetical and Theological Study.* Grand Rapids, MI: Zondervan, 2012.

Campbell, Douglas A. *The Deliverance of God: An Apocalyptic Rereading of Justification in Paul.* Grand Rapids, MI: Eerdmans, 2009.

Campbell, Douglas A. "The Faithfulness of Jesus Christ in Romans 3:22." In Bird and Sprinkle, *Faith of Jesus Christ*, 57–71.

Campbell, Douglas A. "False Presuppositions in the Πιστις Χριστου Debate: A Response to Brian Dodd." *JBL* 116, no. 4 (1997): 713–19.

Campbell, Douglas A. "The Meaning of Πιστις and Νομος in Paul: A Linguistic and Structural Perspective." *JBL* 111, no. 1 (1992): 91–103.

Campbell, Douglas A. *The Quest for Paul's Gospel: A Suggested Strategy.* New York: T&T Clark, 2005.

Campbell, Douglas A. "Romans 1:17—A Crux Interpretum for the Πιστις Χριστου Debate." *JBL* 113, no. 2 (1994): 265–85.

Campbell, Douglas A. "2 Corinthians 4:13: Evidence in Paul That Christ Believes." *JBL* 128, no. 2 (2009): 337–56.

Capes, David B. *Old Testament Yahweh Texts in Paul's Christology.* WUNT, 2nd ser., vol. 47. Tübingen: Mohr Siebeck, 1992.

Carlson, Stephen C. *The Text of Galatians and Its History.* WUNT, 2nd ser., vol. 385. Tübingen: Mohr Siebeck, 2015.

Carraway, George. *Christ Is God over All: Romans 9:5 in the Context of Romans 9–11.* LNTS 489. New York: Bloomsbury, 2013.

Carson, D. A. *Matthew.* EBC. Grand Rapids, MI: Zondervan, 1995.

Carson, D. A., Peter T. O'Brien, and Mark A. Seifrid, eds. *Justification and Variegated Nomism.* Vol. 2, *The Paradoxes of Paul.* WUNT, 2nd ser., vol. 140. Grand Rapids, MI: Baker, 2004.

Catechism of the Catholic Church. Rev. ed. London: Geoffrey Chapman, 1999.

Childs, Brevard S. *Isaiah: A Commentary.* OTL. Louisville: Westminster John Knox, 2001.

Chilton, Bruce D. *The Isaiah Targum.* Collegeville, MN: Liturgical Press, 1990.

Choi, Hung-Sik. "Πίστις in Galatians 5:5–6: Neglected Evidence for the Faithfulness of Christ." *JBL* 124, no. 3 (2005): 467–90.

Chrysostom, John. *The Homilies of S. John Chrysostom.* Vol. 7, *The Apostle of St. Paul to the Romans.* Library of Fathers. Oxford: John Henry Parker, 1841.

Cirafesi, Wally V., and Gerald W. Peterman. "Πίστις and Christ in Hippolytus's *De Christo et Antichristo*: A Response to Michael F. Bird and Michael R. Whitenton." *NTS* 57, no. 4 (2011): 594–603.

Coakley, J. F. *Robinson's Paradigms and Exercises in Syriac Grammar.* 6th ed. Oxford: Oxford University Press, 2013.

The Concordia Bilingual Edition of the Holy Bible, Containing the Old and New Testaments in the English Translation according to the Authorized Version and in the German Translation according to the Original Luther Text. St. Louis, MO: Concordia, 1925.

The Coptic Version of the New Testament in the Southern Dialect. Vol. 5, *The Epistles of S. Paul (Continued), Register of Fragments, Etc.* Oxford: Clarendon, 1911.

Cranfield, C. E. B. *The Epistle to the Romans.* Vol. 1. ICC. Edinburgh: T&T Clark, 1975.

Cranfield, C. E. B. *The Epistle to the Romans.* Vol. 2. ICC. Edinburgh: T&T Clark, 1979.

de Boer, Martinus C. "Apocalyptic as God's Eschatological Activity in Paul's Theology." In Blackwell, Goodrich, and Maston, *Paul and the Apocalyptic Imagination*, 45–63.

de Boer, Martinus C. *Galatians: A Commentary*. NTL. Louisville: Westminster John Knox, 2011.

Dodd, C. H. *The Apostolic Preaching and Its Developments*. New York: Harper & Bros., 1936.

Donfried, Karl P. "Paul and the Revisionists: Did Luther Really Get It All Wrong?" *Dialog: A Journal of Theology* 46, no. 1 (2007): 31–40.

Downs, David J. "Faith(fulness) in Christ Jesus in 2 Timothy 3:15." *JBL* 131, no. 1 (2012): 143–60.

Downs, David J., and Benjamin J. Lappenga. *The Faithfulness of the Risen Christ:* Pistis *and the Exalted Lord in the Pauline Letters*. Waco, TX: Baylor University Press, 2019.

Dunn, James D. G. "Ἐκ Πίστεως: A Key to the Meaning of Πίστις Χριστου." In Wagner, Rowe, and Grieb, *The Word Leaps the Gap*, 351–66.

Dunn, James D. G. *Romans 1–8*. WBC 38A. Nashville: Thomas Nelson, 1988.

Dunn, James D. G. *The Theology of Paul the Apostle*. Grand Rapids, MI: Eerdmans, 1998.

Ellis, E. Earle. *Paul's Use of the Old Testament*. Grand Rapids, MI: Eerdmans, 1957.

Fee, Gordon D. *God's Empowering Presence: The Holy Spirit in the Letters of Paul*. Peabody, MA: Hendrickson, 1994.

Fee, Gordon D. *The First Epistle to the Corinthians*. Rev. ed. NICNT. Grand Rapids, MI: Eerdmans, 2014.

Fee, Gordon D. *Paul's Letter to the Philippians*. NICNT. Grand Rapids, MI: Eerdmans, 1995.

Fee, Gordon D. "Paul's Use of Locative ἐν in Galatians: On Text and Meaning in Galatians 1.6; 1.1; 2.20; 3.11–12, and 3.26." In *The Impartial God: Essays in Biblical Studies in Honor of Jouette M. Bassler*, edited by Calvin J. Roetzel and Robert L. Foster, 170–85. Sheffield: Sheffield Phoenix, 2007.

Fitzmyer, Joseph A. *First Corinthians: A New Translation with Introduction and Commentary*. AB 32. New Haven, CT: Yale University Press, 2008.

Fitzmyer, Joseph A. "The Interpretation of Genesis 15:6: Abraham's Faith and Righteousness in a Qumran Text." In *Emanuel: Studies in Hebrew Bible, Septuagint, and Dead Sea Scrolls in Honor of Emanuel Tov*, edited by Shalom M. Paul, Robert A. Kraft, Lawrence H. Schiffman, and Weston W. Fields, 257–68. VTSup 94. Leiden: Brill, 2003.

Fitzmyer, Joseph A. *Romans: A New Translation with Introduction and Commentary*. AB 33. New Haven, CT: Yale University Press, 1993.

Fitzmyer, Joseph A. *To Advance the Gospel: New Testament Studies*. 2nd ed. Grand Rapids, MI: Eerdmans, 1998.

Foster, Paul. "Πίστις Χριστοῦ Terminology in Philippians and Ephesians." In Bird and Sprinkle, *Faith of Jesus Christ*, 91–109.

France, R. T. *The Gospel of Mark*. NIGTC. Grand Rapids, MI: Eerdmans, 2002.

Furnish, Victor Paul. *II Corinthians: A New Translation with Introduction and Commentary*. AB 32A. New York: Doubleday, 1984.

Gagnon, Robert A. J. "Heart of Wax and a Teaching That Stamps: Τυπος Διδαχης (Rom 6:17b) Once More." *JBL* 112, no. 4 (1993): 667–87.

Garlington, Don. *Faith, Obedience, and Perseverance: Aspects of Paul's Letter to the Romans*. WUNT 79. Tübingen: Mohr Siebeck, 1994.

Gaston, Lloyd. *Paul and the Torah*. Vancouver: University of British Columbia Press, 1987.

Gathercole, Simon J. "Justified by Faith, Justified by His Blood: The Evidence of Romans 3:21–4:25." In Carson, O'Brien, and Seifrid, *Justification and Variegated Nomism*, 2:147–84.

Gathercole, Simon J. *Where Is Boasting?: Early Jewish Soteriology and Paul's Response in Romans 1–5*. Grand Rapids, MI: Eerdmans, 2002.

Goldingay, John. *Psalms*. Vol. 3, *Psalms 90–150*. BCOTWP. Grand Rapids, MI: Baker Academic, 2008.

Gupta, Nijay K. *Paul and the Language of Faith*. Grand Rapids, MI: Eerdmans, 2020.

Hafemann, Scott J. *Paul, Moses, and the History of Israel: The Letter/Spirit Contrast and the Argument from Scripture in 2 Corinthians 3*. WUNT 81. Tübingen: Mohr Siebeck, 1995.

Harmon, Matthew S. *She Must and Shall Go Free: Paul's Isaianic Gospel in Galatians*. BZNW 168. Berlin: de Gruyter, 2010.

Harrisville, Roy A., III. "Before Πιστις Χριστου: The Objective Genitive as Good Greek." *NovT* 48, no. 4 (2006): 353–58.

Harrisville, Roy A., III. *The Faith of St. Paul: Transformative Gift of Divine Power*. Eugene, OR: Pickwick, 2019.

Harrisville, Roy A., III. "Πιστις Χριστου and the New Perspective on Paul." *Logia* 19, no. 2 (2010): 19–28.

Harrisville, Roy A., III. "Πιστις Χριστου: Witness of the Fathers." *NovT* 36, no. 3 (1994): 233–41.

Haussleiter, Johannes. "Der Glaube Jesu Christi und der christliche Glaube: Ein Beitrag zur Erklärung des Römerbriefes." *Neue kirchliche Zeitschrift* 2 (1891): 109–45.

Hay, David M. "Paul's Understanding of Faith as Participation." In *Paul and His Theology*, edited by Stanley E. Porter, 45–76. Pauline Studies 3. Leiden: Brill, 2006.

Hays, Richard B. *The Conversion of the Imagination: Paul as Interpreter of Israel's Scripture*. Grand Rapids, MI: Eerdmans, 2005.

Hays, Richard B. *The Faith of Jesus Christ: The Narrative Substructure of Galatians 3:1–4:11*. 2nd ed. Grand Rapids, MI: Eerdmans, 2002.

Hawthorne, Gerald F. *Philippians*. WBC 43. Waco, TX: Word Books, 1983.

Hebert, A. G. "'Faithfulness' and 'Faith.'" *Theology* 58, no. 424 (1955): 373–79.

Heliso, Desta. *Pistis and the Righteous One: A Study of Romans 1:17 against the Background of Scripture and Second Temple Jewish Literature*. WUNT, 2nd ser., vol. 235. Tübingen: Mohr Siebeck, 2007.

Holmes, Michael W. *The Apostolic Fathers in English*. 3rd ed. Grand Rapids, MI: Baker Academic, 2007.

Hooker, Morna D. "Another Look at πίστις Χριστοῦ." *SJT* 69, no. 1 (2016): 46–62.

Hooker, Morna D. "Πιστις Χριστου." *NTS* 35, no. 3 (1989): 321–42.

Howard, George. "Faith of Christ." In *Anchor Bible Dictionary*, edited by David Noel Freedman, 2.758–60. New York: Doubleday, 1992.

Howard, George. *Paul: Crisis in Galatia; A Study in Early Christian Theology*. SNTSMS 35. New York: Cambridge University Press, 1979.

Hunn, Debbie. "Debating the Faithfulness of Jesus Christ in Twentieth-Century Scholarship." In Bird and Sprinkle, *Faith of Jesus Christ*, 15–31.

Hurtado, Larry W. *Lord Jesus Christ: Devotion to Jesus in Earliest Christianity*. Grand Rapids, MI: Eerdmans, 2003.

Irons, Charles Lee. *The Righteousness of God: A Lexical Examination of the Covenant-Faithfulness Interpretation*. WUNT, 2nd ser., vol. 386. Tübingen: Mohr Siebeck, 2015.

Jerome. *Commentary on Galatians*. Translated by Andrew Cain. Vol. 121 of *The Fathers of the Church*. Washington, DC: Catholic University of America Press, 2010.

Jewett, Robert. *Romans*. Hermeneia. Minneapolis: Fortress, 2007.

Keck, Leander E. "'Jesus' in Romans." *JBL* 108, no. 3 (1989): 443–60.

Keil, Carl Friedrich. *The Twelve Minor Prophets*. Vol. 2. Translated by James Martin. Grand Rapids, MI: Eerdmans, 1954.

Kim, Seyoon. *The Origin of Paul's Gospel*. Grand Rapids, MI: Eerdmans, 1981.

King, Daniel, trans. *The Syriac Peshiṭta Bible with English Translations: Romans–Corinthians*. Piscataway, NJ: Gorgias, 2013.

Kittel, G. "Πίστις Ἰησοῦ Χριστοῦ bei Paulus." *TSK* 79 (1906): 419–36.

Koperski, Veronica. "The Meaning of *Pistis Christou* in Philippians 3:9." *LS* 18, no. 3 (1993): 198–216.

Kugler, Chris. "ΠΙΣΤΙΣ ΧΡΙΣΤΟΥ: The Current State of Play and the Key Arguments." *CBR* 14, no. 2 (2016): 244–55.

Lambrecht, Jan. "A Matter of Method: 2 Cor 4,13 and Stegman's Recent Study." *ETL* 84, no. 1 (2008): 175–80.

Lambrecht, Jan. "A Matter of Method (II): 2 Cor 4,13 and the Recent Studies of Schenck and Campbell." *ETL* 86, no. 4 (2010): 441–48.

Layton, Bentley. *A Coptic Grammar*. 2nd ed. Wiesbaden: Harrassowitz, 2004.

Lightfoot, J. B. *The Epistle of St. Paul to the Galatians*. 1865. Reprint, Grand Rapids, MI: Zondervan, 1971.

Lindberg, Conrad. *The Earlier Version of the Wycliffite Bible*. Vol. 8. Stockholm: Almqvist and Wiksell, 1997.

Lindsay, Dennis R. *Josephus and Faith: Πίστις and Πιστεύειν as Faith Terminology in the Writings of Flavius Josephus and in the New Testament*. AGJU 19. Leiden: Brill, 1993.

Linebaugh, Jonathan A. "The Christo-Centrism of Faith in Christ: Martin Luther's Reading of Galatians 2.16, 19–20." *NTS* 59, no. 4 (2013): 535–44.

Linebaugh, Jonathan A. "Righteousness Revealed: The Death of Christ as the Definition of the Righteousness of God in Romans 3:21–26." In Blackwell, Goodrich, and Maston, *Paul and the Apocalyptic Imagination*, 219–37.

Longenecker, Bruce W. "Πίστις in Romans 3.25: Neglected Evidence for the 'Faithfulness of Christ'?" *NTS* 39, no. 3 (1993): 478–80.

Longenecker, Richard N. *The Epistle to the Romans*. NIGTC. Grand Rapids, MI: Eerdmans, 2016.

Longenecker, Richard N. *Galatians*. WBC 41. Dallas, TX: Word Books, 1990.

Luther, Martin. *Luther's Works*. Vol. 26. Edited by Jaroslav Pelikan. St. Louis, MO: Concordia, 1963.

Martyn, J. Louis. "Apocalyptic Antinomies in Paul's Letter to the Galatians." *NTS* 31, no. 3 (1985): 410–24.

Martyn, J. Louis. "The Apocalyptic Gospel in Galatians." *Int* 54, no. 3 (2000): 246–66.

Martyn, J. Louis. *Galatians: A New Translation with Introduction and Commentary*. AB 33A. New York: Doubleday, 1997.

Matera, Frank. *God's Saving Grace: A Pauline Theology*. Grand Rapids, MI: Eerdmans, 2012.

Matlock, R. Barry. "Detheologizing the Πιστις Χριστου Debate: Cautionary Remarks from a Lexical Semantic Perspective." *NovT* 42, no. 1 (2000): 1–23.

Matlock, R. Barry. "'Even the Demons Believe': Paul and Πίστις Χριστοῦ." *CBQ* 64, no. 2 (2002): 300–318.

Matlock, R. Barry. "ΠΙΣΤΙΣ in Galatians 3.26: Neglected Evidence for 'Faith of Christ'?" *NTS* 49, no. 3 (2003): 433–39.

Matlock, R. Barry. "The Rhetoric of Πίστις in Paul: Galatians 2.16, 3.22, Romans 3.22, and Philippians 3.9." *JSNT* 30, no. 2 (2007): 173–203.

McFadden, Kevin W. "Does Πιστις Mean 'Faith(fulness)' in Paul?" *TynBul* 66, no. 2 (2015): 251–70.

McKnight, Scot. *The Letter to Philemon*. NICNT. Grand Rapids, MI: Eerdmans, 2017.

Metzger, Bruce M. *The Early Versions of the New Testament: Their Origin, Transmission, and Limitations*. New York: Oxford University Press, 1977.

Moo, Douglas J. *Galatians*. BECNT. Grand Rapids, MI: Baker Academic, 2013.

Morgan, Teresa. *Roman Faith and Christian Faith: Pistis and Fides in the Early Roman Empire and Early Churches*. New York: Oxford University Press, 2015.

Morris, Leon. *1 and 2 Thessalonians*. TNTC. Downers Grove, IL: InterVarsity Press, 1984.

Moule, C. F. D. *An Idiom Book of New Testament Greek*. 2nd ed. Cambridge: Cambridge University Press, 1959.

Mounce, William D. *Pastoral Epistles*. WBC 46. Nashville: Thomas Nelson, 2000.

Murdock, James. *The New Testament, Translated into English from the Syriac Peshitto Version*. Piscataway, NJ: Gorgias, 2001.

Murray, John. *The Epistle to the Romans*. Vol. 1. NICNT. Grand Rapids, MI: Eerdmans, 1959.

Origen. *Le Commentaire d'Origène sur Rom III 5–V 7*. Edited by Jean Scherer. Cairo: L'Institut Français d'Archéologie Orientale, 1957.

Oswalt, John N. *The Book of Isaiah, Chapters 40–66*. NICOT. Grand Rapids, MI: Eerdmans, 1998.

Owen, John. *The Death of Death in the Death of Christ*. In *The Works of John Owen*, edited by William H. Goold, 10:139–428. Edinburgh: Banner of Truth, 1967.

Pascal, Blaise. *Pensées*. Translated by A. J. Krailsheimer. New York, Penguin, 1995.

Pifer, Jeanette Hagen. *Faith as Participation: An Exegetical Study of Some Key Pauline Texts*. WUNT, 2nd ser., vol. 486. Tübingen: Mohr Siebeck, 2019.

Quarles, Charles L. "From Faith to Faith: A Fresh Examination of the Prepositional Series in Romans 1:17." *NovT* 45, no. 1 (2003): 1–21.

Rainbow, Paul A. *Johannine Theology: The Gospel, the Epistles, and the Apocalypse*. Downers Grove, IL: IVP Academic, 2014.

Ridderbos, Herman. *Paul: An Outline of His Theology*. Translated by John Richard de Witt. Grand Rapids, MI: Eerdmans, 1975.

Robertson, O. Palmer. *The Books of Nahum, Habakkuk, and Zephaniah*. NICOT. Grand Rapids, MI: Eerdmans, 1990.

Ruhl, Charles. *On Monosemy: A Study in Linguistic Semantics*. Albany, NY: State University of New York Press, 1989.

Schaff, Philip, ed. *Nicene and Post-Nicene Fathers*. Vols. 3 and 5. Grand Rapids, MI: Eerdmans, 1978.

Schenck, Kenneth. "2 Corinthians and the Πίστις Χριστοῦ Debate." *CBQ* 70, no. 3 (2008): 524–37.

Schliesser, Benjamin. "'Abraham Did Not "Doubt" in Unbelief' (Rom. 4:20): Faith, Doubt, and Dispute in Paul's Letter to the Romans." *JTS* 63, no. 2 (2012): 492–522.

Schliesser, Benjamin. *Abraham's Faith in Romans 4: Paul's Concept of Faith in Light of the History of Reception of Genesis 15:6*. WUNT, 2nd ser., vol. 224. Tübingen: Mohr Siebeck, 2007.

Schliesser, Benjamin. "'Christ-Faith' as an Eschatological Event (Galatians 3.23–26): A 'Third-View' on Πίστις Χριστοῦ." *JSNT* 38, no. 3 (2016): 277–300.

Schliesser, Benjamin. "'Exegetical Amnesia' and Πιστις Χριστου: The 'Faith *of* Christ' in Nineteenth-Century Pauline Scholarship." *JTS* 66, no. 1 (2015): 61–89.

Schreiner, Thomas R. *Galatians*. ZECNT. Grand Rapids, MI: Zondervan, 2010.

Schreiner, Thomas R. *Paul, Apostle of God's Glory in Christ: A Pauline Theology*. Downers Grove, IL: IVP Academic, 2001.

Schreiner, Thomas R. *Romans*. 2nd ed. BECNT. Grand Rapids, MI: Baker Academic, 2018.

Schweitzer, Albert. *The Mysticism of Paul the Apostle*. Translated by William Montgomery. 1931. Reprint, Baltimore: Johns Hopkins University Press, 1988.

Seifrid, Mark A. *Christ, Our Righteousness: Paul's Theology of Justification*. NSBT 9. Downers Grove, IL: InterVarsity Press, 2000.

Seifrid, Mark A. "The Faith of Christ." In Bird and Sprinkle, *Faith of Jesus Christ*, 129–46.

Seifrid, Mark A. *The Second Letter to the Corinthians*. PNTC. Grand Rapids, MI: Eerdmans, 2014.

Silva, Moisés. *Biblical Words and Their Meaning: An Introduction to Lexical Semantics*. Rev. ed. Grand Rapids, MI: Zondervan, 1994.

Silva, Moisés. "Faith versus Works of the Law in Galatians." In Carson, O'Brien, and Seifrid, *Justification and Variegated Nomism*, 2:217–48.

Silva, Moisés. "Galatians." In Beale and Carson, *Commentary on the New Testament Use of the Old Testament*, 785–812.

Silva, Moisés. *Philippians*. 2nd ed. BECNT. Grand Rapids, MI: Baker Academic, 2005.

Sprinkle, Preston M. "Πίστις Χριστοῦ as an Eschatological Event." In Bird and Sprinkle, *Faith of Jesus Christ*, 165–84.

Stubbs, David L. "The Shape of Soteriology and the *Pistis Christou* Debate." *SJT* 61, no. 2 (2008): 137–57.

Stuhlmacher, Peter. *Biblical Theology of the New Testament.* Translated and edited by Daniel P. Bailey. Grand Rapids, MI: Eerdmans, 2018.

Taylor, John W. "From Faith to Faith: Romans 1.17 in the Light of Greek Idiom." *NTS* 50, no. 3 (2004): 337–48.

Thielman, Frank. "Paul's View of Israel's Misstep in Rom 9.32–3: Its Origin and Meaning." *NTS* 64, no. 3 (2018): 362–77.

Thiselton, Anthony C. *The First Epistle to the Corinthians.* NIGTC. Grand Rapids, MI: Eerdmans, 2000.

Tilling, Chris. "Campbell's Faith: Advancing the *Pistis Christou* Debate." In *Beyond Old and New Perspectives on Paul: Reflections on the Work of Douglas Campbell*, edited by Chris Tilling, 234–52. Eugene, OR: Cascade, 2014.

Timmins, Will N. "A Faith unlike Abraham's: Matthew Bates on Salvation by Allegiance Alone." *JETS* 61, no. 3 (2018): 598–600.

Torrance, T. F. "One Aspect of the Biblical Conception of Faith." *ExpTim* 68, no. 4 (1956–1957): 111–14.

Ulrichs, Karl Friedrich. *Christusglaube: Studien zum Syntagma πίστις Χριστοῦ und zum paulinischen Verständnis von Glaube und Rechtfertigung.* WUNT, 2nd ser., vol. 227. Tübingen: Mohr Siebeck, 2007.

Vallotton, Pierre. *Le Christ et la foi: Etude de théologie biblique.* Geneva: Labor et Fides, 1961.

Wagner, J. Ross. *Heralds of the Good News: Isaiah and Paul in Concert in the Letter to the Romans.* Leiden: Brill, 2003.

Wagner, J. Ross. "Isaiah in Romans and Galatians." In *Isaiah in the New Testament*, edited by Steve Moyise and Maarten J. J. Menken, 117–32. London: T&T Clark, 2005.

Wagner, J. Ross, C. Kavin Rowe, and A. Katherine Grieb, eds. *The Word Leaps the Gap: Essays on Scripture and Theology in Honor of Richard B. Hays.* Grand Rapids, MI: Eerdmans, 2008.

Wallace, Daniel B. *Greek Grammar beyond the Basics: An Exegetical Syntax of the New Testament.* Grand Rapids, MI: Zondervan, 1996.

Wallis, Ian G. *The Faith of Jesus Christ in Early Christian Traditions.* SNTSMS 84. Cambridge: Cambridge University Press, 1995.

Walters, J. Edward, trans. *The Syriac Peshiṭta Bible with English Translations: Galatians–Philemon.* Piscataway, NJ: Gorgias, 2013.

Wanamaker, Charles A. *The Epistle to the Thessalonians.* NIGTC. Grand Rapids, MI: Eerdmans, 1990.

Warfield, Benjamin Breckinridge. "Faith." In *Biblical and Theological Studies,* 404–44. Philadelphia: Presbyterian and Reformed, 1952.

Watson, Francis. "By Faith (of Christ): An Exegetical Dilemma and Its Scriptural Solution." In Bird and Sprinkle, *Faith of Jesus Christ,* 147–63.

Watson, Francis. *Paul and the Hermeneutics of Faith.* 2nd ed. New York: Bloomsbury T&T Clark, 2016.

Watts, Rikki E. "'For I Am Not Ashamed of the Gospel': Romans 1:16–17 and Habakkuk 2:4." In *Romans and the People of God: Essays in Honor of Gordon D. Fee on the Occasion of His 65th Birthday,* edited by Sven K. Soderlund and N. T. Wright, 3–25. Grand Rapids, MI: Eerdmans, 1999.

Whitenton, Michael R. "After Πιστις Χριστου: Neglected Evidence from the Apostolic Fathers." *JTS* 61, no. 1 (2010): 82–109.

Williams, Sam K. "Again *Pistis Christou.*" *CBQ* 49, no. 3 (1987): 431–47.

Williams, Sam K. "The Hearing of Faith: Ακοη Πιστεως in Galatians 3." *NTS* 35, no. 1 (1989): 82–93.

Witherington, Ben, III. *Grace in Galatia: A Commentary on St. Paul's Letter to the Galatians.* Grand Rapids, MI: Eerdmans, 1998.

Wolter, Michael. *Paul: An Outline of His Theology.* Translated by Robert L. Brawley. Waco, TX: Baylor University Press, 2015.

Wright, N. T. "Faith, Virtue, Justification, and the Journey to Freedom." In Wagner, Rowe, and Grieb, *The Word Leaps the Gap,* 472–97.

Wright, N. T. *The Letter to the Romans.* In *The New Interpreter's Bible,* 10:393–770. Nashville: Abingdon, 2002.

Wright, N. T. *Paul and the Faithfulness of God.* 2 vols. COQG 4. Minneapolis: Fortress, 2013.

Wright, N. T. *Pauline Perspectives: Essays on Paul, 1978–2013.* Minneapolis: Fortress, 2013.

Yarbrough, Robert W. *The Letters to Timothy and Titus.* PNTC. Grand Rapids, MI: Eerdmans, 2018.

Yeung, Maureen W. *Faith in Jesus and Paul: A Comparison with Special Reference to "Faith That Can Remove Mountains" and "Your Faith Has Healed/Saved You."* WUNT, 2nd ser., vol. 147. Tübingen: Mohr Siebeck, 2002.

Yong, Kukwah Philemon. "The Faith of Jesus Christ: An Analysis of Paul's Use of Πιστις Χριστου." PhD diss., Southern Baptist Theological Seminary, 2003.

General Index

Abraham
  faithfulness of, 62–63
  faith of, 60–64, 79–80, 92, 129–31, 199, 216
  faith reckoned as righteousness, 94–95
  as father of all who believe, 80
  as man of faith, 52, 231
  as model of faith, 133
  obedience of, 61–63, 78
  offspring of, 90–91
  as paradigm for Jesus's faith, 81–82
  paradoxical nature of faith of, 131–32, 267–68
  vicarious effect of faith of, 81
adjectival genitive, 161n3
Allen, R. Michael, 258n69, 265n94
already and not yet, 179, 266–67
Anderson, Garwood P., 234n157
anthropological/anthropocentric view of ἐκ πίστεως Χριστοῦ, 27, 250
anthropology, 240, 250–59
"apocalyptic" school of Pauline theology, 33–34, 47, 111
Aristotle, on four causes, 260–61
atonement, liberal view of, 195
Augustine, 54, 159, 191–93, 242

baptized "into Christ," 108
Barclay, John M. G., 48n91, 135n87, 249n25
Barnett, Paul, 165n11, 166n20
Barr, James, 52n2, 57, 72n70, 207, 216
Barth, Karl, 26, 195, 265
Barth, Markus, 45

Bates, Matthew W., 56n21, 58, 59n34, 152n122, 243n11, 254nn45–46, 254n48
Beale, G. K., 172n40
Beker, J. Christiaan, 232n154
believing in Christ, 13–20, 268
  as believing in God, 244–45
  in passive voice, 119
believing "into Christ," 108
believing that Christ, 268
Berger, Klaus, 232n154
Betz, Hans Dieter, 106n8, 126n60, 198n55
biblical theology, 240n4
blindness, as metaphor for unbelief, 177
"body of faith," 54–55, 59, 69, 115, 120, 202, 204–5, 236, 257n61
Bohairic, 189
Bolt, Peter G., 91n129
Bortone, Pietro, 109nn20–21
Bruce, F. F., 126n60
Bultmann, Rudolf, 107, 142n103, 165, 252–53, 259
  anthropological approach to Paul, 32, 49
  demythologizing Paul, 28–30
  on faith as unconnected to history, 46
  on the resurrection, 29
Burton, Ernest De Witt, 55n20, 198n55, 201, 203n74
"by faith," as Pauline idiom for Christ-oriented faith, 97–98, 184–85, 210, 224–33
  and debated genitives, 233–37
"by faith to faith," 229–31

Scripture Index